AI VERSUS IP

The rise of artificial intelligence is challenging the foundations of intellectual property. In *AI versus IP: Rewriting Creativity*, science writer Robin Feldman offers a balanced perspective as she explains how artificial intelligence (AI) threatens to erode all of intellectual property (IP) – patents, trademarks, copyrights, trade secrets, and rights of publicity. Using analogies to the *Bridgerton* fantasy series and the Good Housekeeping "Seal of Approval," Professor Feldman also offers solutions to ensure a peaceful coexistence between AI and IP. And if you've ever wanted to understand just how modern AI programs like ChatGPT, Claude, Gemini, Grok, Meta AI, and others work, *AI versus IP: Rewriting Creativity* explains it all in simple language, no math required. AI and IP can coexist, Feldman argues, but only if we fully understand them and only with considerable effort and forethought.

Robin Feldman is the Director of the AI Law and Innovation Institute at the University of California Law, San Francisco. Over the last decade, she has provided technical advice on AI policy to the US government, including committees of Congress, the Army Cyber Institute, the Government Accountability Office (GAO), the Department of Justice, and other federal and state agencies.

AI versus IP

REWRITING CREATIVITY

Robin Feldman

Arthur J. Goldberg Distinguished Professor of Law,
Director of the AI Law and Innovation Institute,
University of California Law, San Francisco

CAMBRIDGE
UNIVERSITY PRESS

CAMBRIDGE
UNIVERSITY PRESS

Shaftesbury Road, Cambridge CB2 8EA, United Kingdom

One Liberty Plaza, 20th Floor, New York, NY 10006, USA

477 Williamstown Road, Port Melbourne, VIC 3207, Australia

314–321, 3rd Floor, Plot 3, Splendor Forum, Jasola District Centre, New Delhi – 110025, India

103 Penang Road, #05-06/07, Visioncrest Commercial, Singapore 238467

Cambridge University Press is part of Cambridge University Press & Assessment, a department of the University of Cambridge.

We share the University's mission to contribute to society through the pursuit of education, learning and research at the highest international levels of excellence.

www.cambridge.org
Information on this title: www.cambridge.org/9781009646864

DOI: 10.1017/9781009646833

When citing this work, please include a reference to the DOI 10.1017/9781009646833

First published 2025

A catalogue record for this publication is available from the British Library

Library of Congress Cataloging-in-Publication Data
Names: Feldman, Robin, author.
Title: AI versus IP : Rewriting Creativity / Robin Feldman, University of California Law, San Francisco. Other titles: AI v. IP
Description: Cambridge, United Kingdom ; New York, NY : Cambridge University Press, 2025. | Includes bibliographical references and index.
Identifiers: LCCN 2025000519 (print) | LCCN 2025000520 (ebook) | ISBN 9781009646864 (hardback) | ISBN 9781009646840 (paperback) | ISBN 9781009646833 (epub)
Subjects: LCSH: Intellectual property. | Artificial intelligence–Law and legislation.
Classification: LCC K1401 .F39 2025 (print) | LCC K1401 (ebook) | DDC 343.09/998–dc23/eng/20250113
LC record available at https://lccn.loc.gov/2025000519
LC record available at https://lccn.loc.gov/2025000520

ISBN 978-1-009-64686-4 Hardback
ISBN 978-1-009-64684-0 Paperback

AI versus IP

REWRITING CREATIVITY

Robin Feldman

Arthur J. Goldberg Distinguished Professor of Law,
Director of the AI Law and Innovation Institute,
University of California Law, San Francisco

CAMBRIDGE
UNIVERSITY PRESS

CAMBRIDGE
UNIVERSITY PRESS

Shaftesbury Road, Cambridge CB2 8EA, United Kingdom

One Liberty Plaza, 20th Floor, New York, NY 10006, USA

477 Williamstown Road, Port Melbourne, VIC 3207, Australia

314–321, 3rd Floor, Plot 3, Splendor Forum, Jasola District Centre, New Delhi – 110025, India

103 Penang Road, #05-06/07, Visioncrest Commercial, Singapore 238467

Cambridge University Press is part of Cambridge University Press & Assessment, a department of the University of Cambridge.

We share the University's mission to contribute to society through the pursuit of education, learning and research at the highest international levels of excellence.

www.cambridge.org
Information on this title: www.cambridge.org/9781009646864

DOI: 10.1017/9781009646833

When citing this work, please include a reference to the DOI 10.1017/9781009646833

First published 2025

A catalogue record for this publication is available from the British Library

Library of Congress Cataloging-in-Publication Data
Names: Feldman, Robin, author.
Title: AI versus IP : Rewriting Creativity / Robin Feldman, University of California Law, San Francisco. Other titles: AI v. IP
Description: Cambridge, United Kingdom ; New York, NY : Cambridge University Press, 2025. | Includes bibliographical references and index.
Identifiers: LCCN 2025000519 (print) | LCCN 2025000520 (ebook) | ISBN 9781009646864 (hardback) | ISBN 9781009646840 (paperback) | ISBN 9781009646833 (epub)
Subjects: LCSH: Intellectual property. | Artificial intelligence–Law and legislation.
Classification: LCC K1401 .F39 2025 (print) | LCC K1401 (ebook) | DDC 343.09/998–dc23/eng/20250113
LC record available at https://lccn.loc.gov/2025000519
LC record available at https://lccn.loc.gov/2025000520

ISBN 978-1-009-64686-4 Hardback
ISBN 978-1-009-64684-0 Paperback

To my beloved husband, Boris Feldman, who could never be replaced by Claude, Grok, or any other AI.

CONTENTS

ACKNOWLEDGMENTS

I am grateful to Justine Caedo, Mary Cornaby,Vaughn Goehrig, Zachary Henderson, Noah Jones, Merav Magen, Tanziuzzaman Sakib, Arturo Villa, Alex Whisnant, Millicent Wong, and Caroline Yuen for excellent research assistance, and I am particularly indebted to Zachary Henderson as well as Amanda Fish and Caroline Yuen for invaluable insights and for leading the research team. I am deeply grateful to Rotem Alaluf, Professor Emily Burns, Michael Callahan, Dr. Natalie Feldman, Jason Bayer, Charles Tait Graves, Roberta Horton, Professor Yaniv Konchitchki, Taylor Marcus, Yanir Nulman, John Slafsky, Sean Quinn, and Benjamin Zagorsky for their thoughts on development of this book or comments on drafts, as well as the people in industry who were kind enough to answer questions but wish to remain anonymous. I also wish to thank participants in the AI in STEM (science, technology, engineering and mathematics) and Medicine conference panel, the Government, Public Policy, and Artificial Intelligence conference, and the AI Inventorship Listening Session, hosted by the US Patent and Trademark Office. On the publishing side, I am deeply grateful to Cambridge University Press editor Matt Gallaway, copyeditors Beatrice Goddu and Venkatesh Krishnamoorthy, and the eagle eyes of proof reader Dr. Nanette McGuinness. As always, any errors are entirely my own. This work draws from and builds upon my previous works, in particular, "Consumption Taxes and the Theory of General and Individual Taxation," an article published in the *Virginia Tax Review* in 2002, *Rethinking Patent Law*, a book published by Harvard University Press in 2012, and "Artificial Intelligence and Cracks in the Foundation of Intellectual Property," an article published in the *University of California Law Journal* in 2024, with the permission of the publishers when required. Additionally, motivated by the subject matter at hand, I used publicly available large language models, including ChatGPT, Claude, Grok, Meta AI, and Google Gemini, to assist in this book's copyediting process and in exploring the math and science underlying modern AI. For more information on that experience, see the *Feldman Interviews Feldman* podcast "How I Used AI in Writing a Book about AI," available on the AI Law & Innovation Institute's website or in my LinkedIn post.

INTRODUCTION

The Constitution is not a very long document. Yet tucked between the folds that grant Congress the power to establish the post office[1] and to create the lower courts[2] lies the power "to promote the Progress of Science and useful Arts, by securing for limited Times to Authors and Inventors the exclusive Right to their respective Writings and Discoveries."[3] The founding fathers anticipated, it seems, the need to protect the diverse and developing outputs of their newborn country.

The constitutional establishment of copyrights and patents in the United States has since then been supplemented by the common law establishment of trade secrets and their slightly odd cousin, trademarks.[4] Together, copyright, patent, trademark, and trade secret form the basic pillars collectively described as intellectual property (IP).[5]

Across hundreds of years, the core concepts of what we protect and why we protect it have remained relatively stable. Through tectonic technological shifts – the industrial revolution, the digital revolution, and the proliferation of the internet, smartphones, and social media – these core concepts have persisted. But artificial intelligence (AI) poses a different kind of challenge. The collection of emerging technologies and computational methods that fall under the umbrella of artificial intelligence threatens to shake the very foundations of intellectual property law and our idea of what deserves protection.

Much legal scholarship on artificial intelligence,[6] as well as political commentary[7] and even the occasional lawsuit,[8] focuses on how the modern wave of generative AI systems may, through their operations, impinge on intellectual property rights already granted to others. Primary among those concerns lies the fact that generative AI systems pull their training data from information on the internet, much of which may be protected by copyright and thus unlawful to reproduce without consent.[9] Other legal scholarship focuses on whether creations designed or co-designed by AI systems should themselves receive intellectual property protection – a debate that, contrary to the first concern, considers the status of AI systems as creators capable of receiving legal protection.[10] Yet another set of legal scholarship on AI considers safety and ethical concerns, often calling for, or conceptualizing methods of, regulating AI.[11] Despite this range of scholarly discussion, one issue remains largely unexamined: As AI continues to embed itself throughout society, it will progressively break loose the foundations of what we choose to protect with intellectual property, forcing us to reconsider how intellectual property derives its value.

Using the language of the Constitution, our implicit image of the "progress" we hope to "promote," and the standards we use to assess the value of *human* contributions to that progress, are quietly at risk from the accelerating development of AI technology. In particular, AI has the potential to significantly shrink the pool of invention, expression, secrets, or reputation – that is, the areas covered by the intellectual property umbrella. In addition, AI may narrow the protectible space available to human contributors. Moreover, AI has the potential to shrink the value proposition of the intellectual property regimes themselves, by shaking society's faith in the purpose and effectiveness of these legal systems.

The changes wrought by AI create existential questions for society's conception of human invention. The term "existential" is used here, not in the modern sense of threatening something's existence, but rather in the broad sense of philosophical existentialism, as being concerned with exploring the meaning and value of existence.[12] In this case, the concern is the purpose and value of intellectual property, along with its implications for the value of human invention.

As we face this changing landscape, we cannot behave like the proverbial saboteurs, throwing our "sabots" into the machinery in hopes of stopping its gears.[13] The march of technology rarely retreats, and it is in our interest to adapt. We also must be careful to distinguish our fears about AI's possible threats to society[14] from the task of defining the boundaries of intellectual property. The theoretical concepts underlying intellectual property aren't designed to bear such weighty burdens, and the legal doctrines of IP, for the most part, have avoided taking on the heavy mantle of morality in the United States.[15] Instead, society has crafted other forms of regulation – including labor laws to protect workers during the industrial revolution,[16] criminal codes outlawing the possession of burglar's tools,[17] and regulation of federal funding for gene-editing research on humans[18] – to address broader moral and ethical concerns arising from technological changes.

In addition, we should be wary of our all-too-human instinct to insist on the primacy of our own, individual contributions to innovation. Measuring human value by our individual or collective contributions to intellectual property is a mistake. After all, technological advancement is a *product* of human innovation. The artificial intelligence systems humans create may, in some circumstances, be able to produce new creations and inventions better than our own, with the result that intellectual property systems eventually may regard many human contributions as insufficient for recognition. Nevertheless, we should not view this development as self-diminishing any more than when our offspring display greater talents than our own. Yes, their talents may make ours pale by comparison, but they couldn't have existed without us.

Perhaps in that evolved context, we might do well to remember the words of English theologian Robert South that "if there be any truer measure of a man than by what he does, it must be by what he gives."[19] In other words, what we choose to protect must be bounded by the value of the contribution it represents. As AI forces us to recalibrate our conception of what counts as an extraordinary contribution, the outer bounds of protectability will also need to be recalibrated.

Change, however, is not necessarily bad – and many have argued that the United States' intellectual property regimes are overdue for an overhaul.[20] The reach of intellectual property law has expanded dramatically over the past several decades, and this expansion has drawn its fair share of criticism.[21] In the end, AI may operate as a counterbalance, by helping to pare back some aspects of intellectual property law, as well as providing an opportunity for us to plumb the legal and philosophical depths of intellectual property protection in the context of modern innovation.

One can predict much wailing and gnashing of teeth as we step into this next iteration of human-technological interaction. Nevertheless, we should borrow a concept from both existential philosophers and their arch opponents, theologians, to note that the enterprise we are embarking on demands a little humility.[22] The ground beneath us will be unsettled for quite some time, and there is much we don't, and can't, understand yet.

This book proceeds in four parts. In Part I, I offer an overview of modern artificial intelligence systems and technology – what AI is, how it has developed, how it works, and the nature of some ethical concerns with the technology. I also introduce the four primary intellectual property regimes: patent, copyright, trademark, and trade secrets. I begin by anchoring these regimes in the dual (and dueling) philosophies of utilitarianism and nonconsequentialism, along with their legal origins in US law. This background will be essential for understanding arguments made about IP and AI as the book progresses.

Part II surveys some of the current discussions regarding AI and intellectual property – with a special focus on the open and pressing question of whether large language models, by their very existence, commit mass copyright infringement. I also touch on some of the challenges AI poses to authorship (for copyright) and inventorship (for patent). I examine how AI intersects with the IP-adjacent right of publicity – and AI's disturbing ability to imitate the voices and appearance of real people through "deepfakes." In Part III, I describe how AI is set to shrink not only the *pool of materials* eligible for intellectual property protection but also the *value* of intellectual property regimes as we know them.

Fortunately, adapting to the impending changes facing intellectual property does not require a wholesale reimagining of the field. Rather, we can understand pathways forward through the allegory of the diamond, which this book introduces and discusses in Part IV. With that image as the model, I describe how the legal system can trim what is classed as protectible, casting the net only around the remarkable and thereby preserving value.[23] Further, the legal system could restore confidence in both AI and IP through the establishment of a public–private certification body. I conclude that, together, these approaches would mitigate the problems looming ahead for the four intellectual property regimes.

The speed of development in AI poses challenges for any author, and I approach the writing of this book with a bit of trepidation. Technical explanations may have changed by the time a reader reaches a particular page, pending legal cases may have advanced, and new cases may be brewing. To the best of my ability, I have tried to anticipate and leave room for advancements that may occur, despite the profound unpredictability of the field. With that caveat in mind, I turn to the enterprise at hand.

PART I

Background on AI and IP

1 AN OVERVIEW OF ARTIFICIAL INTELLIGENCE

One cannot apply legal rules to any emerging technology without at least a basic understanding of the technology itself. Although the technical nuances of AI are tremendously complex, this chapter provides a foundational understanding of modern AI systems, focusing on the types of systems that likely are most familiar to readers – large language models such as ChatGPT (Generative Pre-trained Transformer).

A word of caution before we begin. Due to the speed of AI development, cutting-edge technologies at the time of this writing may be old news not long after the book's publication. Accordingly, the reader should treat this chapter as a branching-off point for continued learning.

Since computer and cognitive scientist John McCarthy's coinage of the term "artificial intelligence" in 1955,[1] varying definitions,[2] technological changes, popular culture,[3] and growing media attention have led to misleading assumptions[4] about these systems.[5] Any responsible definition must directly exclude these misinterpretations.

One widely used definition of AI refers to *the use of computing systems for automating tasks that would normally require human intelligence.*[6] The definition succinctly captures the crux of the technology. Nevertheless, it is essential to recognize that AI is much more than any single specific technology, program, or use case. Rather, AI is a large and fast-growing interdisciplinary field within computer science, mathematics, and statistics, with its own wide array of subfields, many of which nest and overlap. Although it has become common to talk about AI as a single concept, most modern AI systems are specific applications of a few important subfields: machine learning, deep learning, and deep neural networks. (Generative AI systems, such as large language models, are further nested within these subfields; see Figure 1.1.) It is the recent

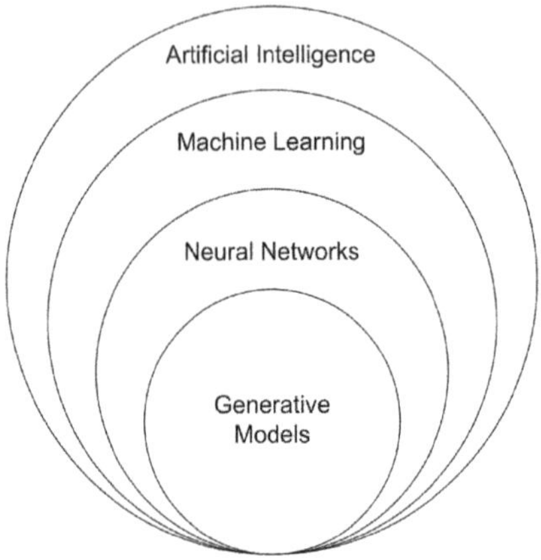

Figure 1.1 A visual representation of some of the subfields contained within the broad field of Artificial Intelligence.

rapid innovation in these particular subfields that is responsible for most of the current debate, discussion, and open questions about the nexus between AI and intellectual property law.

Virtually all modern AI systems – certainly all the ones this book is concerned with – fall somewhere within the subfield of artificial intelligence called "machine learning," which contains the nested subfields of neural networks and generative models. Indeed, machine learning has become so important and ubiquitous that at the time of this writing, any discussion about AI is very likely about machine learning or one of its subfields. In this context, it's important to understand the following: AI is not an entity itself, but a way of completing a task.

Consider the difference between machine-learning programs and traditional programming. In traditional, non-machine-learning programming, the software code is rigid and mechanical, and therefore, the computer can only handle very specific situations. Take, for example, ELIZA, an early computer chatbot developed by researchers at MIT.[7] The inventor described ELIZA in this way:

> The gross procedure of the program is quite simple; the text is read and inspected for the presence of a *keyword.* If such a word is found, the sentence is transformed according to a *rule* associated with the keyword[.][8]

In other words, ELIZA might be programmed so that if a client looking for customer service help enters the keyword "contact," the chatbot will display the customer service email. Notably, when ELIZA encounters a user input that it is not programmed to handle, it will essentially repeat the user input back to the user. At that point, ELIZA's conversational limitations become obvious.[9]

Rules-based programming is responsible for error messages and software crashes, which occur when the device encounters an unfamiliar user input. Since the computer can *only* do what it's been explicitly programmed to do, if a user wishes to vary its functionality, they'll need to manually change its programming.

Machine learning, on the other hand, enables the software to *adapt*. It involves "learning" algorithms and applying them to perform tasks,[10] a process that allows for greater flexibility and wider functionality. While rules-based programming requires manually changing lines of code to improve the software's capabilities, machine learning enables the software to, for example, respond to patterns in the data that the model isn't trained on.

Standard machine learning systems typically require a human to provide the algorithm with highly structured training data – meaning data that is stored and organized in a way that enables the computer algorithm to comprehend it.[11] These algorithm-based systems acquire "knowledge" through processing data relevant to certain tasks, enhancing their performance in those tasks over time.[12] Importantly, this "learning" process is not identical to the process of human learning. Rather than building a *theoretical* understanding of the task it has been set to achieve, machine learning systems identify statistical correlations and patterns in the training data to systematically optimize their output.[13]

Consider spam-email detection. A human developer trains a machine learning system on a vast collection of emails to detect which of them are likely to be spam at a percentage comparable to or better than humans. The machine learning system, however, does not comprehend the emails with all the valences that a person might. Instead, it uses the statistical correlations it has generated from the emails it has reviewed to guide its classification of new, unseen emails.

But these relatively capable, more traditional machine-learning systems are not the focus of the current wave of AI interest. (In fact, machine learning of the kind described above has been around for over half a century.[14]) Instead, the remarkable innovations in artificial intelligence today stem from a powerful and very data-hungry subfield of machine learning called "deep learning."

Deep learning uses computer-based statistical models known as "artificial neural networks" – a subfield nested within machine learning (see Figure 1.1). These models are capable of *updating their depth of understanding each time they see new information.* After being trained on large quantities of *unstructured* data – as opposed to the structured data that the previously discussed systems rely on – these neural networks become capable of making robust predictions and decisions and generating highly nuanced outputs.[15] (As the name suggests, artificial neural networks were inspired by, though they do not replicate, the biological networks of the human brain.[16])

The fundamental idea behind deep learning is that the neural network contains a vast number of parameters, sometimes called "weights,"[17] embedded across multiple layers of interconnected "nodes." These nodes are somewhat analogous to the human brain's neurons.[18] Just as the human brain has biological mechanisms for processing and storing everything we learn – from facts to language to the ability to perceive emotions – deep learning allows AI systems to *store* information and *update* their understanding when they absorb new information. In practice, a given model does this by adjusting its parameters as it is fed more data. This allows the system to optimize[19] its representation of the data it was trained on – just as how the more times a child encounters dogs, cats, and mice, the child gets better at distinguishing and identifying them.

At a technical level, each layer in the neural network extracts different features from the input data, and subsequent layers build on those extracted features. This process helps the AI model refine its understanding – just as a child begins by distinguishing dogs from cats and eventually can distinguish German Shepherds from Labradors. At least for now, networks with more data and layers can learn more intricate, hierarchical patterns in the data.[20] The neural networks used in modern deep learning are almost unfathomably large, with billions, or even trillions, of parameters.[21] Most important, these models are capable of being trained on vast quantities of unstructured data gathered from the internet.[22]

Key differences exist between traditional machine learning, which does not rely on neural networks, and deep learning, which does. First, although both systems use algorithms, the models learn and solve problems differently. Training a traditional machine learning algorithm typically requires hand-built features, and computer engineers must closely monitor the algorithm during the training process. In contrast, deep learning models are capable of "autonomously extract[ing] meaningful features from raw data, learning the most useful features for the task progressively."[23] In other words, they assist in their own training. Second, and perhaps most important, the capabilities and outputs of these two systems vary widely. Traditional machine learning typically yields only simple outputs such as numbers or classifications, while deep learning is capable of producing a myriad of outputs. Some deep-learning outputs are enormously complex, including, but not limited to, robust text and speech.[24]

In general, AI systems can be broadly categorized as falling within two different levels of so-called "intelligence."[25] Simple machine-learning systems are designed and trained for a specific or narrow set of tasks and will, no matter what, operate in limited contexts.[26] On the next level, programs such as ChatGPT are stunning in their ability to comprehensively respond to prompts on a wide variety of subjects.[27] Although they can update their knowledge of a particular task or domain, they do not possess the cognitive ability or flexibility necessary to transfer knowledge to new domains or tasks. In contrast to these is a theoretical class of AI systems that has the ability to understand, learn, and apply knowledge across a wide range of tasks at a level comparable to, and possibly exceeding, human intelligence.[28] Also referred to as "artificial general intelligence," such systems currently do not – *and may never* – exist.[29]

Nevertheless, many AI systems today perform increasingly complex tasks better than humans.[30] For over ten years, the best player of the ancient strategy board game GO has been an AI model. AI-driven robots are beginning to perform surgeries and "can match or even exceed a human in dexterity, precision, and speed."[31] Moreover, as of this writing, there are fully autonomous, driverless taxis picking up and transporting customers without human intervention.[32]

Of course, there is much that AI still can't do. Most feats in the physical realm remain beyond their capabilities. An AI can't yet cook your dinner or make your bed because it lacks the manual dexterity needed. (Breaking an eggshell without destroying the liquid inside, for example, turns out to be an astoundingly difficult task.) Similarly, AI is unlikely to be equipped to handle tasks outside of the environment in which it was trained. Although this limitation may be less visible in the familiar context of chatbots, where the inputs and outputs are merely information, it comes into play when a user asks AI to *do something* for them. Taking digital actions on the user's behalf, especially when multiple steps are involved, is considerably more challenging and mostly beyond AI's current capacity.[33]

The vital difference is the degree of flexibility, breath, and context-switching that a given AI system can manage.[34] This brings us to the kind of AI system most relevant to this book – generative AI. These systems[35] lie at the cutting edge of the most sophisticated deep learning models[36] and are designed to create new content, such as text, images, code, audio, or video when prompted by a user.[37] Among the increasing number of commercial generative AI products, the most well-known is ChatGPT,[38] a chatbot that relies on a deep learning model trained on natural language data. ChatGPT can generate human-like text responses based on user text inputs. In the eyes of many commentators, ChatGPT's public release and global popularity have symbolized the start of a new "AI boom."[39]

This is a good time to address a common misconception about how deep learning models and specifically, generative AI systems, work. These systems have incredible capacities to generate outputs that are similar to, and in some cases that mirror, the data and materials they're trained on (such as images or written works). It is therefore common to believe that AI models conduct something like a database search, followed by a cutting-and-pasting process, to create their outputs. By analogy, imagine an art student with a bag full of magazine clippings who collages new works on request, although one should note that this idea is not at all how these models work in practice.[40] In reality, however, the training dataset is not accessible to the AI system after the training is complete. The bag is no longer accessible to the art student.

The AI system learns from the training data through a process of looking at each item in the training database and updating itself repeatedly. This is somewhat similar to how humans learn: to teach a child the difference between the colors red and orange, the child must learn from examples encompassing different shades of orange and red. While the child will at first confuse the colors often, each new example improves her ability to distinguish them. The child's brain repeatedly updates her conception of "orange" and "red" until eventually, the child is able to identify the colors perfectly even when they appear outside of the example set she was trained on. With a little practice, the child even may be able to mix paints together to *produce* the color orange without a reference.

All of this learning happens in the child's brain, where deep understanding of color is stored biologically. With AI models, however, the "learning" is stored in complex sets of numbers that represent multi-directional locations in relation to other complex sets of numbers.

To understand how various legal doctrines might interact with AI, let's take a look under the hood of a large language model, such as ChatGPT. I'll use a simple analogy, and no math, I promise.

Imagine you want to learn everything there is to know about Washington, D.C. It is a rich and varied city, with the unique status of America's capital, differing neighborhoods, historical monuments, government institutions, and layers of political history. In short, our goal is to create an understanding of Washington that accounts for its many dimensions. A human might begin by exploring all its neighborhoods, speaking with locals, reading historical texts, studying geographic maps, and just generally trying to absorb the patterns and relationships that exist throughout the city's history and landscape.

For our purposes, think of Washington, D.C. as what we want to train our model to understand.[41] Thus, similar to the exploration above, someone programming an AI model would scour the internet to collect every map, photograph, congressional record, government document, historical archive, news article, and policy paper about Washington, D.C.

Don't forget social media posts and gossip rags! We want our model to understand not just the physical description and the history of D.C., but also the feel of the city, its cuisines and cultures, and the subjective experience of visiting and living in the nation's capital.

Try to imagine just how much information we'll have to collect and analyze. There are countless books, articles, websites, and conversations to pore over, and the information contained will be highly diverse. One source might provide a map of postal delivery routes from 1876; another could be a recommendation for a plumber pulled from social media. These texts have been written in various voices and writing styles, presenting different perspectives across different periods of time.

Our goal is to create an understanding of Washington that accounts for its many dimensions, but no project has infinite resources. Thus, before we even begin wandering around the city, we need to make some major design decisions about how we'll set up our map and perhaps coordinate a team to help us. These design choices provide a template for the project – they're fixed once we start, and they'll shape how we learn about the city.

The first design decision involves how we break all of the data into small, manageable chunks that will help us learn to navigate the city. We don't make any decisions about what will be in each chunk of data, just how many chunks we are going to have – a decision that may be driven by the amount of resources we can invest in the project. For example, with large language models, designers might break the data down into individual words, two-word groupings, syllables, or even individual characters.[42] Different chunk sizes will also be better suited for different types of tasks. This initial decision will determine how many unique words or ideas the AI model will understand in the long run (its vocabulary).

Assume that based on our goals, tools, and available energy, we decide to have 50,000 chunks of information on our map. Any given piece could be a landmark like the White House, an attribute like "honest," a detail like "water," or a concept like "government." Each of these 50,000 pieces will become a detail on the map, located by a set of coordinates to help us understand where it lies in relation to the other chunks of data. Imagine sticking push-pins into random locations on the map, with the expectation that we will learn more about each push-pin over time.

But this is no ordinary two-dimensional map, which would have relatively simple coordinates. We get to choose the number of dimensions. Just for the moment, let's assume we randomly choose 300 dimensions. That may sound like a lot, but we'll need that many dimensions to understand the numerous levels of relationships within our data. We don't just want to know that two D.C. diners are a mile apart, we also want to know which one is better rated, and which one was founded during the Civil War. Once we decide to have 300 dimensions, each pin will need a complex set of numbers to give the coordinates for its location in all of the 300 dimensions.[43]

Given that the pins showing the relative locations for all 50,000 of our chunks of data will each need to be identified with coordinates showing 300 dimensions, it would probably help if we were not the only person wandering around, trying to find where everything is in relation to everything else. And now we reach another decision point: how many guides can we recruit and how many expeditions will we send them on?

One should note that the people we hire need no specific knowledge about D.C. or guiding tours. We can hire anyone who can follow basic instructions, even if they have never been to D.C. and aren't in the tour guide business. Let's assume we have hired 100 tour guides who will each engage in 12 map-making expeditions.[44] This is like equipping 100 guides with backpacks full of tools – compasses, notebooks, and cameras – to map D.C. over 12 intense expeditions, each round aiming to uncover deeper insights about the city. Their goal is to create a map so detailed that it captures not just landmarks like the White House, but also the vibe of neighborhoods, the flow of the Potomac, and even the buzz of government in action.

Finally, we decide how many connections or pathways our map can have. The pathways serve to connect our pins across the 300 dimensions, but they aren't just like static streets on a map. They're more like adjustable bridges with what we might call "importance dials" attached to each.

When our guides first arrive in D.C., these pathways are randomly set up, with arbitrary importance values. Some pathways and importance values might initially suggest that the Lincoln Memorial is closely connected to ice cream trucks, while others might weakly link the Supreme Court to the Metro system. It's just entirely random, nonsensical information.

During our training expeditions, our guides continuously adjust these importance dials as they discover the actual relationships between locations. The guides will strengthen certain pathways while weakening others, based on what they observe as they explore. A bigger map with more pathways can learn more, but it's harder to explore. Thus, let's limit ourselves to 100 million pathways.[45]

These choices – 50,000 chunks of data, 300 dimensions, 100 guides, 12 map-making expeditions, 100 million pathways – are locked in before we start wandering around D.C. They represent our template for the mapping process.

As noted, to start the mapping, the 50,000 pins – representing chunks of Washington, D.C. information – are placed completely randomly in our 300-dimensional space. Our guides start with absolutely no knowledge of what's where or how any of the information relates to anything else. It's as if they're stumbling around, trying to figure out anything at all.

When Guide 1 heads out for this first expedition, we offer a completely random group of coordinates. The guide goes to those coordinates, reaches out, and finds nothing. The guide makes small, random adjustments to the coordinates. The guide's fingers finally brush against something solid. They feel the grand, stony edges, and the guide realizes it's the Lincoln Memorial. Now, Guide 1 has found something to work with.

Similarly, Guide 2 jumps to the random coordinates, finds nothing, and adjusts the coordinates randomly until finally sensing something wet and flowing in nature. Guide 2 has splashed into the Rock Creek tributary of the Potomac River. Each of the remaining guides engages in this first baby step. Now that our guides have each found something to work with, the real learning begins.

Remember the information we gathered at the beginning, the original documents of our training data, which we separated into chunks? Guide 1 now picks up one of those original documents, choosing one related to what the guide has found so far, and extracts a sequence of a few chunks. For example, a document describing the Lincoln Memorial might include the sequence "the memorial contains 36 columns symbolizing the number of states in the U.S. when Lincoln died."

Our guide, then, omits the last chunk of the sequence.[46] Using the information currently in the map, our guide tries to predict the missing chunks that say, "when Lincoln died." Of course, the current map shows all 50,000 chunks of our information scattered randomly, with no indication of how each piece of information might, or might not, relate to another piece. As you can imagine, the guide's prediction will be wildly inaccurate – maybe suggesting that the thirty-six columns symbolize the number of states in the United States when Lincoln flew to the moon.

Undaunted, our guide immediately compares the wild prediction with the actual document and observes the error. Learning from this discrepancy, the guide makes precise adjustments to thousands of importance dials, such as strengthening pathways between "Lincoln Memorial" and concepts like "monument," "Abraham Lincoln," and "marble," while also weakening pathways to irrelevant concepts like "flight" or "moon" or "science." The guide might try an entire global shift by adding .5 to all of the dials across all dimensions. At the end of the day, some pathways might be reduced to zero or even negative numbers. In other words, the guide makes a calculated set of adjustments based on information gained through trial and error.[47] Over time, as our guide makes adjustments through trial and error, this guide begins to develops knowledge of the city's monuments and their historical significance.

Meanwhile, Guide 2, who stumbled upon Rock Creek, is going through the same process with a document about waterways, making another guess and then a set of importance-dial adjustments. Guide 2 begins trying predictions for other sequences from other training documents, and adjusting importance dials to refine these predictions. Such adjustments lead to discoveries of connections to "tributaries,"

"Potomac River," "hiking trails," and "Rock Creek Park." Guide 2 begins seeking connections to other water-related pins – like "Washington Tidal Basin" or "Anacostia River channel" – particularly homing in on dimensions that signal "liquid" or "movement." When testing connections to "Supreme Court" or "ice cream vendors," Guide 2 finds minimal relevance, so the guide decreases those pathway-importance dials. Over time, Guide 2 specializes in the city's natural geography, waterways, and park systems.

But then there's a third guide who stumbles into something less solid, more abstract. Guide 3 bumps into the White House, not feeling stone or water, but a vibe – a swirl of activity, power, and rules. Wandering further, Guide 3 hits the Capitol next and then the Supreme Court. Each discovery carries a similar hum – words like "law," "leader," or "decision" echo in the air. This guide doesn't focus on physical characteristics or historical information. Rather, Guide 3 tunes his senses to coordinates that land on locations humming with authority, policy, or administration.

Over time, Guide 3 becomes a master of the abstract. Encountering something like "Congress," Guide 3 doesn't just see a building. Rather, this guide senses Congress' "government-ness," connecting it to "White House" or "legislation" locations. Thus, while one guide excels at monuments and another at rivers, this third guide navigates the invisible threads of meaning, grouping blocks not by touch or smell, but by their intangible similarities.

As all 100 of our guides learn, they carefully reposition each pin in our 300-dimensional space, moving related concepts closer together. The Lincoln Memorial pin gradually shifts toward other monument pins and American history pins. Meanwhile, unrelated concepts like "flight" or "moon" drift farther away. With each training round, our guides refine both the positions of the pins and the strength of connections between them, creating a map with increasingly sophisticated relationships that reflects the true Washington, D.C. In the process, the guides also develop and enhance their specializations.[48]

Although twelve mapmaking expeditions does not sound like very much, it's important to note that there are an enormous number of trials and adjustments in each. For example, the first exploration, which begins with our guides testing out examples from the training data, typically includes hundreds of thousands of sequences.[49] Each guide makes predictions about these sequences, calculates errors, and adjusts dials accordingly. Processing one batch of examples constitutes a single iteration. Our guides complete millions of these iterations during each of the twelve mapmaking expeditions. By the end of just the first expedition, our guides will have processed billions of sequences and made trillions of tiny adjustments to importance dials. And when all twelve map-making expeditions are complete, these countless iterations transforms our initially random collection of pins and pathways into a sophisticated understanding of Washington, D.C.'s complex landscape across many dimensions.[50] Now we have a fully trained model, ready to process input queries from users.

You already have the basic idea of the technology, so this final description will go quickly. Your beautiful map is ready: 50,000 chunks of information are properly pinned with their 300-dimensional coordinates and the 100 million pathways connecting them. This map is now fixed. It is like a printed atlas, with the positions and pathways set in stone. In responding to prompts, nevertheless, the model will be able to use specialized experts who can shift their focus depending on a visitor's question, navigating through the fixed map to provide the most accurate response. Once again, we will use the concept of employing guides to do the work for us. Our old guides are on a well-earned vacation, so we hire brand-new guides with clean, fresh notebooks.

Let's say a visitor approaches with the following prompt: "Find a historical day trip in D.C. that I can take." That question would get broken into chunks such as "historical," "day trip," and "D.C." Fortunately, these chunks are already on the map,[51] each with its own 300-dimensional coordinates, fixed from training. The system can't change the map, but, as we will see, it can decide which parts to focus on.

When responding to the prompt, our team of 100 guides is assembled. Unlike the training phase, in which each expedition had a fresh team building upon the previous expedition's map, these guides now work with the finished map. Again, they process the question through 12 layers of analysis. And in each layer, the guides examine different aspects of the map:

For the first layer, some guides focus on "D.C." and "historical" and immediately highlight the historical landmarks clustered on the map, where chunks like "Lincoln Memorial" and "National Archives" reside. The map shows these landmarks are strongly connected to historical tours.

At another layer, different guides examine whether natural features like "Potomac River" should be included in a historical tour, but quickly determine that the pathways on the map more strongly connected historical sites with "day trip." At a later level, another group of guides identifies connections to government-related historical sites like "Capitol Building" or "White House," noting their historical significance as shown on the map.

As the request moves through all 12 layers, the focus becomes refined. With early layers, guides might explore broadly – briefly considering food spots in D.C. for a "day trip." By later layers, the insights from earlier layers help narrow the focus to historically significant locations. This progressive refinement is key: at each layer, guides can examine different aspects of the map depending on what was learned at previous layers, even though the map itself doesn't change.

After passing through all twelve layers, the guides combine their collective insights to generate an answer: "For a historical day trip in D.C., start by visiting the National Archives to explore the Constitution and the Declaration of Independence. Then head to the Lincoln Memorial to reflect on America's past. Then finish the day with a visit to the Capitol to watch a congressional session and see the government in action."

Guides who focused on landmarks provided the historical sites: "Lincoln Memorial," "National Archives," and "the Capitol." Guides who examined descriptive connections added contextual information: "reflect on America's past" and "explore the Constitution." Guides who studied government-related history ensured relevant political-historical connections were maintained, tying everything together with the "day trip" structure. And voilà! Our large-language model worked, and the user is happy.

Let's briefly review the prompt and response action to highlight the parts of the process that are fixed and the parts that are dynamic. The map's chunks (like "Lincoln Memorial" or "National Archives"), their 300-dimensional coordinates, and the 100 million pathways connecting them are fixed; they were set during training and can't be altered now. The structure of the process – 100 guides working through 12 layers – is also fixed, somewhat like rules of collaboration. But each guide's focus is dynamic. Guides choose which pathways to follow and which chunks to emphasize based on the prompt. If the visitor had asked, "What's a food-focused day trip in D.C.?" the guides would have shifted their attention to culinary-related chunks, highlighting locations such as "Eastern Market" and "Georgetown bakeries." In other words, the guides would have used the same fixed map but with a different focus.

A few observations are worth noting. The model available for users does not contain either the original documents or a mathematical representation of those documents. The 300-dimensional coordinates help identify how small chunks of information from the documents relate to the other 50,000 chunks of information. Recall that those chunks could be syllables, single words, two-word combinations, individual characters, or other small groupings. Nor is it easy to determine the role that various documents might play in training a model, or even which *chunks* of which documents play a role in training or in responding to a particular user's prompt. These issues will be important in Chapter 3, when we examine hot topics in AI and IP.

If the map doesn't store training data (like a specific webpage) but learns patterns (like "government words go together"), how does the phenomenon of "memorization" occur? With memorization, the model responds to a prompt by producing a near-perfect copy of a document in the training data. Given the difficulties of reconstructing the model's pathway – a process involving billions of sequences and trillions of tiny adjustments – scientists are not entirely sure how and why memorization occurs.[52] With the speed of advancement in the field, however, it is entirely possible that a greater understanding will emerge by the time the reader reaches this page. Nevertheless, a few theories exist. First, memorization may occur when information appears too often; like a famous speech painted on a wall in every D.C. neighborhood – the map might etch that exact path so deeply that a guide can retrace it with near perfection. Second, memorization might occur in the opposite circumstance, when a series of words is so unusual or specialized that the most likely patterns among them lead to the reconstruction. Most important, memorization happens when the user asks the model to specifically recreate a particular document.

At the end of the day, memorization is not the norm. Nevertheless, it remains a puzzling and persistent artifact of today's generative AI models.

For those who would like a translation guide, take a look at the chart in this sentence's end note, which shows the terms used in the D.C. map example and the corresponding terms in computer science.[53] And I sincerely hope computer science mavens will forgive me for any oversimplifications.

The metaphor of creating a multi-dimensional map is intended to give readers a relatively accessible explanation of how some modern large language models work. Lost in the simplification, however, is the sense of awe with which computer scientists speak about the emergence of AI, in general, and generative AI, in particular. Engineers are accustomed to saying "we used this component with this strength, because it had to support this weight, etc." AI, however, is not trained in any way connected to the problems we want to solve. We simply ask a general machine to master the task of predicting the next word, letting the machine hone its skills on all the text produced by mankind. The resulting system has somehow intuited many concepts, relations, and higher-level abstractions.

Scientists study the inscrutable workings of the models that emerge. But we don't understand precisely how they are doing what they do, or even perhaps all that they are doing.

The quality, representativeness, and volume of data available today has enhanced the capabilities of modern generative AI by massively increasing the scale of training.[54] It's no surprise, then, that the explosion of collected and digitized data over the past few decades has fueled the rapid expansion of AI systems and their uses.[55] The enormous progress in generative AI also has been fueled by the availability of greater power to process data than ever before.[56] Thus, increased data and computing power have been the drivers of the current AI revolution. In fact, as Richard Sutton explained in his 2019 commentary, *The Bitter Lesson*, all of the major breakthroughs in AI (including the breakthroughs that would lead to generative AI systems) can be traced to leaps in computing and the amount of data available, rather than to the brilliance of the human scientific mind.[57]

Consider the increasingly large number of mathematical calculations[58] needed to train cutting-edge AI models. As an example, 700,000 operations were used to train the first artificial neural network, Perceptron Mark I. In comparison, OpenAI's model, GPT-4,[59] used a stunning 21 septillion operations.[60] (That's the number 21, followed by 21 zeros.) The difference in the amount of computing power is staggering.

Of course, that isn't to say the field has been stagnant for twenty years: innovations and advances in algorithm design and quality have made their mark as well. For example, deep learning models were utterly impractical until 2006, when a paper introduced a method for quickly training neural networks.[61] The basis for most modern neural networks, called *generative adversarial models* – a subtype of generative AI – emerged only eight years later, in 2014.[62] And as recently as 2017, the transformer architecture, a foundational building block for a wide range of state-of-the-art language processing models, propelled AI technology even further.[63]

The advancement in AI capabilities has led to widespread adoption of the technology and created an immeasurable impact on public and private life – for better, for worse, and for both. Numerous powerful AI tools are available to help people create impressive digital works of art.[64] And AI is finding ever-broader applications in healthcare and medicine. These include clinical administrative support, identifying molecules that might target disease states, and creation of digital "twins" of patients, which can provide patients and doctors with "a comprehensive model of potential health outcomes under different scenarios."[65] Across industry sectors, from electronics to biotechnologies, AI systems have propelled innovation forward.[66]

Publicly available generative AI systems also have the potential to help level the playing field for immigrants and those whose native languages differ from the language of the country in which they live. A user need only type employment dates, details, and experiences into a generative AI system and a snazzy resume written in beautifully expressive and grammatically perfect language emerges. The same technologies can help those non-native speakers once they arrive at work, where AI can craft the wording for memos, requests, and self-assessments. This type of freely available tool also can assist those who lack access to expensive job or school entrance counselors.

On the flip side, AI may sometimes calcify existing inequalities. Courts have used machine learning to assist with sentencing decisions, in the hopes that an algorithmic approach would standardize sentencing and eliminate the human tendency for bias. However, concerns have emerged that rather than eliminating bias, AI actually may magnify the bias already existing in the sentencing process.[67] And, of course, AI tools cannot help level any playing field if those who need them most lack access to them and education in how to use them.

AI also has had both positive and negative ramifications for education writ large. In universities around the country, educators are transforming their pedagogy, to both improving teaching methods with AI and grappling with the novel avenues AI provides for cheating.[68]

Regardless of whether one sees the glass as half full or half empty, AI is changing the way we think and the way we live. AI has begun to reshape financial systems, requiring fresh thinking when it comes to governance.[69] Even the US Patent Office has noted that "AI has the potential to fundamentally change how people perceive the world around them and live their daily lives."[70]

Despite such proliferation, major tensions remain concerning the wisdom of barreling full speed ahead into a world dominated by AI. Although modern AI systems are remarkably powerful, it can be difficult or impossible to explain why an AI system produced a given output, which creates a potentially frightening mystery. This opacity flows from the way these models work. Recall that AI models constantly update themselves as they are trained on more and more data, similar to the way a child learns to distinguish between two colors. And just as a child cannot not cite the specific past observation that leads them to identify a color as orange and not red, considering that models are trained on huge collections of data, it may be impossible to identify any *one* piece of training data responsible for a given output.

This class of issues is often called the "black box" problem,[71] given that the user – and even an AI specialist – cannot see inside. The black-box problem remains so challenging that even the software engineers and mathematicians who wrote the initial program may be unable to explain or recreate the AI's decision-making.[72]

There are many reasons to be concerned about a system capable of generating outputs whose origin and evolution we do not understand. For example, an AI system might produce biased results that are inaccurate or harmful, without our ability to trace how or why the system produced them.[73] Moreover, as we increasingly delegate our decision-making to AI systems, a lack of transparency runs in the face of one of the core tenets of democracy – one which is generally regarded as a marker of good governance.[74] That tenet is accountability.[75]

Specifically, accountability confers an obligation to explain and justify one's decisions and conduct.[76] When that obligation is satisfied, society can rest assured that if something goes wrong, proper mechanisms exist to question the relevant decision-makers, ensure they justify their actions, and respond to any improper results.[77] But accountability goes hand-in-hand with transparency.[78] One cannot hold someone (or some system) accountable without being able to examine what transpired. As we increasingly trust AI systems to perform high-risk tasks, how will we hold these AI systems – or their developers, platforms, or users – accountable, especially when the system's decision-making process is a black box?[79]

The importance of establishing well-founded trust in AI systems cannot be overstated. Some readers might recall the shocking incident in which a pedestrian, who was initially struck by a human-driven car, was then dragged for approximately 20 feet by an autonomous vehicle. The vehicle was developed by Cruise, a California-based startup owned by General Motors,[80] and the incident resulted in Cruise losing its license to operate and withdrawing its entire fleet of cars from service.[81] Much of this fallout centered on the company's initial post-incident response.[82] In Cruise's communications with regulators, the company focused on the initial impact caused by the human driver and failed to draw attention to the damage caused by the autonomous vehicle that dragged the injured pedestrian. According to the company's subsequent (and lengthy) internal investigation report, this erroneous decision was a result of "leadership failures and mistakes in judgment."[83] The internal report explicitly stated that "Cruise's senior leadership repeatedly failed to understand the importance of public trust and accountability."[84]

There are already calls for greater transparency and explainability of AI when it is used in public, high-stakes scenarios. For example, the need for independent oversight of AI systems featured prominently in President Biden's Blueprint for an AI Bill of Rights.[85] The Blueprint, which has no legal or regulatory force,[86] set out five principles intended to guide the development and deployment of AI systems.[87] Underlying each of the document's principles is a requirement for transparency and accountability in AI, whether in the form of independent evaluations, reporting, or monitoring.

The desire for accountability with AI systems transcends jurisdictional divides. In the European Union, that desire is given full legal force through an EU regulation, the EU Artificial Intelligence Act (EU AI Act),[88] which automatically binds every member state to a risk-based regulatory framework.[89] The framework contains four levels of risk for an AI system, ranging from unacceptable (systems simply banned) to minimal or no risk (systems freely usable). The EU AI Act imposes a litany of obligations on many entities in the AI value chain, but the lion's share of obligations falls on providers and deployers of high-risk systems.[90]

The EU AI Act places transparency and explainability front and center. Providers of high-risk AI systems must establish ways to monitor their systems after the systems have been deployed in the market, collecting and analyzing data so that the provider can continuously monitor compliance with the Act's provisions.[91] One should notice the ongoing nature of this obligation, which lasts for the lifetime of the AI system. This is not simply a box-ticking exercise. Indeed, the EU AI Act imposes significant obligations on providers when a "serious incident" occurs, which includes any incident that directly *or indirectly* leads to serious harm to a person, property, or the environment, or serious and irreversible disruption of the management or operation of critical infrastructure.[92] A report of the incident must be made "immediately after the provider has established a causal link between the AI system and the serious incident *or the reasonable likelihood of such a link*" and in any case, no later than fifteen days after either the provider or the deployer *becomes aware* of the incident.[93] (The latter requirement ensures reporting whether or not the provider is ready to assume responsibility.) These stringent obligations are aimed at making AI systems more transparent to regulators.

China's AI regulation evidences a similar concern for transparency. The Generative AI Interim Measures, which came into force in China in August 2023, require providers and users of generative AI services to take effective measures to "increase the transparency" of their technologies. In contrast to the US and EU measures, however, China's regulation provides less information on the definition of transparency.[94]

These early attempts at AI regulation by nations across the globe are likely to expand, both in terms of the content of the measures currently in place and the number of nations that choose to impose them. Ultimately, the more advanced an AI system becomes, the greater its potential impact on society – and the more stakeholders will want to have confidence in the soundness of an AI's decision-making process.[95]

Beyond transparency, the breathtaking speed and potential impact of AI inspires many commentators, including those involved in producing and developing cutting-edge AI, to call for deep and thoughtful consideration of AI's future impact on society.[96] Looming questions include whether, and to what extent, AI will: (1) affect the mental, social, and physical abilities of humans;[97] (2) ease or exacerbate disparities between groups;[98] (3) impact various employment and economic sectors;[99] (4) contribute to or mitigate issues related to climate change; and (5) and even "go-rogue" by possibly injuring, enslaving, or destroying human life.[100]

Of course, with the rapid pace of development, it is possible that many concerns with current-generation AI will be resolved. To cite one example, although a host of concerns flow from the sheer size of AI models, many researchers are hard at work developing small-language models. These can be effective, and they require significantly less data and less computing power, making them cheaper and easier to operate.[101] As for the deeply troubling black-box problem discussed earlier, companies are hard at work trying to solve it and some appear to have made considerable progress. For example, researchers at the company Anthropic claim to have "developed a technique for essentially scanning the 'brain' of an AI model, allowing them to identify collections of neurons – called 'features' – corresponding to different concepts."[102]

As captivating as all of these issues may be, this book requests your focus for only one of the infinitely engaging topics surrounding law and AI. The following pages explore the relationship between developments in AI and a fascinating, complicated, and increasingly important set of legal regimes. These regimes span an enormous territory, from the creation of artistic endeavors, to the invention of new technologies, to the development of a company's reputation, to the generation and preservation of a company's most valuable secrets. Collectively dubbed "intellectual property," these legal realms face fundamental challenges from the rise of modern AI. To understand the potential impact of AI, the following section explores the history, development, and theoretical foundations of intellectual property law in the United States.

2 AN OVERVIEW OF INTELLECTUAL PROPERTY

The theoretical foundations of intellectual property in the United States trace back to the nation's founding and are deeply embedded in its legal and historical fabric. If the reader bears with me for a page or two as I describe two moral philosophies, I promise it will get more exciting.

Throughout this history, US intellectual property regimes have predominantly adhered to an approach known as utilitarianism. In a reductionist form, this approach evaluates a potential action by weighing the overall sum of the good consequences against the bad.

In contrast to utilitarianism, some intellectual property regimes reveal occasional influences of a competing approach known as non-consequentialism. Non-consequentialism evaluates a potential action by focusing on key values, regardless of the totality of the outcomes.

At the risk of wildly oversimplifying moral philosophy, utilitarianism considers the "utility," that is, the total outcome of an action, on balance. Non-consequentialism focuses on upholding core values, regardless of whether the total consequences of an action might be positive. The sections below provide classic examples of these theories and describe how they play out in the history and operation of each of the four intellectual property regimes.

2.1 UNDERLYING THEORIES

Understanding the foundational theories of intellectual property begins with the utilitarianism described above, in which an action is justified if the overall societal outcome of the action results in more good than harm.[1] With utilitarianism in its modern context, societal outcomes are often measured by the ability of individuals to satisfy their preferences, particularly in contexts like the marketplace.

Non-consequentialist theories, on the other hand, reject any outcome-driven evaluation. Instead, they argue that certain actions are right or wrong based on their adherence to values such as morality, justice, or individual liberty, irrespective of the consequences.[2] In a non-consequentialist framework, an action that violates a fundamental right or moral standard is impermissible, even if it leads to a greater net balance of good, while an action that adheres to a fundamental right or standard is permissible, even if it leads to a greater net balance of "bad."

Now it gets more interesting.

To illustrate the fundamental difference between utilitarian and non-consequentialist theories, consider the well-known thought experiment, the trolley car dilemma. In this hypothetical scenario, a runaway trolley is headed toward a group of thirty pedestrians. You are given the option to divert the trolley by redirecting it to a different path where it will instead strike one individual standing away from the crowd.

A utilitarian focuses on the total outcome of the action and would choose the course that leads to the most favorable balance of consequences: in this case, diverting the trolley to save thirty lives at the expense of one.

A non-consequentialist, however, focuses on the action or inaction itself. From that perspective, the deliberate choice to take a single life – even if it results in a greater overall good – violates a fundamental moral principle against intentionally causing harm. Therefore, a non-consequentialist might favor inaction, even though thirty people will lose their lives.

The trolley dilemma underscores the central tension between the two moral philosophies. In some cases, however, the best decision may be the same whether one takes a utilitarian or non-consequentialist approach. For example, both utilitarians and non-consequentialists recognize the benefits of redistributive tax policies. Their rationales, however, differ sharply. For utilitarians, the primary concern is maximizing overall welfare. They argue that redistributing wealth, from those with more to those with less, can enhance societal well-being, particularly if the preferences of those with fewer resources are given greater weight.[3] This approach operates in the belief that individuals who have less tend to experience a stronger positive effect from additional resources than those who have more.[4] A single chair may mean more to someone who has no furniture than to a king who has a palace full of hundreds of chairs. Despite this analysis, utilitarians note the limits of redistribution, cautioning that if the transfer of wealth reaches the point at which it discourages productivity among higher earners, it could ultimately reduce total societal welfare, thereby undermining the very purpose of the policy.[5]

Non-consequentialists similarly support redistributive tax policies, but for a different reason. For non-consequentialists, the justification for wealth transfer lies in adhering to norms of fairness and justice, particularly the ethical demand for equality in society.[6] In this framework, redistribution is not simply a tool for maximizing welfare but a moral necessity, independent of the consequences it may produce.

To summarize, the divide between utilitarianism and non-consequentialism lies in how each approach evaluates the morality of actions. Utilitarianism centers on the outcomes, asserting that an action is right if it maximizes the balance of good over harm, with success often measured through the satisfaction of preferences, particularly in contexts like the marketplace. In contrast, non-consequentialism emphasizes the adherence to core values such as justice, autonomy, or individual liberty.

Some readers may feel pulled to different sides of the table depending on the circumstances. Others may complain that the terms within each philosophy are sufficiently malleable for adherents to reach any conclusion they want. (Others just may be glad to emerge from the philosophy section.) Nevertheless, with due apologies to the philosophy mavens, this brief tour provides all the foundation we need for turning to the intellectual property regimes themselves.

2.2 COPYRIGHTS AND PATENTS: A BRIEF TOUR

Of the four intellectual property regimes, we begin with patents and copyrights. US patent and copyright laws are fundamentally grounded in utilitarian principles. Although some scholars argue that early American legal thought reflects a diverse range of ideologies, and certain treaty obligations closely reflect the European concept of moral rights moral rights,[7] the overwhelming consensus remains that US patent and copyright laws serve a distinctly utilitarian purpose.[8] The consensus underscores the notion that patents and copyrights are not merely safeguards for individual creators but vital policy mechanisms designed to promote broader societal benefit by incentivizing innovation and creative expression.[9]

The language of the Constitution reinforces this utilitarian framework by empowering Congress to secure rights for authors and inventors with the explicit goal of promoting societal progress in the realms of science and the useful arts.[10] In philosophical terms, the focus on *promoting progress* indicates that patents and copyrights are intended to function as mechanisms for overall, utilitarian, public benefit rather than for any moral entitlements of creators.[11] The Supreme Court's 1966 ruling in *Graham* v. *John Deere* neatly underscores this interpretation, serving as a reminder that the US patent system functions to offer rewards and incentives that stimulate the production of new knowledge.

> [T]he patent monopoly was not designed to secure to the inventor his natural right in his discoveries. Rather, it was a reward, an inducement, to bring forth new knowledge.[12]

At the heart of this utilitarian rationale lies the free-rider problem faced by inventors: if inventions may be freely used by anyone, inventors may struggle to garner a return from their successful products.[13] And if inventors lose this financial incentive, innovation may decline.[14] By granting exclusive, time-limited rights, patent law shields inventors from "free-riders" who could otherwise capitalize on an invention without contributing to its development.[15] In doing so, patent law protects the American spirit of reaping the fruits of your labor while also harnessing the power of innovation for society at large.

The utilitarian calculus plays a similar role in copyright. Once an author completes a creative work, the minimal costs associated with reproduction present the same type of free-rider problem described with patents. (Think of a priceless work of art, reproduced in poster form to hang on the wall.) Absent copyright protection, creators must contend with competitors who can offer copies of their works at a fraction of the price.[16]

In another negative consequence, absent copyright protections, authors may rush to the market, ultimately devaluing important pre-publishing processes such as editing and revision.[17] In this light, a utilitarian framework underscores the necessity of copyright protections – not merely to reward authors but to ensure a vibrant, creative ecosystem that enriches society as a whole by promoting the production and dissemination of new works.

2.3 TRADEMARKS AND TRADE SECRETS: A BRIEF TOUR

As just described, US patent and copyright regimes are firmly grounded in constitutional language, reflecting their utilitarian purposes to promote societal progress. In contrast, trademark and trade secret laws follow more winding historical and philosophical paths, which are trickier, yet just as necessary to untangle. These subfields evolved through a combination of practical needs and theoretical justifications, embedding elements of both utilitarianism and consequentialism into their frameworks.

To ground our detective work in an example: the prevailing justification for US trademark law today is the consumer "search cost theory."[18] At its core, this theory suggests that trademarks serve a critical function as repositories of information about the source and quality of goods. By allowing consumers to rely on trademarks as a marker of worth, the law reduces the time, effort, and costs associated with finding products that meet one's preferences.[19] This theory – conceived by influential scholars William Landes and Richard Posner – is widely embraced in both academic circles and courtroom decisions,[20] forming the backbone of modern trademark justification.

The utilitarian essence of the search cost theory is evident in its focus on consumer welfare. Trademarks enable consumers to more effectively navigate a marketplace saturated with choices, which, in turn, enhances market efficiency. The rights granted to producers – though substantial – are not the end goal. Rather, they serve as a mechanism to maintain product quality, ensuring consumers can make informed and confident purchasing decisions. As with patent and copyright law, the benefits of trademark protection are framed in terms of the larger societal good.

The search cost theory, however, was only adopted in the late twentieth century, with the result that examining US trademark law exclusively through this theory risks obscuring the rich and varied history that preceded its adoption.[21] In its formative years through the mid nineteenth century, US trademark law was primarily concerned with protecting producers[22] against fraudulent practices[23] such as "passing off"[24] one item as another, in which deceitful actions misled consumers and diverted trade. This early perspective framed trademark law within the context of unfair competition,[25] evidencing a non-consequentialist approach that prioritized the moral rights of producers and the integrity of the marketplace.

The late nineteenth century marked a strengthening of the producer-focused framework. Courts and legal scholars increasingly justified protecting producers from illegitimate trade diversion by elevating property rights – in the form of intellectual property – to the forefront of trademark law.[26] Commenting on this period, Daniel McClure observes that "[t]reating trademarks as 'property rights' became the unifying principle for much legal reasoning."[27] Thus, the era saw trademark law conceptualized in the predominantly non-consequentialist terms of safeguarding producers' interests, protecting property rights, and upholding moral standards within the marketplace.

As the twentieth century dawned, a paradigm shift toward utilitarianism challenged the traditional, natural-rights-based doctrine that viewed trademarks as property.[28] Instead, theorists began to advocate for a model that prioritized the protection of business goodwill[29] and, more importantly, safeguarding consumers from confusion and deception.[30] A shift toward utilitarian reasoning became evident as scholars drew on insights from economics and the social sciences to assess the real-world implications of trademark law for the consumer and the marketplace.[31]

By the latter part of the twentieth century,[32] this paradigm shift reached its zenith. Scholars and courts conceptualized trademark law as a pro-competitive tool designed to enhance market efficiency.[33] This shift enabled the emergence of ideas such as the aforementioned consumer search cost theory. By the millennium, trademark law was viewed as a utilitarian mechanism for protecting both producers and consumers in the broader pursuit of enhancing market efficiency, although strains of property rights continue to play out in the litigations related to certain trademark doctrines, such as claims that someone is tarnishing or diluting a producer's brand.[34]

Turning to trade secrets – the other pillar of intellectual property lacking constitutional origins – we encounter a more muddled legal regime with an even more ambiguous theoretical foundation.[35] At its core, trade secret law seeks to safeguard commercially valuable information that is neither widely known nor easily obtainable.[36] The framework for trade secrets has always been burdened by definitional and conceptual challenges, some of which remain unresolved. In fact, the 1939 Restatement of Torts explicitly acknowledged the difficulty of arriving at a precise definition for trade secrets,[37] with language recognizing the ongoing "muddle" and "disarray" that has consistently characterized this area of law.[38]

One reason for this confusion can be found in the complex origins of trade secret law. Beginning as a state common-law doctrine – that is, based on court decisions rather than legislation – and rooted in the broader context of unfair competition, trade secret law was not initially conceived as a pillar of federal intellectual property protection. Over time, states began codifying trade secret protections, particularly through the federal Uniform Trade Secrets Act. Nevertheless, the resulting body of law remained patchwork. Even the federal Defend Trade Secrets Act, introduced and adopted in 2016, leans heavily on these state doctrines.[39] The result is a legal framework shaped by a range of justifications that often pull in different directions.[40]

These justifications, accumulated through case law, span a broad spectrum. They range from property rights[41] and the regulation of unfair competition, to economic efficiency,[42] to commercial ethics, and even to the encouragement of invention.[43] This array of rationales reflects the multifaceted nature and conflicting principles of trade secret laws, underscoring the challenge of constructing a cohesive theoretical framework for this pillar of intellectual property.

The conflicting prerogatives emerge in the early court cases, which often used a complex blend of justifications for protecting trade secrets. One key example is the *Peabody* v. *Norfolk* case,[44] decided by the Massachusetts Supreme Court in 1868 and widely regarded as the first major dictum on trade secrets.[45] In his opinion, Justice Gray initially highlighted the utilitarian importance of encouraging innovation,[46] but much of his following argument was anchored in the non-consequentialist notion of upholding property rights.[47]

Nevertheless, by the early twentieth century, the property-based view of trade secrets came under scrutiny.[48] Justice Holmes' oft-cited opinion in the 1917 case of *DuPont* v. *Masland* explicitly rejected the property justification in favor of focusing on the bad acts of those who have betrayed the confidence of the trade secret holder:

> The word "property" as applied to trademarks and trade secrets is an unanalyzed expression of certain secondary consequences of the primary fact that the law makes some rudimentary requirements of good faith. Whether the plaintiffs have any valuable secret or not, the defendant knows the facts, whatever they are, through a special confidence that he accepted. The property may be denied, but the confidence cannot be.[49]

Thus, Justice Holmes emphasized that the core goal of trade secret law was not about property ownership, but rather, about *the breach of confidential relations*. This approach shifted the justification for trade secrets from property rights to ethical responsibilities within business relationships, highlighting a different non-consequentialist value.[50]

The Law and Economics movement of the 1960s introduced yet another pivotal reorientation of trade secret law – this time toward a grounding in the economic efficiency of informational markets. Courts and scholars began to reframe trade secret protection, moving away from the justification of natural property rights or ethics to viewing trade secrets as a necessary tool for stimulating innovation. Information, although expensive to produce, could be easily and cheaply replicated. Therefore, information required protection to ensure that market actors had sufficient incentive to invest in its creation. Trade secret law thus became a means of preventing "free riding" – similar to the effects of patent law discussed earlier. As such, trade secret law shifted once again, this time toward a utilitarian justification centered on optimizing the production of information within the marketplace.[51]

Despite its fragmented historical origins, US trade secret law has ultimately converged around a central theme of promoting marketplace competition. As Graves and Katyal observe, modern formulations of trade secret law consistently reflect this competitive focus.[52] One should note, however, that although the market-based justification has gained widespread acceptance, some scholars maintain that the law's historical underpinnings conflict with the modern framework with the result, they argue, that US trade secret law lacks a unifying normative theory.[53]

In brief, all four pillars of intellectual property – patents, copyrights, trade secrets, and trademarks – are currently grounded in utilitarian principles despite meandering paths. At their core, these intellectual property systems exist to promote societal welfare by incentivizing innovation and enhancing market efficiency. Although these regimes protect the rights of producers and creators, that protection serves as a vehicle for achieving broader societal gains.

Notably, US intellectual property regimes generally have resisted invoking morality as a justification for protections. Throughout the country's history, patent law occasionally has denied applications on moral grounds,[54] nixing protection for gambling devices and fraudulent articles.[55] Nevertheless, the United States Patent and Trademark Office (USPTO) gradually abandoned this justification, determining that enforcing morality requirements falls outside of their authority[56] – a stance supported by courts[57] and scholars.[58] In addition, the United States is a signatory to certain international copyright treaties that speak to the moral rights of authors, but these are exceptions to the general rule.[59]

Beginning in 1946, Congress also tried to codify morality provisions within trademark law by barring the registration of immoral, scandalous, or disparaging trademarks.[60] The provision, however, was deemed unconstitutional by the Supreme Court in 2011 in its unanimous *Matal* v. *Tam* decision.[61] The court held that, in the context of trademarks, freedom of speech – guaranteed by the First Amendment – takes precedence over any claims of immorality.[62] Thus, to the extent that trade secret law had been deployed in the service of morality, the Supreme Court decision narrowed trademark's focus to maintaining good-faith behavior in business, rather than imposing broader morality standards.[63]

On the whole, therefore, the intellectual property system lacks the framework for examining any of the weighty moral concerns posed by artificial intelligence, leaving ethical decision-making to other realms. In this book, we will do the same, given that the structures at hand are too rickety to support these discussions, while remaining mindful of the need to address such critical topics in their place and time.

More broadly, intellectual property regimes have largely moved away from all non-consequentialist stirrings, including moral rights and producer rights, as well as any overarching property rights framework. Instead, today's intellectual property regimes prioritize utilitarian goals related to promoting societal progress. We will see these utilitarian goals play out as the book explores how the rapid expansion of AI puts pressure on the realms covered by the intellectual property umbrella – invention (patent), expression (copyright), business information (trade secret), and reputation (trademark).

AI is already straining what we value, how we value it, and whether the intellectual property system can continue supporting that value in the face of so much upheaval. These questions will be of critical importance to the future of intellectual property, yet they have received little attention. But first, how could one possibly write a book about AI and IP without examining the fascinating issues captured in today's headlines? This leads us to the current hot topics.

PART II

Hot Topics in AI and IP

3 DO TRAINING MODELS INFRINGE COPYRIGHT?

ChatGPT burst onto the national scene in November 2022.[1] Since then, public attention has been riveted on debates over artificial intelligence and intellectual property. We've seen an avalanche of literature, commentary, speculation, and litigation, particularly related to large language models[2] but also regarding similar models for music, videos, and imagery. Throughout this whirlwind, discussion has centered heavily on the copyright regime,[3] but additional issues include patents, inventorship, and rights of publicity.[4]

Copyright has been the primary focus of contention for the simple reason that modern large language models are a generative kind of AI tool, that is, they generate content. Specifically, they are capable of producing text, images, sounds, videos, and more in response to some human input, typically referred to as a "prompt."[5] The outputs of these AI systems can look quite creative – so much so that for many AI-generated works, it is an open question to what extent they should be entitled to copyright protection on account of their originality. From the opposite perspective, they might also be susceptible to copyright enforcement actions due to their possible infringement on other works.

The outputs aren't the only aspect of generative AI that has inspired the flurry of debate and discussion. Crucial to the controversy is how these models are trained.[6] (Recall the discussion about deep learning and neural networks from Chapter 1: the model is first trained with starting information, the patterns and probabilities are developed in that process, and then the model is deployed to respond to a prompt.) The most complicated questions revolve around whether the act of training these models results in copyright infringement.[7]

This leads us right to the doorstep of the most prominent and consequential controversies that concern AI and copyright infringement. Before describing these, a few paragraphs of legal primer are in order: How does copyright law work in practice? The following is a tremendously condensed tour of the key doctrines as they apply to the question of whether large language models engage in copyright infringement.

In technical terms, copyright law protects original works of authorship fixed in a tangible medium of expression. Originality is key to deciding if a work is entitled to copyright protection. One might think originality means creativity, particularly in a field related to creative expression, but that is not what it means at all. Rather, originality just means the author created it, rather than copying.

As for the amount of creativity, copyright law requires remarkably little. In the words of the Supreme Court, "the requisite level of creativity is extremely low" and works will qualify for copyright as long as they have "some creative spark, 'no matter how crude, humble or obvious' it might be."[8] The amount of effort makes no difference, either. Whether the work took ten years to create, or ten seconds, copyright law cares only that the work contain at least a "modicum" of creativity.[9] Thus, a laborious but uncreative compilation of pre-existing information probably would not yield a copyright, while a particularly creative or original grouping of those same facts probably would.[10]

As discussed in Chapter 2 of Part I, a copyright gives the legal owner the right to prevent others from making unauthorized copies of protected material without permission.[11] Those rights are subject, of course, to the all-important doctrine of fair use, which serves as a limit on the power of the copyright owner.

Fair use, currently codified by Congress in the Copyright Act of 1976[12] but venerable in its origins,[13] represents the proposition that in some circumstances, it may be societally beneficial to allow copying of copyrighted material. Fair-use determinations are fact-intensive and hinge on four factors specified in the Copyright Act. A court balances the results of these factors together, a muddy practice that can make outcomes difficult to predict.

The first factor examines the purpose and character of the use, particularly whether the use is of a commercial nature. For example, copying excerpts from a work for the purpose of commenting on that work likely constitutes an appropriate use; making bootleg copies of a movie to sell at the local flea market likely does not.

The full wording of the Copyright Act's first fair use factor requires consideration of, "the purpose and character of the use, including whether such use is of a commercial nature or is for nonprofit educational purposes."[14] The language could be read to suggest that any commercial use, outside of one for non-profit educational purposes, would automatically fail the first factor. Nevertheless, the Supreme Court has explained that even commercial endeavors may constitute appropriate uses under the first fair use factor. According to the Justices, the question is whether the commercial activity falls within the general purposes of fair use, which are listed in the Copyright Act's preamble as including criticism, comment, news reporting and others, as well as whether they constitute a purpose that is "transformative."[15]

Consider the 1994 Supreme Court case which featured a rap song pitted against a classic rock-music ballad. The rap group 2 Live Crew had created a parody of Roy Orbison's song "Oh, Pretty Woman." The Supreme Court held that the parody constituted an appropriate purpose and satisfied fair use, despite the commercial nature of 2 Live Crew's work. Specifically, the court explained the inquiry under the first factor as constituting whether the accused work "adds something new, with a further purpose or different character, altering the first [work] with new expression, meaning, or message; it asks, in other words, whether and to what extent the new work is 'transformative.'"[16] Given the line of case law that has developed, the first factor in modern fair-use cases often turns on the transformative nature of the use.

The second factor considers "the nature of the copyrighted work" itself. For example, traditionally creative works such as literature and art receive a higher level of protection than more technical works such as computer programs. The third factor examines how much of the original work is used, and the amount that is considered *too* much may depend on the other factors, including the purpose of the copying.[17] For example, a comedian making a parody of a work for entertainment might get away with a lot, while a commercial competitor might infringe by copying even a small but critical amount. Finally, the fourth factor considers the effect the use may have on the potential market for the original. Courts are especially sensitive when the new work can be said to commercially supersede the original's market by competing with it.[18]

A technical concept emerges in applying the fair-use factors, one that has special relevance to generative AI. That concept is known as "intermediate copying." In simple terms, intermediate copying occurs when a work is copied *not* for its own sake, but *in order to aid or facilitate some other goal* – whether that goal is to create an all-new work that explicitly does not infringe on the original, or to learn about computer software in order to design compatible materials.[19] For example, computer-game companies have examined a competitor's code in an effort to make their own product compatible, as opposed to simply trying to copy the competitor's game.[20] Although courts generally agree it is possible for intermediate copying to constitute fair use,[21] the case results vary.[22] Even within the gaming context, some courts have found intermediate copying to be fair use under the case's particular circumstances,[23] while others have not.[24]

In the current context, we know that the training of generative AI models often involves scraping[25] publicly accessible data – whether text, images, videos, or other forms of content (see Chapter 1). This data is then methodically fed into the model to teach it.[26] The goal of this data-hungry training process is, of course, to enable the model to provide high-quality outputs once training is complete.[27] Thus, whether intermediate copying has occurred in the training process and if so, whether that copying constitutes a transformative use in the first fair-use factor, likely will play a leading role in decisions on how copyright law applies to generative AI.

In addition to the basic concepts within fair use, certain normative considerations are likely to set the stage for any case law regarding whether generative AI infringes copyrights. As discussed in the Introduction and Chapter 2, copyright law in the United States is rooted in the constitutional goal of promoting innovation. ("To promote the Progress of Science and useful Arts."[28]) If generative AI is permitted to continue developing without inhibition, the technology may promote innovation at a speed and scale hard to imagine just a few years ago.[29] This is all the more likely given its broad application to a wide range of disciplines and industries.[30] Put simply, the very existence and continued improvement of generative AI furthers the Constitution's stated goal of promoting innovation.[31]

Moreover, at least for now, generative AI requires vast amounts of data, up to and including attempts to compile all text-based data that is publicly available on the Internet.[32] Arguably, if training data were limited to public domain data, as well as data for which a license has been negotiated, models of this scale would not be able to exist. As discussed in the solution section of this chapter (Section 3.2), for example, it would no longer be possible to train models using collections of scraped data from the Internet, such as those produced by Common Crawl.[33] Data for training would have to be individually checked to confirm it is in the public domain or licensed, posing a prohibitive burden and cost. Thus, only a tiny fraction of copyrighted data would make its way into the models, severely limiting their efficacy.[34] (Note that in Chapter 6, I will propose a way to address precisely that problem.)

Despite these public benefits, there is a tense relationship between the promise of generative AI and the consequences it may have on human-driven innovation. One view among scholars and commentators holds that if courts believe generative AI constitutes fair use, the decision would stymie creativity by decreasing the incentives for people to produce creative works.[35] Others think it would boost creativity, because generative AI reduces the skill barriers to creation.[36] A third theory is that, although generative AI may increase the quantity of creative works, it will ultimately decrease their quality, especially in the long run.[37] A version of this argument worries that in the future, most creative works available on the Internet will be AI-generated, and as a result, most future *training data* will be AI-generated too. The concern is that training AI on artificially generated data might be bad for the technology's continued improvement. This loop would create an "inbreeding" problem that could theoretically result in the worsening of generative AI over time.[38] It's hard to know what combination of downstream effects there will be, but we can be sure that legal practitioners and AI technicians will be contemplating these possibilities in the coming months and years.

Against this normative background lies the question of what to do with emerging technological inventions. Although some might argue that AI presents a uniquely dramatic technological shift, it is certainly not the first time courts have faced copyright claims against new technologies. In recent decades, the Supreme Court generally has chosen not to block technologies with ostensible societal benefits, absent legislative guidance. In the Betamax case,[39] for example, the Supreme Court considered whether home videotape recorders infringed on television studios' copyrights. In a 5–4 decision, the Court reasoned that a "home videotape recorder was capable of substantial non-infringing uses," and therefore, the manufacturers' sale of such recorders did not constitute copyright infringement.[40] In further support of its ruling, the Court pointed to its own prior practice, noting that "[t]he judiciary's reluctance to expand the protections afforded by the copyright without explicit legislative guidance is a recurring theme [,]"[41] and explaining that "[s]ound policy, as well as history, supports our consistent deference to Congress when major technological innovations alter the market for copyrighted materials."[42]

In the years following Betamax, the Supreme Court has declined review for several similar cases. In each scenario, new, potentially copyright-infringing applications of technologies were deemed fair use by lower courts. To use one example from 2007, the Supreme Court let stand a Ninth Circuit ruling that the Google search engine's display of thumbnail images was fair use given that those thumbnails were "highly transformative."[43] The court took into account the fact that "Google incorporates the entire image into the search engine results[,]"[44] and gave its decision "in light of [the search engine's] public benefit[.]"[45] A decade later, the Supreme Court once again declined certiorari in a major copyright case, this time in the matter of Google Books.[46] There, the Second Circuit's key holding determined that Google's creation of, and reliance on, a database containing entire copies of copyrighted texts *was* fair use. The court reasoned that the purpose was sufficiently transformative, and "the copying of the totality of the original [...] is literally necessary to achieve that purpose."[47] Here, too, the court's focus on public benefit is palpable.[48]

Yet the Supreme Court has not always ruled in favor of fair use in these cases. Consider a file-sharing platform called Grokster.[49] Grokster's technology, built on billions of files exchanged per month across peer-to-peer networks, was more decentralized than prior file-sharing services[50] – a characteristic that made enforcement actions against it more difficult.[51] Notwithstanding that difficulty, an investigation revealed that Grokster openly encouraged infringement by routinely inviting its users to download copyrighted works. Perhaps it should come as no surprise that in a unanimous opinion, the Supreme Court held that when a technology *intends* to promote copyright infringement, the distributor is liable for the infringement perpetrated by that technology's users.[52] Although the Supreme Court did not itself conduct a fair-use analysis – perhaps it felt the evidence was too flagrant to require one – the Court made clear that technology companies promoting *others* engaging in blatant copyright infringement using their platforms were on the hook.[53] In the end, the Grokster case sends a message: Don't try to be too clever. Understandably, the Supreme Court may be suspicious of technologies that appear to be little more than burglars' tools designed to pick a legal lock.

As courts turn their focus to whether generative AI models constitute copyright infringement, how will the court view these new technologies? Are generative AI models likely to be viewed as an exciting innovation with potential public benefit, as little more than burglar's tools designed to pick a legal lock, or as something else entirely. The following section will explore these questions further.

3.1 CURRENT CASES

We've seen a whirlwind of litigation so far asserting copyright infringement against producers of generative AI models. The infringement claims generally arise from (1) the way companies train their models and (2) the outputs those models ultimately produce. For example, in *New York Times* v. *Microsoft* (in which both Microsoft and OpenAI are defendants), the *New York Times* alleged that the defendants infringed on *The Times*' copyrights in several ways, including by (1) making and storing copies of *The Times*' copyrighted works to train their models and (2) producing outputs that closely mirror, sometimes verbatim, *The Times*' copyrighted works.[54] Having just read the brief tour of fair use, the reader won't be surprised that, in its memorandum supporting a motion to dismiss the case, the defense dedicated space to

"Longstanding Fair use Principles."[55] The motion remained undecided at the time of this writing.

Other disputes take a similar tack. In each of *Alter* v. *OpenAI*,[56] *Doe* v. *Github*,[57] and *Leovy* v. *Google*,[58] plaintiffs allege, among other things, some combination of copyright infringement by using and storing copyrighted works for model training purposes, and infringement based on similarities between the output of the large language models and the copyrighted works. So far, there have been dozens of complaints filed against AI companies on similar grounds,[59] and at the time of this writing, none of these cases has reached a final judgment. Nor do we have any guarantee the cases will *ever* reach a judgment, given that dismissals and settlements are always a possibility. It may be years before we see even one published district court judgment,[60] and even longer before we begin to see the circuit courts weigh in. This is to say nothing of when, or if, we will hear from the Supreme Court.

Of course, legal and policy thinkers aren't letting their pens run dry while the many cases run their course. Over the past few years, intellectual property scholars have expressed their views prolifically on whether, how, and to what extent copyright law and the doctrine of fair use applies or should apply to machine learning, deep learning, and generative artificial intelligence. The views vary widely. Some have argued that the courts need not slog through the factors of fair use. Rather, the first and fourth fair use factors (purpose and effect on the market) weigh so strongly against the possibility of ever finding fairness with these technologies that fair use simply should not be applied in generative AI cases.[61] Others argue that generative AI models could be constructed, trained, and used in a way that would reliably support fair use, but that fair use analysis should never be assumed, and should continue to involve a careful, case-by-case analysis.[62] Still others assert that because AI models are trained on "unprotectible meta-knowledge"[63] and not on copyrightable subject matter, copyright infringement claims levied against model training practices "should be dismissed at the front gate . . . rather than through the backdoor of fair use[.]"[64]

A fourth line of scholarship suggests that courts should adopt a "prompt-based model of copyright." This would shift the focus from the material used to create the model and towards the prompt a user enters.[65] Despite the variation in these views, they contain a common refrain. They all suggest that we should be careful to avoid the trap of "overzealous rights enforcement," which risks "undermin[ing] the democratic and egalitarian potential of generative AI."[66]

The generative AI cases themselves provide a good sandbox for readers to develop or test their own views. The cases differ from each other, and they likely differ from future cases, as well. Nevertheless, these lawsuits on the whole present a series of endlessly interesting questions for the courts to decide.

The easiest of the copyright issues falls within the first steps of the training process, when as much as a quadrillion bytes of data may be scraped from the Internet to use in training the model. Let's assume copyright owners are able to prove that at least some amount of their protected material existed within the vast expanse of harvested data. If so, when the engineer downloads the information, that download likely constitutes a "copy."

We are talking about the moment before the system even begins the process of breaking down the data and using it to help develop patterns and probabilities. Rather, just the simple act of downloading can constitute copying. Thus, regardless of whatever other actions in the training process constitute copying, most likely, we have already encountered it. That's what makes this the easiest question.

Copying, however, is not the end of the story. The more salient question concerns whether that copying constitutes fair use. As to that question, the training process for generative AI is reminiscent of the intermediate copying cases described before in the context of computer gaming and compatibility.[67] According to these cases, intermediate copying occurs as part of a process towards a goal *other than* simply copy the work. In the gaming context, the goal was *not* to copy the competitor's game but to ensure compatibility.

As noted in the prior section, courts generally agree that intermediate copying may constitute fair use. The results can vary, however, depending on the circumstances,[68] and one examines those circumstances under the fair-use factors.

To apply those factors in our setting, recall that the first fair-use factor considers the purpose and character of the use, with modern cases focusing particularly on whether the purpose of the use is transformative. A transformative purpose, the Supreme Court has explained, involves adding something new "with a further purpose or different character."[69] Thus, in our setting, the question will be whether the courts consider the creation of generative AI systems to be transformative. On the one hand, courts might view generative AI as similar to search engines displaying thumbnail-sized images or the Google Books project uploading copies of library books. On the other hand, the Supreme Court could choose to drastically reduce the space that has been given to emerging technologies, particularly by the appellate courts. Most important, one should stress, is that these are new and evolving areas of law, parts of which have been decided only at the appellate level, rather than reaching the Supreme Court.

Moving on, the fourth fair use factor, regarding the effect on the copyright owner's market, may be a more delicate question for generative AI models to handle, at least at some stages in the process. When considering effect on the market, there's a difference between a new work that directly *substitutes for* an original work[70] (likely problematic) and a new work that creates additional options for consumers while depressing the market for the original work.[71] If someone writes a brilliant parody making fun of a popular song, fewer people may buy the original as more people buy the parody. But copyright law would consider this as fair use, given that a parody comments on, but does not substitute for, the original.

Similarly, an AI model that gives users new ways to obtain unprotected material, for example, putting together a sample itinerary for a trip to Italy, may be engaging in fair use, even if the Italian Tourist Bureau would rather that users visit *their* website to view the advertisers.

From a more subtle perspective, suppose there is a bustling market for human artists who create custom logos for companies at a high fee. Thanks, in part,[72] to being trained on all the logos publicly available on the internet, a generative AI model then becomes capable of reproducing *completely novel* logos within seconds. The market for human-created logos collapses, drastically reducing the cost of purchasing a new logo (and presumably reducing the value of preexisting logos as well). That is a negative market effect, but not because the AI model is offering any copies.

On the other hand, the most difficult case for a generative AI model exists when the model's responses to prompts contain an extensive amount of protected expression, such as when the prompts exhibit memorization. I will consider memorization in greater detail below, but it is worth noting that such memorization presents a direct challenge to the original work's market potential. When a generative AI model reproduces copyrighted works that the owner keeps behind a paywall, that response substitutes for the owner's market.[73]

The second and third fair-use factors are likely to fall in the direction that the courts move with the other factors above. The second fair-use factor considers the nature of the original work, with traditional creative works receiving greater protection than computer software. The third fair-use factor considers the amount of the work copied – in other words, if one claims fairness, one should not take more than is necessary.

If a court finds that the purpose of a generative AI model is sufficiently transformative, then copying the full amount of the work in creating the training data may be necessary to accomplish that transformative purpose. Courts have found that when taking the entire amount is necessary for an appropriate use, the activity can constitute fair use.[74] The nature of the original work could be applied with the same logic – that is, the transformative purpose of generative AI could not be accomplished without inputting all types of works. On the other hand, if courts find that creating a generative AI model fails to constitute a sufficiently transformative purpose, the other factors likely will fail, as well.

The analysis above considered the copying through the simple inputting of the original data. The next question concerns whether the model itself should be considered to contain copies of the original work after it has been fully trained.

For most people, it may be tempting to say that the AI model must contain copies of the work, or at least a paint-by-numbers version of the work. But hopefully, readers will have some sense by now that the information contained in a generative AI model is quite different from, and far more sophisticated than, a simple snapshot, xerox, or paint-by-numbers version of the work. Rather, as described in Chapter 1, an AI model's billions or trillions of parameters are each a mathematical structure that assigns different levels of importance to patterns and connections that might appear in the prompt. There are no one-to-one correlations between the structures and the inputted data. Rather the billions of structures emerged as the training process bounced varying pieces of data off each other to find the patterns and connections.

Each structure contains the instructions needed to run the transformation process in which the input (prompt) interacts with this and other structures to eventually become the output (response). In other words, these cannot be characterized as computer files of copyrighted work.

Thus, in my view, the model itself does not contain "copies" of the original works. Nor is the model running repeated copies of those works when it performs the transformations on the prompt that a user enters. From this perspective, copyright owners would have difficulty successfully asserting a claim against the model itself, as opposed to the training of the model.

We now move to the stage in which the model runs the user's prompt repeatedly through the billions or trillions of sets of instructions in the model to predict and build each piece of a likely appropriate response. If the response does not directly contain a significant amount of the original work's protected material, the copyright owner has little to complain about.

Now, however, we move to the most challenging part of the copyright analysis. As discussed in Chapter 1,[75] generative AI models have been known to exhibit memorization. That is, although the models do not contain anything like a copy or even some form or an "encoded"[76] copy, they nonetheless exhibit the ability at times to reproduce training data nearly, although not entirely, verbatim.[77] I say not entirely, because there seem to be small variations from the original work.

Does this mean that the model somehow *does* contain a copy? From a human perspective, it's hard to see such side-by-side comparisons of output and *not* conclude there must be some sort of stored copy somewhere – and that is more or less *The Times*' argument as expressed in the complaint.[78] Nevertheless, recall, once again, that a given model's billions or trillions of parameters are just numerical structures, each with probable levels of connection to certain patterns or connections and each containing instructions for the transformation processes that will be used to develop a response to the prompt.[79] Moreover, the same prompt can yield different outputs each time the model is run – sometimes slightly different and sometimes drastically so.[80] Given these facts, perhaps the most one could say about the model itself is that the parameters might (although scientists do not yet completely understand why) contain mathematical structures that could potentially recreate a given work, at some times, for some prompts, although not always.

This framing still would not lead to the conclusion that the model *contains* a copy of the work, but it does lead to another important moment in the analysis. When a generative model responds with a largely exact copy of the original work, does that response constitute copying? As with the original question, this seems to be reasonably manageable. When a generative AI model (or any technology) produces outputs which, considered alone, would amount to copyright infringement by a human, then the standard copyright rules should apply.[81] In the *New York Times* case, we have a commercial model that produced a work substantially similar[82] to a preexisting copyrighted work. *The Times* should be able to enforce their copyright, unless, of course, the defendants can convince the courts that fair use should apply. That analysis would return to the four fair-use factors, particularly the first factor, related to the transformative nature of the technology, and the fourth factor, concerning whether the model's responses substitute in the market for the original work.

Although the fair use doctrine lists each of the factors separately, the doctrine does not look for a particular tally or accounting. Rather, courts consider all of the relevant factors, weighing them together to reach a result. In that sense, fair use is more of an art than a science. Thus, at the end of the day, the generative AI cases may turn on how heavily courts weigh the minority of memorization responses – ones that have the potential to substitute for the original work in the market – against the transformative nature of the majority of the unproblematic responses that the technology provides.

3.2 COURT, CONTRACT, AND TECHNOLOGICAL SOLUTIONS

Given the novelty and complexity of the issues, only a fool would try to predict how a court will rule. As a reminder, here are four of AI's highly unusual characteristics: (1) Generative AI models tend to be trained on data that is copyrighted *and* not copyrighted, and it is difficult to unscramble the two strains after the fact. (2) The models themselves do not store copies of copyrighted data, though they occasionally exhibit the ability to *remember* that data, in a way that even the model makers do not fully understand. (3) The same AI model can be used for a wide array of purposes, including but in no way limited to facts-based question-and-answer queries, math tutoring, proofreading, and short-story writing. (4) AI outputs can range from "completely novel" to "verbatim reproduction," and everything in between.

And of course, the reader should take all the analysis and speculation above with a full tablespoon of salt. The Supreme Court's composition has changed considerably from the periods of any of the cases described above. Justice Thomas is the only current Justice who was on the Court for Grokster, and none were members for the Betamax decision.[83] Moreover, some of the Court's most important fair-use rulings were far from unanimous: the Betamax decision was decided 5 to 4.[84] When it comes to predicting how the courts will handle novel issues such as copyright and AI, no one has a crystal ball.

Whatever the courts rule, the implications will be significant. Deep learning and generative AI's technical workings are deeply intertwined with copyright.[85] Therefore, a ruling on the question of copyright infringement will affect the speed and trajectory of the technology's development and may determine its continued existence. It would not be the first time a court ruling sent a new technology into a tailspin: consider Napster, a revolutionary system for sharing music files that launched in 1999. Although the case never reached the Supreme Court, Napster's demise began when a district court in San Francisco denied fair use and held that the company must prevent users from sharing any copyrighted works – a requirement Napster could not meet.[86] Only time, and the courts, will tell.

Although the courts are likely to decide in some capacity, the major parties could preempt the courts, resolving their disputes in other ways. By choosing to settle out of court, the parties could avoid the risk of establishing unfavorable legal precedents.

The major artificial intelligence companies, however, may prefer to see these cases through to their conclusion, given that a settlement would involve only the copyright holders who are part of each particular case. Settling, therefore, may only be a stopgap, falling short of solving the issue for all possible claimants, now and in the future. Although risky, taking the issue through the courts may offer a more secure and long-term solution.

Nevertheless, resolution by contract may ultimately provide the smoothest route, if a reasonable approach can be hammered out. One option involves reaching a payment-flow deal between the creative content industry and the AI industry.[87] The parties could agree to limitations on the production of outright, identical copies of the works, along with a mechanism to provide royalties for use of the works in training data. Courts could enforce these limitations in case of transgression.

Models do exist for this. The market could handle a royalty system that would benefit large and small players alike, and it has done, so even when a limited use does not justify the effort necessary to obtain a copyright license. Consider how the market has handled song royalties, going all the way back to the days when a coffee shop might have played the radio for background music. In those days, a particular artist's song might drift over the airwaves multiple times a day as different servers started their shifts and tuned in to different stations. The transaction costs necessary for the coffee shop to keep track of the songs played, and their frequency, not to mention tracking down the artists in order to pay them for their original work, would be prohibitive. Despite these challenging circumstances, non-profit rights organizations emerged, known as ASCAP (American Society of Composers, Authors and Publishers) and BMI (Broadcast Music, Inc.). These entities provide a classic model for collective rights organization, serving as a link between music copyright holders and businesses (such as the coffee shop mentioned above) that play their music: issuing licenses, tracking use, and arranging royalty distribution even if it is small.[88] Coordinated bodies like these could create a system that generates a small level of payment for copyright holders – and paying up each time would be cheaper for AI companies than the risk of a massive infringement fine.

Without such a broad contract deal, only the large players, such as major record labels or publishing houses, are likely to reach contractual agreements with artificial intelligence developers. The transaction costs are worth it for the big players on both sides, given the amount of content and the value that content presents. For small players, however, the cost of reaching a deal would be more than its probable return. Think of a small, solo artist and a neighborhood hardware store. Neither would be likely to arrange such licensing deals alone. Thus, a universal payment model would be better for all.

For some copyright holders today, it may be difficult to swallow any type of agreement with the generative artificial intelligence industry. Some copyright owners might be concerned with the principles at stake, not the transaction costs of reaching an agreement. Other copyright owners may view the use of their works in massive sets of training data as intangible yet existential incursions on their creativity. Still others may object to the imitation of their signature practices – even though such style and imitation are not protected by copyright, as described below.[89]

Unfortunately, throwing one's shoes into the machinery is more whimsical than effective. Although reaching a deal with infringers may seem odious to some, it may ultimately be preferable to the alternatives. A well-worn adage from a 1916 political cartoon, although cynical, is particularly apt. To paraphrase, even when someone says, "it's not about the money, it's the principle," it's the money.[90] In other words, principles may yield – or at least be satisfied – when dollars are on the table.

The adage also aligns with the theoretical underpinnings of intellectual property in the United States. As discussed in Part I, these foundations are almost entirely utilitarian in the economic sense of the term. A reasonable and contractual payment system, that offers economic benefit to society at large, fits within the theoretical orientation of the US intellectual property regimes.

Apart from potential contractual solutions, technical solutions may crop up in the near future. One category of technical solutions involves copyright owners erecting their own defenses: making it harder for AI companies to find and use their copyrighted data for training purposes. Already, many companies request removal of their data from the Common Crawl, so that it cannot be used in this or another manner.[91] Instead of finding everything in this free one-stop shop, those who train model would have to seek data from some less convenient, less-inclusive, or more expensive source. Companies could also put more of their data behind paywalls,[92] or try to limit the amount of time data appears on the internet.

A third possibility is to render one's copyrighted data unusable for model training. Such tools already exist: A company called *Nightshade* has developed a tool that they claim turns a company's copyrighted materials into a kind of poison pill. If used as training data, it can permanently damage an AI model.[93] I suspect we may see this type of approach deployed with increasing frequency, though not without potential legal pitfalls. These technologies foreshadow what may eventually escalate into a kind of AI training-data arms race, with each side trying to develop technological ways to gain the upper hand or at least limit the other's technologies.

Another category of technical solutions focuses on how the technology will appear to judges and laypeople – in other words, trying to make it easier for courts to find fair use. Although this is only loosely technical, a company could ensure that all its internal and external communications provide crystal-clear evidence that the intended purpose of its AI model is transformative. An AI company that consistently focuses on promoting the generation of *novel* outputs, demonstrating a clear intention that the model *not* be used to create infringing works, would be in a much better position than Grokster, which actively promoted infringement.[94] In the same vein, AI companies would be wise to take a leaf out of Google Books and find ways to limit output size to snippets[95] – if not in all cases, then at least when an input appears likely to result in an output of copyrighted material.

It might be difficult to limit the length of material used in the training process itself, but there may also be self-monitoring mechanisms available to AI companies to limit their infringement. Unlike search engines, which traditionally search for a particular string of words, generative AI systems can answer queries that simultaneously relate to different parts of a text, identifying patterns. This typically requires training on the full text. The training process, however, has a better chance of claiming that the use is "transformative" and meets the definition of fair use if, at the end of the day, the answer to a user's query is not substantially similar to the original work.[96] With this in mind, generative AI models could be developed in which the system runs each answer through a quick test, similar to those currently available to detect plagiarism. Copyright owners might then argue that running the response through a plagiarism check entails making a "copy," but the model company would have a strong argument that its action constituted fair use.[97] The purpose of retaining the database would be to *prevent* copyright infringement, providing an appealing argument that the purpose of use is an appropriate one and that the action does not harm the copyright owner's market.

Model-makers may even find ways of training that do not require copying at all – a technical speculation that goes well beyond the scope of this book. Nevertheless, it is at least conceivable that future developments may enable model training by merely examining the contents of a link without downloading those contents or making anything that could be construed as a copy.[98]

I have no doubt that by the time this book comes off the press, we'll see many more innovations, solutions, and countermeasures around AI and copyright questions. Some of them may simplify things, while others will inevitably introduce new complications. No matter what, the field will be active – and unpredictable – for the foreseeable future.

4 IP FOR AI CREATIONS?

Apart from the copyright-infringement questions discussed above, other debates focus on the other side of the coin: whether creations designed or co-designed by AI systems should themselves receive intellectual property protection. Such is the duality of AI. Like a human, AI can be both an infringer and a creator.

So far, issues related to AI as a creator have arisen only as a matter of copyright law (within the topic of authorship) and patent law (within the topic of inventorship).[1] Within the two intellectual property realms, AI as a creator appears in the context of two hot-topic legal questions: The first asks whether, as a legal matter, artificial intelligence itself should be recognized as the author of a copyright-protected creation or the inventor of a patented work.

At least for the moment, the legal perspective on the first question is abundantly clear. Current intellectual property law does not permit AI to be the legal author of a copyrighted work[2] nor to be the legal inventor of a patented one.[3] Even the most advanced AI models are still, at the end of the day, just computer software,[4] and there is considerable historical and legal precedent establishing that only *humans* can be authors or inventors. The US Copyright Office has been crystal clear on this point,[5] and courts have held that statutory standing for a non-person to sue under The Copyright Act must be explicitly granted by an Act of Congress.[6] Similarly, the US Patent and Trademark Office has stated it "recognizes that [...] an AI system may not be named an inventor or joint inventor in a patent or patent application,"[7] referring to a 2023 Federal Circuit opinion that explicitly held as much in saying that, "only a natural person can be an inventor, so AI cannot be."[8] The current outlook could not be clearer than that.

In my view, both the Copyright Office and the Patent Office have adopted the appropriate approach, not only legally, but also practically and normatively. As I explained in public testimony to the Patent Office in May 2023, "both in terms of the incentives given to people by listing them as the inventor of a patent and in terms of the susceptibility to deterrence presented by rights controlled by others, it is neither socially desirable nor entirely coherent to list AI on patents."[9] After all, "would we really want to assign a patent, as an initial starting point, to an entity that cannot be deterred from encroachments on the rights of other inventors, such as patent infringement, patent misuse, or any other form of sanctionable behavior?"[10] These same arguments apply to copyright authorship as well.

Proponents do, indeed, exist for the notion that AI models should be recognized as authors or inventors. Some scholars see practical benefits in changing the law to allow copyright for AI-created works, such as ensuring there are sufficient incentives to use generative AI.[11] And to date, at least two countries – Australia and South Africa – have recognized an AI system as an inventor under patent law at least once.[12] In the case of Australia, however, that recognition didn't last when the high court later reversed the decision.[13] At the end of the day, legal academics seem to be largely united in their rejection of AI systems as inventors.[14]

The arguments in favor of authorship or inventorship recognition are fascinating from a philosophical and theoretical point of view, and they may well have merit in the far-flung future, if and when AI with human-level intelligence moves from science fiction to reality. But for now, there will always be a human being *somewhere*: Humans have a hand in creating AI models, and humans are the ones who use them.

This leads us to the second hot-topic legal question: Should works created in whole or in part by generative AI receive a copyright or patent *at all,* and to whom should it be given? Specifically, should a patent or copyright go to the person or people who used the AI system to design the work, or to the maker of the AI model? We'll examine some of the possible answers to this question first in the context of copyright authorship, and then in the context of patent inventorship.

4.1 COPYRIGHT AUTHORSHIP

In early 2023, the US Copyright Office issued a statement (2023 Statement) clarifying its practices for registering works "that contain material generated by the use of artificial intelligence technology."[15] Citing a wealth of case law,[16] the Copyright Office reaffirmed the foundational requirement that a work must be authored by a human to be protected by copyright.[17] But the Office also took pains to note that works created with the assistance of artificial intelligence *are not automatically ineligible* for copyright protection. Eligibility "will depend on the circumstances, particularly how the AI tool operates and how it was used to create the final work. This is necessarily a case-by-case inquiry."[18]

The Copyright Office's choice of the term "AI tool" makes an interesting statement in itself. As the public contemplates AI in the form of Hollywood's fictional characters from movies such as *The Terminator* and *I, Robot*, the 2023 Statement frames AI in an entirely different light. Specifically, the wording highlights the fact that inventors and creators use all kinds of tools, from pencils and oil paints, to marble-cutting machines and inkjet printers, to spell-check programs and pitch-correction software. From that perspective, AI isn't a mythical force or entity; it is simply another tool that humans use.

On the topic of how much the human must participate, the Copyright Office is adamant that merely writing the prompt is not sufficient to secure copyright protection.[19] According to the 2023 Statement, when a person inputs a prompt, the AI technology "determines the expressive elements of its output." As a result, "the generated material is not the product of human authorship" and is not protected by copyright.[20] The Copyright Office has consistently affirmed this view in its Review Board decisions, as well.[21]

Despite the "prompt" limitation, the 2023 Statement breaks new ground by announcing that the Copyright Office will, indeed, register work that *includes* AI-created content and by providing explicit guidance for the application process.[22] Specifically, an applicant should describe the authorship contributed by a human and disclaim any content that is more than *de minimis* and AI-generated.[23] In other words, the Copyright Office has opened the door to some copyright protection in relation to AI-generated works, even if the opening is only a tiny crack.

The Copyright Office's policy has already led to registration of various works that were partially generated by AI. One example, titled "A Single Piece of American Cheese," has made headlines recently.[24] Although the striking work defies a prose description, the best I can explain is that it features an artificial human face composed of stained-glass-type segments of geometric shapes, along with spaghetti for hair, spaghetti strings descending onto the neck, and a piece of yellow cheese melting at the top of the hair. The human artist secured copyright for the unified image by carefully documenting how he selected and arranged the work using numerous AI edits to the original, AI-generated image, including directing the so-called "inpainting" of features.[25]

Nevertheless, is there any situation in which a work created *only by prompting* a generative AI model could be copyrightable? Here are some sample scenarios as food for thought, but they are only the stirrings of the potential questions on the horizon: What if the prompt is a thousand words long and provides highly specific instructions? And what if AI models become capable of so much precision that it is possible to eliminate most of the "randomness" involved in the output, so the result almost entirely adheres to the specific input? Or suppose an AI model enables an artist to issue unlimited, highly targeted prompts that can change an image or work in granular ways? It's plausible that novel scenarios such as these and others may yield different scenarios of copyrightability, but nothing in US law has reached that point yet.

Of course, scholars of copyright law have strong views on how copyrightability will or should ultimately work in the context of AI. Arguing for a "limited prompt-based approach," Mark Lemley asserts that it is just the prompt, and not the work itself, that deserves copyright protection. Generative AI makes "the cost and difficulty of producing the actual output"[26] much lower, he suggests, implying there is much less need for copyright protection.[27] Nevertheless, Lemley concludes that "coming up with the right prompt to generate what you want will sometimes be an art form in itself."[28]

In contrast, other scholars have argued that works created by computers (and specifically AI models) *should* be copyrightable, in part because of the difficulty of distinguishing works that were made by a human from those made by a computer.[29] Notably, scholars writing even before the launch of modern generative AI offered thoughtful, nuanced views on the copyrightability of machine-generated works. In her 2011 article, Annemarie Bridy suggested that "the programmer of generative software is the logical owner of the copyright in the works generated by his or her software[,]" because that person is, "after all, *the author of the author* of the works."[30] Here we are again, caught up in the nesting structure that comes with all things AI.

Nevertheless, copyrightability has always turned on human authorship and creativity – a focus that is unlikely to change. Right now, the great majority of creative works produced by generative AI involve minimal human input, so it isn't surprising that the Copyright Office has consistently rejected their applications.[31] Moreover, as impressive as current-generation AI models are, their outputs are scattershot. Provide the same AI model with the same prompt one hundred times, and you'll end up with a range of wildly different outputs.[32] This may soon change, however, and AI models may become so responsive to user input that they can be applied as precisely as an artist's paintbrush. If that future comes to pass, it's easy to imagine that the law will adapt to treat AI tools no differently than it treats paintbrushes, cameras, and all the tools of artists today.

4.2 PATENT INVENTORSHIP

Both The US Patent and Trademark Office and the courts (including the Supreme Court), so far, have been clear that "the patent system is designed to encourage *human* ingenuity[.]"[33] Accordingly, the Patent Office, much like the Copyright Office, has expressed its intention to focus "the patentability of AI-assisted inventions on the human contributions." This supports the office's policy objectives "by incentivizing human-centered activities and contributions, and by providing patent protections to inventions with significant human contributions while prohibiting patents on those that are not invented by natural persons."[34]

Taking a similar approach to the Copyright Office, the Patent Office stressed that AI-assisted inventions "are not categorically unpatentable."[35] More specifically, the Patent Office in 2024 provided three fictitious examples of inventions that either incorporate, or were invented with, the assistance of AI tools. One hypothetical invention uses artificial neural networks to detect anomalies, for example to detect malicious packets trying to break into a computer network;[36] another involves AI-based methods of analyzing and separating desired human speech from extraneous background speech;[37] and a third proposes a novel tool for treating fibrosis.[38] For each of these hypothetical cases, the Patent Office discussed claims that theoretically could be patentable, while identifying others that would be unpatentable because of the particular relationship of an AI system to the claim.[39]

Notwithstanding these commendable efforts to see through the weeds, it is difficult to imagine a near-term future that is *not* rife with complicated line-drawing and bad incentives. For inventors committed to acting in good faith, it will inevitably be difficult to know just how much a human inventor can harness the power of AI systems without irreversibly crossing a line. The consequences of such an error could be enormously costly, with the potential that an application for a blockbuster invention – one that could generate billions of dollars in company value, if the patent application succeeds – could be judged unpatentable for containing insufficient human ingenuity after it has been made public, meaning that the invention is thrust into the public domain, available to anyone.[40] Fear of such a result inevitably will incentivize inventors to intentionally under-disclose the extent to which they used AI systems in the research and development process.[41] I explore this subject further in Chapter 6, where I propose some potential solutions to these challenges.

As AI systems develop, it is always possible that they will be viewed more like tools, no different from hammers, nails, computers, or computer-aided design software. Although the tool analogy is powerful, it is an imperfect one and vulnerable to the argument that AI systems are qualitatively different from paintbrushes or AutoCAD.[42] Notwithstanding that inventors have always benefited from the creation of innovative tools, few modern tools have had the potential to invent on their own – at least, not without some significant human guidance.

There are rough analogies in prior technology, but nothing even approaches the potential at hand in AI. For example, in writing about human genes roughly a quarter century ago, I pondered how the law might treat an instruction manual that could operate on its own.[43] After all, both human genes and software are a set of instructions that carry out a function.[44] As difficult as it was to fit the innovations of that time into legal boxes, modern AI struggles even further to fit within those confines. Not only can AI follow instructions, it can improve or even develop those instructions on its own – using its own extensive rounds of trial, error, and refinement based on the mass of knowledge available to it.[45]

In short, these hot-topic issues related to copyright authorship and patent inventorship are unlikely to be solved with ease, at least not anytime soon. On their own, today's AI models may only produce artworks that are somewhat crude or inventions that embody limited novelty. However, if AI becomes capable of brilliant and truly novel inventions, as well as stunning and completely new poetry or works of visual art, society may be increasingly uncomfortable maintaining the view that the human contribution, as measured by the amount of user input, reigns supreme.

5 RIGHT OF PUBLICITY AND DEEPFAKES

While this book is primarily concerned with the relationship between artificial intelligence (AI) and the law of intellectual property (IP) – that is, patent, copyright, trademark, and trade secret law – AI is having profound effects on IP-adjacent areas of the law, as well. Of particular concern is the set of doctrines known in modern lingo as "the right of publicity." If the concept seems hazy and unfamiliar, you're in good company. The doctrines are far from robust, both in terms of the underlying theory and in terms of how they are applied. Nevertheless, AI has pushed these fledgling doctrines into the limelight, particularly with the emergence of using AI to create troubling "deepfakes."

Historically, the right of publicity has been broadly understood as the "right to control the use of one's identity and image, and variations of that image in commercial use."[1] The phrase "right of publicity" appears to have entered the federal legal lexicon in 1953,[2] although the right itself had been around for decades, at the time.[3]

In general, the right of publicity has been couched in the doctrines of privacy and unfair competition.[4] As Jennifer Rothman explains, "[f]rom the start there was a property-based conception of the right of privacy [. . .] understood as a right of self-ownership."[5] Over time, however, language related to the right of publicity has drifted towards the utilitarian view of intellectual property rights,[6] describing the right of publicity as encouraging entertainers to invest in their performance abilities so that the public can have the benefit of those performances. In other words, we reward the successful entertainer not because the entertainer has some form of property right, but as a vehicle to foster entertainment for society's benefit.

For example, the 1977 *Zacchini* v. *Scripps-Howard Broadcasting Co.* case concerned an entertainer whose act consisted of being shot out of a homemade cannon. Over the protest of the performer, a television station filmed and aired the entire act. Although the Supreme Court focused on whether the First Amendment protected the television station under the circumstances (it did not), the Justices, as a side note, also discussed the underlying state law claim as arising from the goal of benefiting society, the same as patent and copyright:

> Ohio's decision to protect petitioner's right of publicity here rests on more than a desire to compensate the performer . . . [it] provides an economic incentive for him to make the investment required to produce a performance of interest to the public.[7]

The Justices went on to note that "[t]he same consideration underlies the patent and copyright laws" and that although such laws might "perhaps" consider rewarding the rights-holder as a secondary consideration, the primary intent is to benefit the public.[8] Once again, we hear the strains of the utilitarian theory of intellectual property, but this time in the context of the emerging right of publicity doctrine.

Today, there is no federal statute guaranteeing the right of publicity, although many states have had right-of-publicity laws on the books for decades.[9] The lack of a federal statute, however, may change. Thanks in part to some of the threats posed by AI, Congress began considering a right-of-publicity statute in 2024. Known by the acronym, the *NO FAKES Act*, the bill protects citizens against unauthorized digital replicas, and provides steep statutory penalties.[10]

The furor over deepfakes touches today's generative AI models. In May 2024, OpenAI launched a voice assistant that enabled users to receive outputs from ChatGPT through synthetic, AI-generated voices.[11] One of these AI voices, named Sky, bore a striking resemblance to the voice of actress Scarlett Johansson. Not long after users began to comment on the uncanny resemblance between Sky's and Ms. Johansson's voices, OpenAI took Sky offline. The company has maintained that any similarity to Johansson's voice was coincidental and unintentional[12] – but notably, Open AI had attempted to contract with Johannson to voice one of its chatbots during the development process. She'd turned them down.[13]

Many state right-of-publicity laws appear capable of handling situations like this one, where there is a clearly identifiable commercial harm. For example, in 1988, the Ninth Circuit ruled that "when a distinctive voice of a professional singer is widely known and is deliberately imitated in order to sell a product, the sellers have appropriated what is not theirs and have committed a tort in California."[14] But few of us are celebrities, and not all harms related to misappropriating one's name, image, and likeness are purely commercial – as anyone who has seen an effective deepfake will understand.

If one is curious about the dystopian side of current-generation artificial intelligence, deepfakes are a great place to start. A deepfake is a kind of computer-generated media that depicts a person – whether through an image, video, or audio – in an extremely realistic way.[15] A deepfake may depict persons both fictitious and real.[16] Deepfakes are becoming increasingly convincing, making it more and more difficult for a human to differentiate between media that does truly depict a person, and media that is synthetic.[17] An AI chatbot like Sky, which can sound uncannily human, is a type of deepfake – but there are other more insidious examples too. In March 2022, a deepfake of Ukrainian president Volodymyr Zelenskyy began circulating on social media. In this deepfake video, President Zelenskyy appears to be surrendering to Russia and commands Ukrainian troops to lay down their arms.[18] While the video wasn't perfect, Professor Hany Farid, an expert in digital media forensics, said it "is the first [deepfake] we've seen that['s] really got some legs, [and] I suspect it's the tip of the iceberg[.]"[19]

It isn't just deepfakes' consequences for public image use and geopolitics that have people worried; they also create new and frightening opportunities for bad actors to commit sexual exploitation and sex-related cybercrime. This has already begun: According to one 2019 study, a staggering 96 percent of all deepfakes are pornographic in nature.[20] Unsurprisingly, makers of sexually explicit deepfakes often target celebrities; Taylor Swift was a victim of one in January 2024.[21] Worse yet, creating deepfakes has become so easy that virtually anyone can be victimized. School-aged children are sometimes targeted by their peers.[22] These real and potential harms have provided some of the momentum for the congressional *NO FAKES* bill.[23]

From a technological perspective, it is clear that AI systems will become increasingly capable of creating digital replicas of human beings that blur the line between the real and the fake. Lawmakers and enforcement agencies are struggling to keep up with these developments to ensure society avoids the threat of a world filled with digitally fabricated media.[24] To quote a 2018 article on the subject, researchers, legal scholars, and technological experts may face the task of "[c]onvinc[ing] the greater public, as well as lawmakers, university technologists, and tech companies, that a reality-distorting information apocalypse is not only plausible, but close at hand."[25]

As described in Section 2.3, intellectual property regimes have largely avoided shouldering the burdens of weighty moral questions. In addition to beefing up the right of publicity with legislation such as the NO FAKES Act,[26] policymakers should keep in mind that intellectual property regimes are not designed to bear such burdens. Moreover, the modern theoretic framing of the intellectual property regimes generally supports the utilitarian goals of promoting the progress of the creative arts and innovation, as well as an efficient and effective marketplace. This framing lacks the breadth and heft to support broader issues of human morality that arise in the context of AI.

We come now to the end of the hot topics regarding AI and intellectual property – ones that have filled headlines and captured the attention of scholars and commentators alike. These provide a wonderful entry into a deeper set of issues that hovers quietly below the surface. Specifically, as AI reaches its tendrils into all aspects of society, it threatens to undermine the question of what – in the context of IP – we choose to value in the first place. The remainder of the book now turns to the issues of what we value, how we value it, and whether the intellectual property system can continue supporting that value in the face of the AI revolution.

PART III

The Deeper Problem for IP

6 SHRINKING THE POOL

Around the turn of the millennium, Lawrence Lessig published a groundbreaking book[1] that he immortalized with the title *Code Is Law*.[2] Lessig posited that the architecture of the internet – that is, its software and hardware – operates in the same manner as legal codes since it directs, regulates, and limits human behavior.[3] He argued that changes in the internet's code could threaten basic values reaching back to the Constitution.[4]

Although perhaps not as far-reaching as the changes Lessig had in mind,[5] recent shifts in AI are challenging our conceptions of what we protect and the value of human contribution to progress. Intellectual property regimes have largely assumed the centrality of humans to the innovation and creativity process. The rapid expansion and progress of AI challenges that human-centered assumption, putting pressure on what we value. In this context, this chapter analyzes the difficulties unfolding in three out of the four areas of IP – patent, trade secret, and copyright. Specifically the chapter shows how AI promises to reduce the pool of inventions, secrets, and creations these doctrines regimes can protect.

6.1 PATENT

Patent validity is conditional on satisfying five pillars of patentability: patentable subject matter, novelty, nonobviousness, utility, and disclosure.[6] Among these, obviousness is one of the most commonly litigated issues,[7] and it has been variously called the "fundamental gatekeeper to patenting"[8] and "the ultimate condition of patentability."[9]

One can think of obviousness as an outgrowth of novelty. With novelty, we ask if the elements of an invention listed in a patent application precisely match each and every element of a preexisting invention, no more and no fewer. If the match is precise in that manner, the application will be rejected for failing to prove the idea is novel.[10] Obviousness, however, moves one step further. Perhaps the invention isn't precisely the same as the preexisting one. Nevertheless, for those who are skilled in the field, the change is obvious based on what has come before, or a combination of preexisting things. In this manner, the test of *nonobviousness* requires an inventor's creation to be truly inventive – something that would be worthy of the government's grant of a powerful patent – rather than mere routine tinkering based on existing knowledge.[11]

At the core of many decisions about nonobviousness stands the mythical PHOSITA, an unhelpful acronym that stands for "Person Having Ordinary Skill in the Art." (This phrase comes directly from the Patent Act itself.[12]) Rather than asking whether the invention would be obvious to a layperson like you or me, the court asks whether the invention would be obvious to someone who knows about the relevant area of technology. Note that a PHOSITA is not the world's leading expert, but rather someone with a level of skill considered ordinary in the relevant art. In this way, the term PHOSITA is similar to the concept of the "reasonable person" in other doctrinal realms – a generalized version of an individual within a particular grouping. These generalized fictions are similar to the character of *Everyman* from the fifteenth-century morality play, which was designed to teach that good deeds are the only thing a person can take on the journey to judgment at the heavenly gates.[13]

The necessity for generalization, of course, results in a fanciful creature.[14] After all, it is difficult to imagine that any one person, even fictitious, might somehow manage to fully represent an entire group of people. In fact, some scholars have criticized the reasonable person as problematic for its ability to be overinclusive or underinclusive especially with respect to gender[15] and race,[16] creating a figure that may be unhelpful for the situation at hand.

The problem is worse with PHOSITA since the concept reaches well beyond one individual representing a category of people to one individual representing multiple categories of people. For example, many patent cases turn on prior art from different areas of technology, raising the question of whether an inventor would be sufficiently "motivated" to combine those pieces of prior art from such different fields.[17] Thus, PHOSITA is an amalgamation of generalized people from different fields, who are then generalized again to mesh the categories together in the case of a new invention.[18]

For example, imagine the invention of the Slinky, a toy made in the shape of a spring that can propel itself down a flight of stairs. To determine whether the invention is obvious, the patent examiner, or the trier of fact in a court case challenging the patent, asks whether a PHOSITA would find it obvious to make the mental leap from the knowledge that exists to the new invention.

The prior art from which the invention draws need not specifically name each component. Rather, the prior art could contain information that would lead an inventor to try a limited series of items within a single category.[19] To offer a simple example, prior art for a new recipe could include a writing suggesting that, to sweeten pastry, one should add sugar or artificial sweetener; it would not need to specify whether to add sugar, Splenda, Equal, or Sweet 'n Low. If testing out the various members within the category of "sugar or artificial sweetener" offers a "reasonable expectation of success," then the prior art covers all the members of each category and the new invention is obvious.

With the Slinky (see Figure 6.1), a PHOSITA would include someone skilled in the art of toymaking. The prior art relevant to a Slinky, however, might include knowledge from many fields including the art of creating (1) mattress and upholstery springs, (2) the coils of automotive shock absorption systems, and (3) the motion dynamics of devices like the Newton's cradle, and perhaps others.

As an aside for those who are intrigued by the last sentence's reference to a Newton's cradle, the device consists of a row of five smooth metal balls hanging from pairs of strings attached to a frame. When the first ball is pulled aside and released, its impact with the row of balls causes one at the other end to fly off, leading to a long-lasting cycle of single balls flying off each end, with the balls in between remaining largely motionless.[20] Named after Sir Isaac Newton, the invention continues to be used across physics classrooms as a

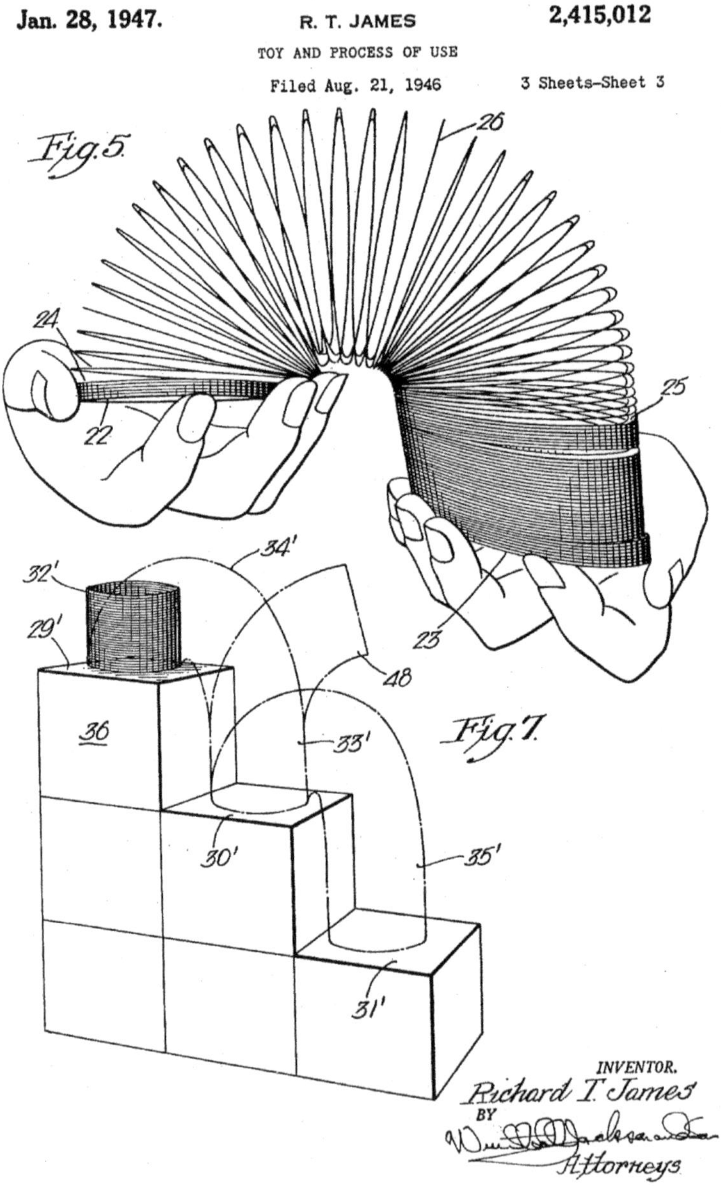

Figure 6.1 An image from the original 1940s patent of the Slinky.

demonstration of the conservation of momentum and energy, as well as a toy in many homes and offices.[21]

Returning to patent law's conception of a person having ordinary skill in the art, the necessary composition of PHOSITA will depend on the examples of prior art that the party challenging the patent – and therefore asserting its obviousness – presents to the court. As Judge Learned Hand explained with great foresight in 1950, to be successful: "[T]he inventor must [become] a mythically omniscient worker in his chosen field. As the arts proliferate with prodigious fecundity, his lot is an increasingly hard one."[22]

To complicate matters, there is no clearly accepted definition of PHOSITA in the doctrine.[23] Capping it all off, practitioners wage humorous wars over spelling: should the acronym be PHOSITA, POSITA, POSA, or even PSITA? The Supreme Court has yet to opine on this weighty matter.[24]

The standard for determining obviousness – as opposed to the definition of a PHOSITA – involves yet another tug-of-war. This one takes place between the Supreme Court and the Federal Circuit, which hears the patent appeals from all district courts throughout the country. The saga begins with the Federal Circuit's long-established test for obviousness: For pieces of prior art to combine and thereby render an invention obvious, the prior art must contain a "teaching, suggestion, or motivation" to combine. This is known as the TSM test, another nonhelpful acronym to add to our collection.[25]

The Supreme Court fired the first salvo in the 2007 case *KSR*[26] by criticizing the Federal Circuit's use of the TSM test.[27] The message contained in that salvo was anything but clear, however. The Supreme Court neither rejected nor replaced the TSM test, but rather explained that the Federal Circuit had "captured a helpful insight"[28] with its test, one that can be applied so that it "take[s] account of the inferences and creative steps that a person of ordinary skill in the art would employ."[29] Nevertheless, the Justices warned against allowing helpful insights to become rigid and mandatory formulas,[30] providing a not-so-subtle hint that the TSM formula had lost sight of the underlying concept being tested.

The Supreme Court's decision on obviousness emerged when the Federal Circuit and the Supreme Court also were engaged in a protracted tug-of-war over another doctrine: patentable subject matter. There, as with obviousness, the Justices overturned a Federal Circuit test as helpful but too rigidly applied. On remand in the patentable subject matter case, the Federal Circuit concluded that applying its test more flexibly led to the same result, and continued to apply its old test much the same way as before. In response, the Supreme Court later returned to replace the Federal Circuit's patentable subject matter test with one of its own.[31]

Returning to obviousness, despite the loud hint from the Supreme Court – a hint that mirrored its message in patentable subject matter – the Federal Circuit has continued to apply the TSM test, penning case opinions that are decidedly lacking in fealty to the Supreme Court's dictates.[32] The Supreme Court Justices, however, never returned to the doctrine of obviousness. Moreover, the composition of the Court has shifted considerably since the 2007 KSR decision.[33] In 2007, the Supreme Court Justices were Chief Justice Roberts, and Justices Steven, Scalia, Kennedy, Souter, Thomas, Ginsburg, Breyer, and Alito, of whom only Chief Justice Roberts and Justices Thomas and Alito remain today. Thus, the modern history of the doctrine of obviousness reads like the cliffhanging, season-ending episode of a series that was canceled and then restarted with new screenwriters. The Supreme Court may, indeed, return to the doctrine of obviousness in the near future, but the concluding episode remains a mystery.

Into this domain strides modern AI, with the capacity to seriously disrupt obviousness. At the simplest level, an AI model has far more access to available information than any PHOSITA, and its ability to interpret that information is vastly more sophisticated.[34] Consider the types of information AI can draw upon to find examples of prior art. For the purpose of obviousness, prior art examples must be available to the public and may include printed publications, such as: US patents or applications that are public; foreign patents or applications that are public; and books or journal articles in the United States or abroad.[35] Prior art also may include publicly available sales brochures, catalogues, and manuals.[36] Scholarship has noted examples of caselaw allowing even more obscure publications to serve as vehicles for demonstrating obviousness, such as "poster boards displayed at conferences, industry whitepapers, proposals circulated at working group meetings of technical standards bodies, doctoral dissertations, and postings on internet discussion forums."[37]

Basic internet searching already provides much fodder for those wishing to challenge an invention's patent as obvious; generative AI's ability to find relevant prior art provides a much more powerful tool in that quest than internet searches. In particular, courts have an easier time crediting a written document as prior art than crediting, for example, the testimony of an expert concerning what those in the field would consider routine.[38] This preference for the written word makes AI's ability to find written prior art especially valuable.

In addition, before the recent explosion of AI, most search tools were limited to scanning for particular wording. Thus, the accuracy of the results relied on a human's ability to guess the precise wording that might have been used in the source. Modern AI systems are far more sophisticated. An AI model may be able to hunt for a written source that contains precisely the document "suggestion" one needs, not by searching for specific words, but by tapping into its massive neural network trained on huge amounts of publicly available information that might express the idea in a myriad of different ways.

AI also provides a more sophisticated ability to understand and combine different areas of prior art. Recall that the current obviousness test looks for a *T*eaching, *S*uggestion, or *M*otivation to combine different areas of prior art. Without AI, a competitor attempting to challenge a patent might have to develop or hire expertise in multiple areas, applying that expertise to search out the documents containing the motivations to combine. But AI has the ability to "learn" what exists in those fields and find plausible written examples of the motivation from the vast array of written materials.

AI could even be trained on the types of examples and logic that prior courts have accepted to prove obviousness and then use that information to predict whether a court will accept one piece of prior art over another. Of course, the AI is only as strong as its operator,[39] and better prompts yield better results.

Modern AI systems do much more than improve upon traditional search tools. Consider whether a court should categorize AI itself as "having ordinary skill in the art." After all, the concept of ordinary skill in the art is intended to test whether the inventor is trying to patent something that is merely obvious to those in the field who are themselves creative. In that context, recall that the term "AI" can include, not only the large language models that are so familiar to everyone, but also systems trained to produce new ideas from general knowledge.[40] Scientists have a long way to go before creating AI models that can produce breathtakingly and entirely new innovations. However, the field may be a little closer to developing AI that can create new combinations or variants by assimilating current knowledge. If AI can invent something claimed in a patent application by working through the existing body of knowledge, and humans have the ability to use AI, then the claimed invention does not require much of an inventive leap from what already exists in the body of knowledge.[41]

One could argue that including AI within those skilled in the art conflicts with the statute, given that AI is not "a *person* having ordinary skill in the art."[42] That conceptual problem, however, is easily avoidable. For example, one could simply conceptualize "a person having ordinary skill in the art" as including "a person using AI as a tool."[43] After all, inventors use all types of tools. Why should we suddenly imagine invention as a process devoid of the latest tools?

Some scholars argue that under current law, "a creative AI system cannot be the P[H]OSITA."[44] They cite Supreme Court language in *KSR* that PHOSITA is "a *person* of ordinary creativity, not an automaton."[45] They also cite language from an older Federal Circuit case, *Standard Oil*,[46] explaining that a PHOSITA "is also presumed to be one who thinks along the line of conventional wisdom in the art and is not one who undertakes to innovate."[47] Presumably, these works read the judicial language as suggesting that a PHOSITA must be human. In addition, it must be a human who applies nothing more than "ordinary" creativity, not an "automaton" such as AI, churning away on endless iterations to search out a solution at the behest of a human with invention on the mind.

That interpretation, however, misses the discussion surrounding the Supreme Court's quote. In *KSR*, the Supreme Court rejected what it termed the Federal Circuit's "constricted analysis,"[48] in which a PHOSITA would look only at prior art designed to solve precisely the same problem. Instead, the Justices concluded that a person of ordinary skill would think more broadly. As the Justices explained,

"Common sense teaches, however, that familiar items may have obvious uses beyond their primary purposes, and in many cases a person of ordinary skill will be able to fit the teachings of multiple patents together like pieces of a puzzle."[49]

When the Justices conclude a few sentences later that "A person of ordinary skill is also a person of ordinary creativity, not an automaton," the emphasis is on "creativity," posed as the opposite of an automaton that just plugs in what has gone before without thinking.[50] In other words, the Supreme Court rejects the Federal Circuit notion, borne out in cases like *Standard Oil*,[51] that a PHOSITA is merely a conventional thinker. Instead, the highest court holds that the PHOSITA is, indeed, one who engages in creativity.[52]

Nor does the Supreme Court's "automaton" language prescribe anything as to the extent to which AI might be involved in a PHOSITA's presumed creativity. The statutory language specifies "a person"[53] and one would expect such persons to exercise their creativity by using the latest tools in the field – including AI. As one practitioner commented to the USPTO:

> Just as the existence of test tubes impacts the level of a person of ordinary skill in the chemical arts, and just as the existence of general-purpose computers impacts the level of a person of ordinary skill in the software arts (and many others), so [too] would AI affect the level of skill in the arts where it can be made useful.[54]

A PHOSITA with AI in hand will substantially raise the bar for what counts as nonobvious for all inventions.[55] In doing so, the march of modern AI will make it much harder for new inventions to convince a patent examiner that the invention is nonobvious, and, if the patent is granted, much easier for challengers to make a convincing case of obviousness. The entire notion of what constitutes an invention becomes increasingly difficult to satisfy.

The impact of that shift could be enormous. AI alters the definition of invention by introducing a more powerful and omniscient evaluator than a beleaguered government patent examiner or a human competitor. This will be true no matter who or what is responsible for carrying the ball on the invention – human or AI. Even if an AI model itself is the primary innovator, other competitors armed with AI will be able to challenge the patent much more effectively than ever before in history.

The impact on *human* invention, however, will be particularly noticeable. As humans expand their use of AI tools and the capacity of AI increases, the space for what a human contributes to any invention may dwindle. The ability of a solitary human to invent without the aid of such tools may shrink even more.[56] In that context, the flash of genius, which has been an essential concept in patent law, could mean less and less.[57] Human flashes of genius may have difficulty fending off AI's ability to demonstrate, through its accumulation of available knowledge, that the blueprint for the invention was out there all along – and that human ingenuity wasn't necessary after all.

Some scholars have suggested that we could create a formal, two-track patent approval system for AI versus non-AI inventions. By separating the two, we could evaluate each in the context of its peers, almost like an accelerated class in high school. Following this approach, when an AI either invents or is used as part of the invention process, the standards for patentability would be higher than the standards applied to human inventions.[58] With a two-part standard, humans would only have to compete with each other.

Such a system might work well in the beginning, but as AI tools become commonplace, the rule inevitably will lose its definitional power. It may become a little like asking the inventor of a new pharmaceutical whether their process involved any standard lab materials. In virtually all cases, the truthful answer would be "yes."

Moreover, obtaining truthful answers to the question "did you use AI" may be challenging for the Patent Office. With no simple way to test veracity, and with a lower standard for human-only inventions, inventers will be sorely tempted to cheat. A rule that invites evasion should give lawmakers pause, given that it will complicate the job for those who enforce the rules and for the legal system itself. Thus, constraining AI inventors to their own category is unlikely to solve the problem.

In short, AI alters the contours of inventive space. Human inventions will seem less and less remarkable as AI's ability to find and combine far-flung and disparate pieces of prior art improves. This will demonstrate the obviousness of many claimed inventions, rendering them unpatentable and shrinking the space for protectible innovation. Although the changes will impact both inventions created with the help of AI and those without, the space for human innovation will experience the greater contraction.[59]

6.2 TRADE SECRET

Patents and trade secrets are often presented as opposite modes of intellectual property.[60] For example, the sine qua non in patents is public disclosure. In the essential bargain of patent law, the patent holder receives the powerful patent right in exchange for disclosing the invention to the public and dedicating it to the public domain when the patent expires.[61] In contrast, trade secrets revolve around keeping information secret.

Despite this and other differences, the onslaught of artificial intelligence is likely to disrupt trade secrets in a manner analogous to the impact on patent law. As with patents, AI significantly reduces the amount of information that will be protectible given that foundational definitions become critically embattled.

Let's start with the concept of secrecy. What does "secret" mean, especially in the context of AI, and just how secret must the information be? The federal definition is a good guide, and it mirrors the approach adopted by most of the states. In defining the term "trade secret," federal law specifies that:

> [T]he information derives independent economic value, actual or potential, from not being generally known to, and not being readily ascertainable through proper means by, another person who can obtain economic value from the disclosure or use of the information.[62]

In less convoluted language, one could say that the information's value flows from the fact that it is not generally known to those in the field and cannot be readily ascertained by proper means.[63]If a trade secret fails the test of secrecy – in other words, if the cat is out of the bag – trade secret protection is not available. In fact, under trade secret doctrines, deriving someone else's trade secret from your own research or reverse engineering it from the final product does not constitute misappropriation of a trade secret.

The fundamental importance of secrecy and what constitutes a proper means of discovery can best be understood in the context of the innocent user, one who releases information without knowing its protected origins.[64] Suppose an angry company employee publishes an article that details the company's secret formula, claims to be the inventor of the formula, and declares that the formula is dedicated to the public domain for everyone to use." Those who republish and use the information, without realizing that the information was acquired improperly, have no liability. The company could choose to file a suit against the angry employee who released the secret, but the employee may have no assets for the company to pursue. As for the secret, it's too late. Once a secret is known (or readily ascertainable), it's no longer a secret.

Scholars have explored the impact of AI on trade secret law primarily in the following context of accidental exposure of secrets. For example, to what extent is AI likely to cause companies to lose their valuable trade secrets, if employees use AI to accomplish workplace functions and inadvertently release secrets in the process?[65] Imagine that an executive enters information from a company's strategy document into a new generative AI system along with a prompt asking for slides,[66] or a junior analyst inputs company financial information requesting that the AI organize it into a spreadsheet. Now that the information has entered the AI's system, it has the potential to become future training data. With that one small prompt, the information may have left that company's private informational sphere. Once that happens, depending on the AI system and within varying timeframes, competitors might be able to retrieve the information by asking the AI for information on another company's strategic plans.[67]

Levine explores this problem in detail, culling examples from press reports during the first year after ChatGPT's public release in 2022.[68] Consider the following event that occurred at Samsung:

> One employee copied buggy source code from a semiconductor database into the chatbot and asked it to identify a fix.... Another employee did the same for a different piece of equipment, requesting "code optimization" from ChatGPT. After a third employee asked the AI model to summarize meeting notes, Samsung executives stepped in. The company limited each employee's prompt to ChatGPT to 1,024 bytes.[69]

The company presumably was concerned that the information could be used as training data for later iterations of the AI. Competitors might be able to access Samsung's trade secrets by asking for sections of Samsung's code or equipment information.Worse yet, imagine if the meeting that the Samsung employee asked ChatGPT to summarize had included Samsung's strategic plans for the coming decade. If the meeting notes later found their way into training data, a query asking for Samsung's strategic plans might bear fruit. Even less specific disclosures could prime the pump for generative AI systems to connect the dots on a company's trade secrets.[70] AI has an astounding ability to glean information about a company – or a person – from seemingly innocent and disparate disclosures. As Ana Nordberg explains:

> correlating information from multiple sources might reveal valuable information concerning strategic market positioning decisions and ongoing research projects [as well as inferring information on pricing, client list, suppliers, distribution routes and networks, manufacturing capability and processes].[71]

Trade secret law, however, faces a more fundamental challenge to its territory: The ability of AI to come up with a trade secret independently. Imagine that every single one of a company's employees and contractors used AI systems with perfect competence and diligence. Not a single drop of the company's trade secret information has leaked onto the internet or into an AI model in any way. Even in that mythical paradise, trade secret law faces a serious challenge. If AI can generate the same solution or set of information contained in a trade secret, and can do so entirely independent of any leakage of information from the company, the trade secret may not be protectible. Specifically, as creative AI becomes increasingly adept at solving problems, one may be able to ask an AI model to solve a problem or assemble a set of information that a company protects as its trade secret.[72]

Consider a company whose advertisements claim the product includes an inexpensive (and secret) way to solve the problem of noisy leaf blowers. A creative AI, at least at some point, might be able to independently develop the solution to that problem.[73] If so, a competitor wishing to invalidate the trade secret protection, or prove that the product does not deserve trade secret protection in the first place, could task the AI with developing the solution.

Or imagine an agency that specializes in recruiting for a particular type of position and maintains lists of possible candidates – people who are at the top of their fields and might be interested in switching jobs – along with the hiring approach that might appeal to them. The agency may have spent years developing the relationships that give them the information contained in these lists. Despite that long, human investment, AI may be able to derive the same information from culling the Internet and analyzing tone shifts in social media, as well as searching posted or reposted conversations, public writings, appearances, or even unprotected email. If anyone using AI can independently derive the trade secret or a list of solutions including the trade secret, the information could be deemed readily ascertainable, thereby failing the definition of "secret."[74]

One might also ask whether evidence of one person's prompts, combined with one specific AI system, is enough to support the claim that the information is readily ascertainable. At least at this point in the development of AI, the skill of the driver determines the performance of the vehicle.[75] In other words, is the information readily ascertainable just because one person crafting the prompts managed to reach that particular information?

Under trade secret law, the fact that a single competitor independently came up with the trade secret does not render the information either generally known or readily ascertainable.[76] Thus, evidence that one person reached the secret using AI could suggest that the information was ascertainable, but perhaps not "readily" so. One might argue further that the AI's result flowed from unusual talent possessed by the particular AI operator. If so, the fact that one genius could derive the secret using AI might not support the conclusion that the information is "readily" ascertainable.[77]

Just as patent law employs a hypothetical person of *ordinary* creativity – not one at the top of the field – to determine if a claimed invention is patentable, so too does trade secret law consider ascertainability from the perspective of someone with *average* skill in the industry. In both cases, the hypothetical person used as a standard is not a genius or an outlier.

All of these considerations, however, are premised on the notion that the AI's output is heavily dependent on the skill of the user and the AI product. That is certainly the state of the art – but only the state of the art today. Assuming AI technology continues to progress in leaps and bounds, it may increase its capacity to operate with lower levels of human skill. Over time, different users and different AI models may be able to generate a reasonably similar set of results, increasingly the likelihood of AI independently generating what are now trade secrets.

In short, as with patents, AI has the potential to significantly shrink the pool of what counts as worthy of protection, carving off and dooming a large section of currently protected trade secrets that will no longer withstand a challenge. That impact may be most noticeable through the shrinking human contribution to trade secrets.

6.3 COPYRIGHT

Chapter 3 delved deeply into copyright's fair use defense, in the context of hot-topic, generative AI cases. The discussion below contains a few additional doctrines needed to understand how AI may also shrink the pool of work subject to copyright protection.

Copyright protection is relatively easy to obtain. One doesn't need to endure the gauntlet of rigorous examination,[78] as required for patents. Rather, for a work subject to copyright protection, the author need only capture the work in a tangible medium of expression.[79] In other words, the moment I write something down, save it in my computer memory, send it in an email, sketch it in a notebook, or make a video of it with my phone, the material is protected. One should also recall from Chapter 3 that copyright requires only a "modicum of creativity" – a measure that that is considered quite low.[80]

Although copyrights are vastly easier to obtain than patents, copyright protection is far less complete.[81] As explained in Chapter 3, the doctrine of fair use tempers copyright protection with other important values such as free speech, the ability to criticize, and the transformative nature of certain uses.[82]

Even if a work is protected, copyright extends only to certain elements of the work. For example, copyright does not protect the facts embedded in a work, and it doesn't protect titles or short phrases.[83] Most important, copyright protects only the particular expression of the idea contained in a work, rather than the idea itself, which is a decidedly fuzzy line.[84] For example, a classic explanation of the idea/expression distinction involves William Shakespeare's immortal play, *Romeo and Juliet.* Modern copyright would likely protect the dialogue, the plot sequence, and the particular characters of the play. Copyright would not, however, protect the idea of two star-crossed lovers from feuding families who die tragically.[85] Those points would constitute the idea rather than how it is expressed.

Although the Shakespeare example seems simple enough, the distinction has proven devilishly difficult in practice.[86] Establishing definitive tests to identify which part of the work qualifies as an idea and which part qualifies as expression has eluded great minds for centuries.[87]

Even expression can escape copyright protection through additional doctrinal limitations. For example, if there is only one way, or a limited number of ways, to express an idea, the "merger doctrine" holds that the expression cannot qualify for copyright protection.[88] After all, how else does one say, "write your name on the box top, tear it off, and mail it in"?[89] Similarly, the "scènes à faire" concept disallows the protection of certain settings or representations that would be essential for conveying the subject matter. Consider a scriptwriter for a war movie set in Germany during World War II. It would be hard to portray military life in Germany at the time without a scene of soldiers raising their glasses at a German beer hall while singing a rousing rendition of the Nazi party anthem known as the "Horst Wessel."[90]

Copyright does, however, provide two different routes for proving copyright infringement: by showing direct evidence or by showing that the accused copier had access and the work is substantially similar.[91] In other words, if one can't show that the accused copier was seen standing over a Xerox machine that was spitting out pages of the book, one can show that the accused copier had access to the book and that the copier's work was substantially similar.[92] Moreover, the accused copier need not have intended to copy; rather, copyright law accepts the notion of "subconscious copying."[93] With subconscious copying, copiers may be morally certain they are the original authors of new works. Nevertheless, if a copier had access to the copyrighted work, *and* the new work landed too closely to the original, the copier will be liable for infringement.[94] For example, in the classic case of subconscious copying, a court decided that George Harrison of The Beatles unconsciously copied the Chiffons' song, "He's So Fine" in writing his song "My Sweet Lord."[95]

The notion of copying in general, and subconscious copying in particular, strays into one of copyright doctrine's muddiest quagmires. What is the difference between direct inspiration and copying? Generations of art students have honed their craft by sitting in a museum and sketching the works on view. If a student's later work bears some resemblance to the museum pieces, where does influence or inspiration end and copying begin? Of course, art students may choose museums precisely because the works are old enough that any copyrights have expired – though this may attribute unusually careful levels of calculation and knowledge of copyright law. Nevertheless, it would be hard to claim that no artist, musician, writer, or other producer of creative work was ever influenced by the works of people they admired.

The muse dilemma is where AI may open deeper cracks in the copyright realm. Recall that a copyright holder who does not have direct evidence of copying must show that the copier had access and that the resulting work is substantially similar to the original. On the one hand, AI may make it easier for a copyright holder to prove that the accused copier had access.[96] AI's ability to extract and analyze data from multiple sources can help copyright holders show with greater precision exactly what a copier might have been exposed to. To channel the dystopian, surveillance society in George Orwell's novel *1984*, AI may be able to pinpoint that an artist accused of copying a song likely was standing in a particular Starbucks on a particular day ordering a triple espresso when the song played over the speakers.

Although AI may help copyright holders prove copying, accused copiers may benefit even more in searching for ways to defend themselves. The ability of AI's neural networks to ingest and search for massive amounts of information could help an accused infringer argue that the "copyrighted" work itself too closely mirrors other works on the same topic. Moreover, AI's ability to discern patterns and connections among vast numbers of works ultimately may help accused copiers argue that much of the copyrighted work today is itself, merely copies of prior works.

If an AI trained on a data set that does not include the creative work at issue can produce a reasonable facsimile of the work when given appropriate prompts, can the work be considered sufficiently deserving of copyright protection? Consider the following: Today's AI already can mimic writing and other creative modes with eerie accuracy. AI systems also can provide "predictions" based on analyses of patterns discerned in past information. Suppose we ask an AI to write an article reporting the results of a US presidential election a month before the election in the style of a particular *New York Times* writer – we'll call the writer Charles Dickens. (Dickens not only wrote extraordinary literature during the nineteenth century, but he was also a journalist.[97]) Even today, an AI system might be able to produce a Charles Dickens-style article detailing the *future* election results by predicting which candidate will prevail, by knowing the writer's own patterns, or even just by understanding the *New York Times*' editorial preferences. If we open the *New York Times* the morning after the election, and Dickens' real article looks much like the writing produced by the AI a month before, what does that say about Dickens' work? We know the facts in the article are not protectible. Moreover, one cannot copyright a style, but only a particular example of expression captured in that style. If an AI can fully create some works in advance, what will be left for authors? On the other hand, if we strengthen AI by jumping in to protect styles, the future will lack the ability to bring new schools of art – impressionism, cubism, photorealism, pointillism, etc. The first person to work using a particular style would own the field.

There is an irony to this potential avenue of defense against an accusation of copying: even if it is successful, it further limits the rewards to human creativity. The more AI helps accused copiers defend themselves from copyright infringement accusations – by showing that the work they're accused of copying is not original when compared to masses of prior material – the more that analysis reverberates for artists themselves. Less room is available for new creativity if our work is truly held up before the mirror of so much that has come before. Can our own creative work survive the level of increasingly intense comparison to all of the muses from whom we may have learned, no matter how innocently or opaquely that learning may have occurred? Artists who can press beyond the boundaries of any muse or influence are likely to be a more limited bunch than the range of those whose works receive copyright today.

In short, across copyright, patent, and trade secret, the arrival of modern AI reduces the capacity of inventions and creative work to survive scrutiny in their quest for protection. Whether in the patent, trade secret, or copyright regime, AI raises the bar for what qualifies as new or secret and enhances a challenger's ability to find a prior art or prior muse that renders the work unprotectible.

Shrinking the space available for invention – and human invention in particular – is only one of the challenges AI brings. Ever more fundamental problems arise as AI begins to challenge the underlying value proposition of intellectual property: AI threatens to limit IP's traditional power to confer value to the invention, expression, secret, or reputation being protected. In Chapter 7, I describe the value proposition problem in detail.

7 SHRINKING THE VALUE PROPOSITION

Every intellectual property right is an intangible. Consider the right to control making copies of a work. We know it as a "copyright," but it is not something you can touch with your hands and feel the boundaries of: It's not like a pencil, or a notepad, or an elephant. Instead, such legal rights – and indeed, the entire system of intellectual property rights – are intangibles.

As a general matter, all legal rights are intangibles, but they often protect quite tangible things. Laws against theft protect my watch, while laws against assault protect my nose. In other words, the legal right may be intangible, but the protected items can be tangible things I can touch.

Life in the intellectual property world is more complicated than that. What do intangible, intellectual property rights protect? They protect things that are, themselves, intangibles. For example, the patent system protects an invention,[1] which is somewhat like an idea. You can reduce the idea to practice and produce a tangible item, but that is just a single embodiment of the idea. It is not the idea itself, which remains no more than an abstract notion, free of physical boundaries.

In the same vein, the copyright system protects the expression used to describe an idea,[2] the trade secrets system protects business secrets,[3] and the trademark system, essentially, protects reputations.[4] All of these things – inventions, expressions, business secrets, and reputations – are themselves intangibles. You can certainly hold a piece of paper with the secret formula scribbled on it; a soda can with the logo printed on it, or a paperback book in which you can read expressive writing. Those are just individual embodiments, however, not the thing protected itself; they are not the secret or the protected expression.

In short, the subjects of protection in the examples above – the idea, the secret formula, the process, and the expression – are intangibles that exist outside of anything we can hold in our hands. Thus, the intellectual property system is an intangible legal concept tasked with guarding intangibles.

AI has the potential to shrink the value proposition of intellectual property by shaking society's confidence regarding both the legal concept and the things protected. The fact that both are intangibles requires particular care in parsing through the issues, and the following sections of the chapter explore each of these intangibles, in turn.

7.1 THE VALUE OF THE REGIME

The impact of AI on the value of intellectual property should be understood by examining both the value proposition of the system itself, and the value of that which it protects, both of which are intangibles. At either level, however, one should begin by understanding a remarkable ability within our society: We are able to bestow value on things that do not exist simply by creating a myth that everyone believes. In other words, things we cannot see or touch have value simply because we believe they do. Before examining the concept of mythmaking in the intellectual property regimes, let's start with something basic: money.

7.1.1 Money and Myth

The global economy is sustained by a simple myth: people believe in the fiction that the paper or coins in your pocket actually have value.[5] As explained by Nobel Prize-winning economist Milton Friedman:

> [P]rivate persons accept [money] because they are confident that others will. The pieces of green paper have value because everybody thinks they have value. Everybody thinks they have value because in everybody's experience they have value.... The United States could barely operate without a common and widely accepted medium of exchange ...; yet the existence of a common and widely accepted medium of exchange rests on a convention:

our whole monetary system owes its existence to the mutual acceptance of what, from one point of view, is no more than fiction.[6]

Quite simply, it is only our collective belief in the value of money that grants it the status of "the root of all evil" (as noted in the King James version of the Bible)[7] and the driving force that "makes the world go round" (as noted in the musical and movie, *Cabaret*).[8] Or, as a country western song explains, "Money can't buy everything. Well, maybe so. But it could buy me a boat."[9]

If humans simply stopped believing money had value, the global economy would collapse. We'd find our pockets full of little more than shreds of paper and shiny disks.

Such fictions are commonplace in the law, where they act as tools to conceptualize elusive and intangible things.[10] Consider the Supreme Court's *Wayfair* decision, concerning the taxability of retailers who exclusively operate online and have no physical presence. As one scholar notes, the Court "felt the need to express a view that data's intangible nature can still be conceptualized as tangible under the law."[11]

Or consider the legal notion of a corporation. We think of "the corporation" as something we all know and understand. Nevertheless, a corporation is a long-standing legal conception of something that, truth be told, is entirely fictional and intangible.[12] Society has endowed it with rights, obligations, and an identity – an entity some consider close to personhood.

This form of mythmaking undergirds the problem faced by all four intellectual property regimes. As described at the beginning of this chapter, the intellectual property system consists of intangible legal rights guarding different forms of intangibles. As with all intangibles, the value rests on a shared conviction that the thing exists and that we know what it is. And, of course, we must also believe that whatever its definition, the thing has value and we know how to assess that value. Unfortunately, AI threatens to profoundly undermine the value of the myth-based system we call intellectual property, both at the level of the system itself and at the level of what the system protects.

Consider first the intellectual property system itself. For our purposes, the most stunning impact of AI on the value of intellectual property relates to whether we need the system at all. More precisely, the question is whether we need one particular part of the system – trademark. The next section (Section 7.1.2) examines the trademark question in depth.

7.1.2 Trademark: Will the Myth Survive?

The trademark system has worked reasonably well for centuries. Some scholars even trace trademark back to ancient[13] practices in which tradespeople would put a mark on the goods they created. Despite this lengthy pedigree, AI threatens to undermine the entire value proposition of the trademark system.

Under its modern conception as described in Chapter 2, the trademark regime operates to reduce consumer search costs by allowing consumers to rely on the positive reputation of trademark holders they trust. Past theories of trademark rested on notions such as protecting the morality of the marketplace, or the interests of producers, from deceptive practices. Without trademark rights, charlatans could more easily trick consumers into believing that an inferior item came from a respected source.

Modern trademark problems flow from concerns about disinformation and misinformation.[14] Consumers, saturated with information from the internet and social media, are driven to look beyond the trademark for information about a product's source and quality. This depletion of consumers' trust in the trademark seriously undermines the role and value proposition of the trademark system.[15]

The emergence of AI compounds and magnifies these trends. Consider misinformation and disinformation. AI enhances the ability of bad actors to obfuscate information and mislead a consumer as to a commercial item's quality and source. Retail giants like Amazon, along with brand-name producers, are plagued by the diversion of sales from name brands to subpar or even counterfeit goods by those who pose as the trademarked seller or a third party selling the trademarked product.[16] For example, a consumer might search Amazon for "Lululemon yoga pants" and find that the first item on the list *appears* to be the Lululemon product but is actually a cheap knockoff from an unknown brand. It can require scrolling past multiple listings to reach the desired product and brand.

Further concerns flow from AI's magnification of fake positive reviews, as well as from influencers and evaluators who may appear neutral but are paid by producers and thus have an interest in declaring the product a "must have" or "one of the top-ten."[17] Although paid evaluators and fake reviews existed before AI, AI can vastly improve the ability of bad actors to send susceptible buyers targeted messages, identify types of brands more vulnerable to such practices, and find the most effective pathways to unethically market their products.[18]

Of course, online retailers can engage in behavior similar to influencers; Companies might pay Amazon to list their product first as a "sponsored product" or as a product "other consumers have purchased." Such approaches are reminiscent of the brick-and-mortar practice in which one brand buys space on an eye-level shelf or the end of an aisle to better attract consumer attention. If we don't object to buying shelf space, should we object to sponsored or featured products online? Federal consumer protection regulations do treat the two categories differently. For example, since 2002, the FTC has required that search engines say when something is a sponsored product. By contrast, brick-and-mortar stores need not disclose that a product placed at eye level or at the end of an aisle is sponsored.[19] The stipulation for online promotion may flow from a recognition that the potential for confusion and misdirection may be greater in the fast-paced and sometimes bamboozling world online.[20]

Describing the potential for other nefarious schemes, Jon M. Garon suggests that sophisticated bots and massive disinformation campaigns could devalue or undercut a trademark by "cybersquat[ting] on the training data."[21] In this way, a competitor could register a mark inappropriately (for example, registering Mercedes.com when you are not the automotive company, Mercedes-Benz) or use a mark that closely approximates a holder's trademark. Bots could then inflate the number of clicks on the fraudulent mark's product, resulting in distorted training data that causes AI to make inaccurate recommendations.[22] Bot-click techniques also could distort the data or recommendations for current cites or evaluators, suggesting that more people are buying a product or posting positive reviews, when all of that information is generated by bots. The impact would unfold in real time, creating a shifting landscape that would be difficult to police or remedy.

Similarly, some bad actors are able to hijack a seller's listing on platforms such as Amazon, tricking the consumer into purchasing a counterfeit item of inferior quality.[23] Thus, hijackers create a copy of the seller's product. By claiming to sell the actual product, the copier secures a spot on Amazon's listing as another seller of the product, the same as a legitimate reseller. Amazon may locate the coveted "add to cart" icon with the seller offering the lowest price, and most buyers go with the default seller chosen by Amazon. Thus, if the hijacker offers a cheaper price, sales will be diverted there.

Hijacking, however, hurts the genuine seller more than if sales were simply diverted. Consumers who receive a low-quality good (or receive nothing) may mistakenly go back to the real company's site, or to evaluator sites such as Yelp, posting poor ratings and bad reviews.[24] Modern AI has the ability to help choose targets more effectively, amplify the effects of the hijacking, or help hijackers jump around quickly to avoid detection. As noted with the other nefarious schemes above, hijacking can poison AI's training data for future rounds so that the producer's product is captured as one with low quality or poor service ratings.

Many of these shady practices above would constitute trademark infringement, if the trademark holder could easily catch and prosecute the perpetrators. However, competitors need not step over the line of trademark infringement to undermine the trademark system. Concepts like "consumer confusion" lie at the heart of modern trademark cases,[25] and AI may portend a more sophisticated ability to inject some level of confusion without triggering a claim of trademark misappropriation. One can imagine programming an AI to first analyze case decisions on infringement and then design a trademark that comes close to a competitor's mark but has a low risk of constituting infringement. Thus, AI may make it easier for competitors to come achingly close to the line of trademark infringement without stepping over it.

The boundaries and foundations of the trademark regime could be reinforced through its expansion, so that borderline behavior is delineated as inappropriate. In that way, today's gray area becomes tomorrow's infringement. But as with all whack-a-mole games, it can be tough to stay ahead.

Other bad-faith behaviors – ones that leap over the lines of legality – could also undermine the value of the trademark system. From a national security perspective, one might worry about the ability of foreign states to sponsor disinformation campaigns intended to shift consumer purchasing behavior.[26] Concerns about state-sponsored misinformation campaigns are making headlines these days in the context of manipulating public opinion[27] but conceivably, a state also could try to shift consumer purchasing behavior to benefit its own interests. For example, one could imagine a nation that relies on producing generic medicines stoking fears that generic medicines produced in another country suffer from quality-control problems. Similarly, one could imagine a nation creating a back-door method of accessing electronics that allows eavesdropping. To increase the number of users who bought the compromised products, the nation could use the above AI-supported techniques to divert consumer attention – especially effective if the product was offered more cheaply. In this way, a given nation could subsidize US consumer spending in the pursuit of compromising those consumers.

To state it broadly, AI helps create a better thief. The outcome is unsurprising. One could not reasonably expect AI to enhance efficiency and effectiveness only for those who wish to do good. Moreover, the history of technological advancement contradicts any suggestion that new technologies only benefit good actors.

Other forms of AI influence may also reduce the value of the trademark system. Michael R. Grynberg argues that the importance of trademarks may fade in the face of AI for two reasons.[28] First, AI can inexpensively gather a wealth of information in a heartbeat, analyzing quality in more depth than the "relatively simple signals embodied in brand names."[29] Sources such as reviews, seller product information, and message board discussions, which would require a consumer to pile up search costs, can be scanned and evaluated in a few seconds by an AI.[30] This may be thought of as similar to AI's capability to collect documents of prior art in the patent context.

Even sites like Amazon, Alibaba, and Rakuten create a third-party filtering of goods. The phenomenon is reminiscent of the role of department stores or big box stores, but, as noted, it is far easier to make mistakes or to mislead consumers online.

In addition, AI's power combines with the explosion in social media to point consumers' eyes in directions other than the trademark for obtaining information about product quality. (And perhaps it's a two-way street: AI technology has helped spark the social media revolution, as well.) Consumers already pay less attention to trademarks or disregard them entirely. As Daniel Seng points out, the reputation of an online platform, such as Amazon, and the platform's own rating system, "have largely replaced the traditional forms of trust from dealings with physical platforms and known traders."[31] Garon makes similar observations, suggesting that AI-generated product recommendations are interfering with the role of trademark and traditional brand management and that AI will entirely replace the role of trademarks as a source for identifying goods and services.[32]

Imagine the role of trademarks in purchasing decisions of the future. Will any of us buy books anymore because they are by a certain author or from a particular publisher, or will we only seek out sources such as Goodreads, Oprah's recommendations, or BookTok[33]? Will you choose Nike running shoes because you like the Nike fit and durability, or will you go with what your trainer suggested? And if your trainer is active on a social media platform, will you look further on that platform for product recommendations? In the modern era, it would be unsurprising if you decided to switch to On Clouds shoes if your favorite movie star or influencer enthusiastically recommends them. Although this kind of advertising has existed for a very long time, AI has the power to speed up and manipulate the process.

On the whole, the trademark system faces significant challenges to its time-honored position of signaling the quality of goods and services. Instead, AI has helped give consumers alternative sources for comparing products and evaluating the quality of goods, all with an ease that reduces search costs.[34]

This is not to suggest that trademarks – and the trademark system – will disappear entirely. Producers and products still need names. Even third-party evaluator sites, such as Goodreads and BookTok, have names of their own, and the names are trademarked. Nevertheless, names and other trademarks may no longer need to do as much work as they did before in capturing the consumer's attention and staying in the consumer's mind, and trademarks may play a much smaller role in communicating value. If it's true that we just don't need it as much anymore, then the value proposition of the trademark system itself has undoubtedly declined.

We will return to the value proposition of the intellectual property regimes, themselves, in Section 7.3. For now, though, we turn to the value of the individual items protected by intellectual property.

7.2 THE VALUE OF THINGS PROTECTED

As described at the outset of this chapter, intellectual property regimes are no more than intangible concepts. They are legal tools society has created to protect an invention, expression, secret, or reputation. The things protected – inventions, expressions, secrets, and reputations – are also intangibles. You can certainly hold in your hand a piece of paper with a poem written on it, a notebook containing a secret formula, or a USB flash drive with a movie on it. Those, however, are just single, tangible embodiments; the things protected remain intangibles that cannot be confined in the three-dimensional realm. Instead, the paper in your hand constitutes no more than a copy of the poem. The poem lives on, even if the piece of paper flies away in the wind.

Thus, intellectual property law consists of intangible legal rights protecting intangibles. It is to the second level, the intangibles protected, that we now turn.

In the land of intangibles stacked on intangibles, a shared understanding of meaning becomes particularly important. If we lose confidence that we all understand the nature of the thing that is being protected, the entire structure begins to crumble. As the following section describes, achieving that shared understanding can be challenging, even in the best of circumstances.

7.2.1 The Trouble with Language and Shared Understanding

To communicate effectively, all societies need a certain level of commitment to – and shared understanding of – those things that we believe exist.[35] The need for a shared commitment operates whether we are talking about something abstract or something concrete. For example, it just as important that we collectively believe *truth* exists as it is that we collectively believe *wood* exists – even while one of these may be easier to agree on than the other.[36]

These shared understandings help us grasp and categorize the world around us and enable us to communicate with one another coherently. Without them, we run into problems. If, for example, John believes sidewalks are infinitely expandable, then he may have difficulty explaining to a police officer – who believes in the finite nature of space – why he tried to drive his car on the sidewalk.

Language, with its concomitant uncertainties and indeterminacies, is not always a helpful handmaiden.[37] And indeed, the indefiniteness of language has been the subject of much academic commentary across the centuries.[38] As I have discussed in various past works, "The nature of language is such that once the truth is enshrined in it, the words chosen are subject to twisting and turning in a myriad of directions."[39] Despite our best efforts, "[l]anguage will always be subject to varying interpretations, no matter how clear and plain one tries to make it."[40]

Our common understandings aren't static either. Language evolves, as do our experiences and cultural conversations.[41] Nor is the law any stranger to the indeterminacy of language: those who draft and interpret contracts, not to mention caselaw and legislation, are intimately familiar with the difficulties of assigning meaning to words.[42]

Despite definitional difficulties, cultural experience and context can often endow a word with a shared understanding. When a colleague says, "I'm going out to get a sandwich – would you like one?" most people don't expect to receive a hot dog. If shared understandings were to break down, however, confidence in the definition of things we are talking about, and their value, would surely suffer. This is the world we are entering with AI.

7.2.2 How AI Challenges Our Shared Understandings

Complications that arise from the rapid development of AI are challenging our ability to identify and value the vast content protected by intellectual property. In that maelstrom, intellectual property may lose its ability to protect the value of something if one cannot reliably evaluate it in the first place.

Consider the interactions between producers and consumers of items embodying an intellectual property right – for example, a copyrighted book. Today's consumers have few reliable avenues to determine the origin of what they are looking at, whether the product or information is of value, or for that matter, whether anything about it can be trusted. Similarly, producers no longer have an efficient and trusted way to communicate that information. The situation creates an information desert – a bleak and barren expanse of nothing but shifting sand.

I have written about "information deserts" in other contexts.[43] The notion begins by asking what parties who are entering a particular informational arena would want to know. In the case of the many things protected by intellectual property – such as information, creative content, and inventions – a consumer might want to know: (1) What is it? (2) What is its origin? (3) What is its value? and (4) How much can I trust it?

Suppose I buy a book on US–China diplomatic relations that recounts interactions between the nations' leaders over the last decade. Can I be certain the book was written by a human, rather than an AI system? If it was written by or with the help of an AI system, can I trust the accuracy of its information and sources? Furthermore, might some or all of the facts in the book be the inaccurate results of AI "hallucination"?

Even if there are sources cited, perhaps the sources themselves are the subject of disinformation or misinformation campaigns, which AI can facilitate more effectively than ever. Suppose a particular "fact," "understanding at the time," "possible motive," or "frequently discussed interpretation" is really a piece of disinformation. Say it comes from a foreign-state-sponsored campaign using AI systems to widely and strategically distribute a supposed fact or interpretation until it eventually enters the mainstream, after which it can become a citable source. It may take a lot of time and effort for a reader to figure that out. By the time someone exposes the lie, the distortion may have already permeated society, and the truth may be irrelevant or obsolete.

For reliability, I might turn to my old friend trademark, looking for the name of a publisher I know and trust. But how many readers actually rely on publishers to find the books they read anymore? As one news site commented (without empirical sources, I should note):

> Until a few years ago, publishers wielded power over readers' selection of books though [*sic*] in-store promotions and newspaper reviews. Now readers increasingly order their books online or download them onto electronic reading devices, write their own reviews and get ideas for what to read next from peers online.[44]

With due apologies to my distinguished publisher Cambridge University Press, readers seem to be relying less and less on the hallowed publishing houses, whose reputations are protected by trademark.

As for the book I am thinking of reading, maybe I could rely on reviews or reviewing sites I know. But can I depend on those? How do I know they are legitimate? Could a slew of positive reviews on a book review site I love have been generated by AI bots? Could my favorite reviewer be sponsored by, or at least be receiving "free gifts" from, product marketers? Taking it a step further, is it possible that my favorite "person" who writes reviews is actually an AI that has been trained on data about me, such as which sites I visit, how long I spend on a particular image or website, and more?[45] For most people, understanding the complexities and incentives that surround copyrighted works in an era of AI is overwhelming – and it's not getting any easier.

The challenges AI brings to the copyright system reach far beyond the uncertainty of whether using generative AI constitutes copyright infringement, whether works generated by AI will receive copyright protection, or whether copyrighted works will become less protectible due to generative AI – although these factors could undermine the value of copyrights. Rather, the problem looming on the horizon concerns authorship. How can one have confidence in the value of work covered by copyright if one cannot determine the extent to which the work is a product of someone or something other than a human author? On a more fundamental level, this harkens back to the question of confidence in the value of the copyright system itself.

One can try to reinforce the system in the face of this uncertainty by conceptualizing a copyright holder as a creator who used AI as a tool and whose reputation rests on their ability to use and evaluate that tool.[46] Because AI is so complex, however, it may be unclear how much any individual or organization can understand and evaluate AI's role in a given creative process. It may be true that AI can test, evaluate, learn, and adjust more rapidly than a human can follow – true even for those who created the AI. They, too, may struggle to fully understand what the AI has done and how good the result is.

As a result, consumers may lack faith that a copyright holder is able to properly judge the quality of an output when AI tools are used.[47] In addition, as AI becomes easier to use, it may become irresistible for users to adopt AI faster than they can police its quality.[48]

The examples above demonstrate a few of the copyright aspects of determining the value of the content of a book and deciding whether one wants to read it. The current state of AI risks leaving potential consumers, users, and creators of copyrightable works wandering in an information desert. Valuing an individual work becomes difficult when one cannot readily identify what the work is or the identity of its creator (human or AI), what ingredients or sources it relies on, and thus how much one can trust it.

Of course, these are not necessarily new problems. Many technological innovations prior to AI have enhanced the mechanisms for fraud and value confusion. Nevertheless, AI has supercharged the problem. The ability to use AI to gather information, target preferences, create misinformation and disinformation, and sow uncertainty about a work's origins presents a new set of challenges and adds a new dimension to prior challenges. Moreover, the emergence of generative AI models, such as ChatGPT, exacerbates challenges to the reliability of information. The black-box nature of the transformation system may defy attempts to specify the origin, or multiple origins, of the reply to the prompt.

Some of the uncertainty regarding influences – and the extent of those influences' contributions – were bubbling under the surface of copyright long before AI appeared on the scene. As discussed in Section 3.3, authors and artists are influenced by works around them all the time, and virtually any item can permissibly serve as a muse, as long as the inspired work does not come too close to the inspiration.[49] As noted in Section 7.1.2, AI has an increasing capacity to learn how to approach the legal line without stepping over it. Wherever the legal lines are drawn, AI could be programmed to ensure that the words, style, or tone adapted into a work stopped short of the legally recognized line of copyright infringement. Of course, human creators could do that now. Any writer or artist could hire an army of attorneys to check the work for potentially infringing uses of any work to which the artist may have been exposed. But today, that inquiry would be prohibitively expensive – not to mention extraordinarily difficult to accomplish. In contrast, AI can do even more than that in the space of a few seconds.

Some of these concerns potentially could be mitigated as technology evolves. For example, perhaps generative AI will develop so that its sources can be tagged and traced – or at least, marked to indicate that a given source cited isn't the result of a hallucination. AI theoretically could develop so that it might spit out a footprint of the path it traveled, accessible to anyone who cared. Although theoretically possible, such a solution might significantly hinder an AI or its users. Worse yet, the record might simply be ignored, rendering such an exercise useless.[50]

A similar problem plagues the various proposals to strengthen confidence in AI through disclosure. Voices ranging from scholars[51] to members of Congress[52] are recommending that authors should provide notice when AI has been used in the process of creation. And in the EU, providers of AI systems that are designed to interact directly with humans are, or soon will be, required to inform users that they are interacting with an AI system.[53] In the United States, the Copyright Office itself has gone a step further, requiring that authors seeking copyright protection disclose the inclusion of AI-generated content and provide an explanation of the human author's contributions to the work.[54]

One can already see examples of press articles providing notice that the work was drafted by AI. For example, the media company CNET has reportedly used the following disclaimer: "This article was generated using automation technology and thoroughly edited and fact-checked by an editor on our editorial staff."[55]

If we take the disclosure route, however, companies may be tempted to create blanket disclosures that do not actually provide much information. For example, companies could choose to always note that any article may have been researched or drafted by or with the assistance of AI – thereby providing little substantive information.

Such blanket disclosures can become useless, if sufficiently widespread. Consider the Proposition 65 warnings in California. Enacted in 1986, Proposition 65 requires that businesses "provide warnings to Californians about significant exposures to chemicals that cause cancer, birth defects or other reproductive harm."[56] The result is that most office buildings, residential apartment buildings, and other commercial locations contain a Proposition 65 notice warning that the premises may contain these chemicals. One could hardly survive, however, without entering a single office, residential, or commercial building, and it's difficult to tell which premises may in fact be dangerous.

At the end of the day, there is no evidence that California citizens pay any attention to these warnings. Press and academic commentators have noted that the ubiquitous warnings are simply ignored.[57] The *Los Angeles Times* reported on an investigation that concluded California consumers are "overwarned, underinformed and potentially unprotected" by the abundance of Proposition 65 warnings.[58]

Even when disclosures are more definite and explicit, consumers are likely to pay little attention when warnings are ubiquitous. Ask anyone who has ever bought a pack of cigarettes whether they paid attention to the warnings on the packaging.

To the extent we are trying to shore up the value of things protected by intellectual property, the real question is whether blanket warning signs can help reassure the public about the quality of products in general. That is tough to accomplish if the public is ignoring everything. It's hard enough for a warning to be effective in relation to tangible things, like packs of cigarettes – but it's even harder when it comes to intangibles, the fundamental concern of intellectual property. Most important, how effective can a warning be when an AI system itself might intentionally or unintentionally undermine that warning by giving the impression of being more reliable, accurate, or ethical than it actually is?

In short, when it comes to intangibles, a key part of the value relies on a shared conviction that the intangible represents something and that we have a reasonable idea what that something is. To the extent AI alters the public's confidence that they understand the contours and value of an item protected by intellectual property, the value proposition of that specific item declines. On the whole, AI is creating uncertainty about key valuation issues throughout the types of items protected.

7.3 AI'S EFFECTS ON CERTAINTY AND QUALITY

As any economist will attest, uncertainty undermines value. Just watch the stock market react to general uncertainty about the economic climate in general, or the stability of an individual company in particular. Similarly, as AI introduces many forms of uncertainty about the provenance and reliability of works protected by intellectual property,[59] the myth surrounding the intellectual property regimes, themselves, may suffer. After all, how valuable is a regime, if we cannot figure out the value of the things it is supposed to protect. As a result, AI may undermine the value of the regimes as a whole, not just the value of the items protected.

In addition to concerns about sources and origins, AI has a more insidious effect on quality, which threatens to weaken the value of the intellectual property systems. For example, generative AI may make life easier for writers and artists, but it does not necessarily improve the quality of the output. At least right now, the written content that AI assists with and produces is often more banal and less insightful – let alone less humorous or personable – than the work a decent writer can produce. The tendency for AI to produce mediocrity (or at best, uninteresting conformity) is likely to change over time, as the capabilities of AI become more refined. Nevertheless, although computers have always been better than humans at tasks that require skills such as identifying patterns and quickly processing information – they have lagged far behind humans in the more subtle qualities of intuition and judgment, which computers have yet to "learn."[60] The same may also prove true for artistic and linguistic creativity, as well as novel analysis of thought.

Of course, there are many mediocre human writers out there too. But as more mediocre content is produced, the average quality across the copyright system diminishes. When everything becomes mediocre, that, too, can undermine the value proposition of intellectual property. If society is creating the potential to earn a reward for something that is, on average, lower quality, the value of the entire exercise is reduced. It raises questions concerning what we, as a society, are rewarding and whether the measure of the potential reward still correlates with the value the thing provides.

Finally, much like to the threat faced by copyright, trademark also faces the threat. AI already offers the promise of quickly and inexpensively created trade names and other types of trademarks. However, conversations with industry insiders suggest that the secret sauce of a wildly successful trademark flows from human instinct in a way that AI cannot replicate. If that assessment is valid, the poorer quality and less effective AI-invented trademarks may reduce the overall quality of the field. As with copyright, AI has the potential to make trademark design easier and cheaper, while degrading the quality – and subsequently, the value – of the trademark regime.

How can consumers have confidence in the value of a trademark if they cannot determine the extent to which the goods are the product of something other than the trademark holder? Moreover, in the case of AI participation, how can they have confidence in the ability of the mark holder to thoroughly understand and judge what the AI might have done?[61] These issues undermine the system's ability to provide the value for which it was created.

In sum, the intellectual property system offers protection for the invention, expression, secrets, or reputation protected. In each case, the value rests on the myth that each system has value, and that we have a shared understanding of the items protected. AI has the potential to shake society's confidence at both levels, thereby shrinking the value proposition of patents, copyrights, trade secrets, and trademark.

PART IV

Pathways Forward

The onward march of AI poses fundamental challenges for the entire intellectual property system. For patent, trade secret, and copyright, the challenge flows from AI's interaction with and influence on the definition of protectible creations and information. As discussed earlier, the discordance risks significantly shrinking the pool of what is subject to protection by patent, trade secret, and copyright.

In addition to shrinking the pool of things subject to intellectual property protection, AI is eroding the value proposition of intellectual property, both on the level of the intellectual property regimes themselves and on the level of the items protected.

Regarding the value of the regimes, themselves, trademark is likely to suffer particular impact. In combination with social media and other alternative methods of conveying information on source and quality, AI threatens to unseat the trademark system as the king of product information. If alternatives flourish, society may need trademark far less than it has in the past.

Trademark, however, is not alone in suffering a loss of value on the level of the regime. Looking across the other three regimes, each may suffer if we cannot figure out the value of the things the regime is supposed to protect. In addition, AI also may have an insidious effect on creative and inventive quality, which could weaken the value of the intellectual property systems as a whole.

Moving from the level of the regimes themselves to the level of the things protected, the value of protected items rests on our shared conviction that we can define basic characteristics of the things protected – such as their origins and reliability – and that we know how to value them. To the degree that AI shakes public confidence in these shared understandings of these items, it could weaken the value of each of these inventions, expressions, and secrets..

In short, to the extent AI shakes our faith in the value of these regimes, it begins to dissolve the myth that sustains the intellectual property systems, along with their ability to grant value to an individual invention, expression, business secret, or reputation. Thus, AI stands to profoundly impact intellectual property by shrinking the value proposition of all four regimes.

The final chapters explore methods of buttressing the value of these four systems by trimming the rights to reinforce them and by restoring public confidence. Describing these pathways requires a brief allegory.

8 THE ALLEGORY OF THE DIAMOND

In a television tale set in Regency England, a capricious queen, with a penchant for towering hairdos, presides over glittering social seasons in which young, eligible maidens vie for the hand of eligible bachelors.[1] Each year, the queen declares one maiden to be the season's "diamond" – an exceptionally rare, stunning, and refined young woman, who therefore becomes the most sought-after commodity. (I use the consciously ironic style of the series as my muse.) The show is, of course, the immensely popular *Bridgerton*, whose third season ranks among the top-ten most-watched Netflix series of all time.[2]

The show is not unique in its use of this gem – diamonds have long been an archetype of rare qualities and exceptional value. Adding to that mystique is the diamond's role in romantic engagement, where it symbolizes the sought-after, life-long commitment of marriage. Of course, the diamond's lofty perch has come under assault with the arrival of its lab-grown kin, which are easier to produce and difficult to distinguish from "the real thing."[3] The price of natural diamonds has fallen amidst uncertainty over the origin of gems and their long-term value.[4] And as the mystique fades, some brides are turning to other gemstones to express their individual style.[5] The author is not aware of research tying the fact that some brides have moved away from diamond engagement rings to the reduction in value of diamonds from the emergence of lab-grown diamonds.[6] Nevertheless, consumer preferences – and therefore value in the market – can be influenced by intangible associations and imagery.[7]

The saga of the beleaguered diamond provides the perfect allegory for AI's potential impact on intellectual property – and as I describe below, the diamond's story points to pathways for ensuring the long-term strength and viability of the intellectual property system. Together, the following two solutions could mitigate the problems described, with some regimes benefiting from the application of both. Most importantly, the two solutions also mesh with the foundational theories each regime relies upon.

9 PRESERVING VALUE BY LIMITING

As any monopolist (or economist) can tell you, the best way to increase value is restrict supply.[1] To take our analogy from the previous chapter, the diamond industry traditionally preserved the high price of diamonds by limiting the amount of product flowing from diamond mines into the market.[2] And therein lies a simple pathway for shoring up the value of intellectual property: Law could limit the supply of products subject to protection, casting the net only around the more remarkable and more protectible products, thereby preserving value not just for those products but for the longevity of the system itself.

In fact, limiting supply could mesh well with the kinds of markets that will inevitably emerge in a post-AI world. In particular, markets for certified human-made goods, which, by virtue of their artisanal nature, may end up holding considerable value. We've seen this phenomenon before. Consider earthenware goods: once upon a time, all bowls, plates, and cups were handmade – and their quality was often measured by their perfection and symmetry (which only a master could achieve by hand). Enter modern manufacturing, and overnight, the rich could buy machine-made symmetrical goods that far outstripped the masters'. The price of artisan goods plummeted, and it wasn't long before manufactured tableware was the norm; eventually, the handmade industry functionally collapsed. Nevertheless, the core lesson of the Allegory of the Diamond lies tucked within the humble earthenware saga, too. Once modern manufacturing became ubiquitous, unique products became increasingly harder to come by – even while humans still valued them. This desire for the one-of-a-kind breathed life back into the collapsed handmade market. Today, humans are willing to pay more for "unique" artisan goods, even though their manufactured counterparts might be "functionally" superior. Paradoxically, in a world of perfect manufactured goods, it is the imperfections of artisanal goods that we often seek out and value most.

AI has captured the popular imagination just as manufacturing once did. For now, we'll continue to see "AI" used in all kinds of labeling and branding to increase a product's draw for consumers. (Even golf club makers are adding "AI" markers to their golf club names.[3]) But if history serves as a guide, we may soon see the emergence of a kind of artisanal creativity movement, where creators will proudly advertise their blogs as "100% human-written," or their products as "100% human-designed." Of course, that assumes consumers have any reliable way to verify such claims – an issue I explore later on. For this section, however, the focus remains on preserving the value of goods protected by intellectual property through limiting the number of goods that receive the coveted prize.

The title of this chapter, Preserving Value by Limiting, is not intended to suggest that the limits haphazardly imposed by AI are the appropriate ones. Yes, the rapid expansion of AI may make some information and some creations – ones that currently receive protection – impossible or impractical to protect. That, in itself, shrinks the pool of protected content. But it can do so in ways that may be counterproductive to the goal of preserving value. As discussed above, AI makes trademark fraud easier, and its ability to rapidly and cheaply create mediocre works or products that fall within copyright and trademark could reduce the value of items under protection in both realms. And, of course, the use of training data undermines the protectability of copyrighted works.[4] In contrast to the haphazard boundaries developed by the current battles between AI and intellectual property, the boundaries shaped by the law should be considered and appropriate: limitations that operate to preserve value in the face of the AI revolution.

Preserving value for the diamonds of intellectual property would require trimming some protectible content that falls on the periphery of intellectual property's protected spheres. But perhaps it is time to trim intellectual property. Scholars have expressed concern for some time about the proliferation of intellectual property rights. Some bemoan the modern tendency to "propertize" everything about information,[5] while others decry the increasing tendency of some intellectual property regimes to favor producers over consumers and create systems of private controls that can stymie technological innovation and artistic creativity.[6]

For example, recall that any expression fixed in a tangible medium can be protectible, as long it contains a "modicum of creativity."[7] Moreover, the bar for a modicum of creativity remains so low as to be almost nonexistent. Against this backdrop, the expansion of electronic communication brings an explosion of material subject to copyright, from emails to computer code, datasets to Instagram photos, YouTube to TikTok videos, and any written social media posts longer than a short phrase.[8] Although the average person may not think in these terms, every email, text, and TikTok is potentially subject to copyright protection.

A similar situation is unfolding with trade secret law. For example, employers and pharmaceutical companies have expanded the material they suggest is covered by trade secret protection. These assertions are largely untested by the courts. In response, scholars have argued that the use of trade secrets has expanded well beyond the territory supportable by theory or precedent.[9] Moving to patent law, the sheer number of patents issued has more than doubled since the turn of the millennium.[10] Once again scholars and even some Supreme Court decisions have chimed in to express their doubts about patent validity issues ranging from obviousness to subject-matter coverage to disclosure.[11] For the pharmaceutical space, the proliferation of follow-on patents – particularly ones that protect minor modifications of a patented drug – has raised particular concern about the quality of patents and the ability of improper patents to block out downstream competition.[12]

Trademark law also has expanded, with the development of doctrines related to trademark dilution, including blurring and tarnishing, both of which are the subject of debate.[13] Tarnishment occurs when another seller uses the trademark with a line of goods that has either a negative connotation or a lower level of quality that the trademarked line. For example, imagine a line of pet-odor carpet sprays called CoCo Kenel – as a play on the perfume company Coco Chanel. This type of use can potentially harm the trademark holder's mark by associating the two in the consumer's mind. Blurring occurs when another seller uses a famous trademark on a line of unrelated goods, for example, using Microsoft's name on a line of mattresses.

Finally, some companies have been able to expand the coverage of intellectual property regimes by contracting for larger coverage. These issues may arise in trade secret contracts, in which the secret-holder defines the area of protection to include the catch-all phrase "confidential information." This type of language can sweep in protection for information that does not rise to the level of a protectible trade secret. Similarly, some patent and copyright contracts expand coverage to items that fall outside the definition of protectible inventions and creations, for example by extending protection even if the invention fails to receive a patent, or if the book merely copies what is already in the public domain.[14]

As with the diamond allegory, it is rarity that enhances reward; expansions of supply are likely to undermine value.[15] Thus, the modern expansion of intellectual property rights, whether welcome or controversial, likely reduces the allure of each protected work. To offer a simple example, imagine that the definition of what is a protected molecule has expanded, resulting in a proliferation of patented molecules to test against a particular disease state. If you charge too much for your molecule, a developer will turn somewhere else; but if yours is the only game in town, your pricing power is greatly enhanced. In the same vein, if the market is crammed with low-value products, the search for the diamond becomes more difficult (and costly) for consumers. And if you have to kiss a lot of frogs to find the prince, the mystique and allure of frogs – not to mention frog-kissing – declines considerably.

The modern expansion of intellectual property rights meshes well with the changes required to preserve value in the face of the AI onslaught. The adaptations won't require wholesale reimagining of the various regimes. First, taking a closer look at the patent and copyright regimes reveals doctrines that are largely ignored but have great potential for measuring the value of the human contribution to a protected work and appropriately limiting the pool. We can begin with the patent system.

Within the five elements required to sustain patentability lies the sadly ignored doctrine of "usefulness." One would not have expected the doctrine to languish so extensively, given its pedigree. The Constitution dedicates one of the few words in the intellectual property clause to this concept, referencing the grant of power to Congress "[t]o promote the Progress of Science and useful Arts."[16] In the legislative context, the usefulness requirement appeared in the opening of the Patent Act of 1793[17] and continues to occupy a prominent position in today's Patent Act, which specifies:

> Whoever invents or discovers any new and *useful* process, machine, manufacture, or composition of matter, or any new and useful improvement thereof, may obtain a patent.[18] (emphasis added)

Nevertheless, as Risch explains, "usefulness has been largely ignored, [becoming] the toothless and misunderstood 'utility' doctrine, which requires that patents only have a bare minimum potential for use."[19] This is not to suggest that courts have never used the utility doctrine when overturning patents, but the doctrine's applications are few and far between.[20]

The development of a robust doctrine of usefulness could result in a significant trimming of the inventions that are deemed patentable. Along these lines, scholars have suggested restricting patents for inventions that do not improve on other things on the market,[21] patents that would cost the consumer more than the invention costs to make,[22] or patents for which there is no social usefulness. These types of approaches could form the beginning of a useful doctrine of usefulness.[23] Only the truly inventive – the rare find amidst the fool's gold – would be eligible for protection.

Limiting patent protection to the true gems could help shore up the value of patents, from the perspective that scarcity increases value. Moreover, it could blunt other negative impacts of AI described above. Recall that if the conceptualization of a person having ordinary skill in the art includes that person using AI, the sophistication of widely available, modern AI tools could threaten the protected status of many inventions through its ability to more thoroughly comb through vast libraries of knowledge. Limiting protection to the more inventive end of the scale makes it less likely for a PHOSITA, even one using AI as a tool, to find the invention preexistent in prior art or even to dredge something out to demonstrate obviousness.

One might also consider shifting the analysis of prior art away from scrutinizing minute aspects of documents to provide more emphasis on the testimony of those who actually use and invent current art. That shift would move the locus of the analysis away from the stronghold of AI and closer to the human realm.[24]

Moving beyond patents, the copyright regime houses its own feeble doctrine that could be strengthened in service of preserving value. Specifically, copyright protection applies only to those works containing a modicum of creativity. In the definitive modern case on the topic, *Feist v. Rural Telephone Services*, the Supreme Court explained that "the requisite level of creativity is extremely low; even a slight amount will suffice."[25] The Justices then use a variety of phrases to indicate that the minutest morsel of creativity will suffice, explaining that failing the test would require that "the creative spark is utterly lacking," the creativity is "so trivial as to be virtually nonexistent" and the work is "devoid of even the slightest trace of creativity."[26]

Admittedly, creativity is a tricky notion to define with any degree of clarity. Russ VerSteeg makes a valiant attempt in a 1993 piece in which he turns to philosophers, cognitive scientists, and psychoanalytic theorists in search of a definition.[27] In the end, VerSteeg concludes that the law should just avoid the inquiry altogether and merely satisfy the creativity analysis by comparing the degree of difference between the work and prior works to which the author had access.[28]

Justin Hughes also bemoans copyright's current iteration of the creativity doctrine. He argues that the Justices in *Feist* ask judges to search for creativity "by detecting small amounts with the accuracy of a Geiger counter" and ignore "Justice Holmes's thundering admonition in *Bleistein* … that judges are *not* to make aesthetic judgments."[29]

In its purity of form as identified by the Supreme Court, however, the modicum-of-creativity doctrine only barely manages to serve as a gatekeeper for copyright. In an era in which every thought dashed off from the top of one's head as an email, text, or social media post is the potential recipient of copyright protection, a higher threshold for creativity is certainly needed.[30]

Helpful models do exist in the academic literature, some of which suggest focusing on the tools used by the creator or the creator's process.[31] Describing these and other proposed approaches, let alone choosing among them, would be several chapters' worth of writing all on its own. For the purpose of this book, I simply note that a more robust doctrine – and specifically, one that trims the forest of works subject to copyright protection – could enhance value by focusing protection on works of greater creativity *without* wading into aesthetic judgments. That shift alone, however, is insufficient to mitigate the broader, more far-reaching effects of AI described above. The solution will require more, as described in Chapter 10.

In contrast to the patent and copyright regimes, no dormant or moribund doctrines stand out in trade secret law as a handy vehicle for enhancing value. This may occur, in part, because there is a dearth of legal precedent – especially given the recent flowering of trade secrets and the passage of federal legislation to provide federal and civil trade secret rights. Nevertheless, there are opportunities to strengthen doctrines within trade secret in a manner that might reduce trade secret proliferation and focus the rights on more valuable information, thereby enhancing the value of the entire regime.

The basic principles that would benefit from sharpening include that: (1) Trade secret functions to police market-competitive boundaries and guard against misappropriation. It should not serve a tool for open-ended concealment;[32] (2) The fact that a company would suffer competitive harm if information were released does not mean, in and of itself, that release of the information would implicate trade secret rights. The information might not rise to the level of a trade secret in the first place;[33] and (3) Price terms negotiated in an adversarial process between two parties cannot later be claimed by both as a joint invention.[34]

Shrinking the pool in the manner described above not only would enhance value in the abstract: It also would address the concern that AI can readily develop whatever information humans develop or assemble to assist their business. If AI can easily and independently develop the solution, then perhaps that solution is, indeed, of lesser value and less deserving of protection – assuming that the AI also can choose the best of several options.[35] In any event, these concerns are consistent with the underlying doctrines and theoretic concepts of the regimes, and it is possible to clarify and further apply the doctrines to begin addressing them.

Returning now to all four intellectual property regimes – patent, copyright, trademark, and trade secret, the breadth of each of these regimes could be better bounded, in ways that would focus on protecting only those things that lie at the core of the protection goals and theories. Limiting supply in this manner would strengthen the value of each gem that received protection, which would help shore up each regime in the face of the AI revolution.

10 PRESERVING VALUE BY CERTIFICATION

I consider myself not just a techno-optimist, but also a techno-realist.[1] For example, emerging technologies such as artificial intelligence can bring extraordinary advancements for society and individuals alike.[2] They can also, however, bring their fair share of challenges, and for AI, one of those problems is trustworthiness.

As described in Chapter 9, we can preserve the value of individual intellectual property regimes by shrinking the pool of items that receive the coveted prizes of patent, copyright, trademark, or trade secret. More can be done, however, to shore up the foundation of the entire intellectual property system, particularly for copyright, trademark, and to some extent patent.

One possible solution to the problem has been around for well over a century in the context of brick-and-mortar goods. For example, consumers across many generations have known of the eponymous Good Housekeeping Seal of Approval. Launched in 1909, the Good Housekeeping Seal of Approval is an emblem indicating that a product has been evaluated by the Good Housekeeping Institute and deemed trustworthy.[3] Above all other consumer rating services, this one has become a household name and even a general term for something of reliable quality. (International readers might be more familiar with the Forest Stewardship Council's (FSC) 100 percent mark that indicates a product is made entirely from responsibly managed, FSC-certified forests.) It's worth considering how a trusted certification like this might help AI companies earn the confidence of consumers – and it's easy to see why earning that confidence is so important.

10.1 PRIVATE APPROACH

As described above, both the copyright and trademark regimes suffer from confusion over the value, source, and reliability of the product. For copyright, questions include: Does an AI-assisted system, or other product or service powered by AI, draws from reliable training data? Does the work actually belong to the AI-assisted source providing it, or does it infringe on someone else's work? Beyond generative AI models like ChatGPT, one cannot even discern whether the creation was produced by humans, AI, or some combination of both. For trademark, one also cannot readily discern whether the product actually was made by the trademark holder and whether it lives up to the trademark holder's quality. Perhaps the product offered is simply stealing the genuine product's designation, replacing it with something of inferior quality. This desert of information leads to a reduction in consumer confidence, a loss of faith in the myth underlying the system, and resulting damage to the value propositions.[4] As a result, both of these regimes could benefit from a reliable third party offering – a certification that speaks directly to some or all of these concerns.

Even the patent regime could benefit from a certification system, in that a certification body could identify whether a product was produced with the assistance of AI at all. In the patent context, some scholars have suggested that the existence or degree of AI content should determine the level of scrutiny required for patentability or the standards applied.[5] For the purposes of this chapter however, the idea is that a certification body could contribute to reliable consumer information. Some consumers may value a product designed and produced without AI, similar to how many consumers currently value the labels handcrafted, organic, or non-GMO (free of genetically modified organisms). The certification body could ensure compliance with its definitions of an "AI-free" product. More than simply creating a niche product of higher value – hence higher price – for consumers willing to pay for it, an AI-free certification could help restore consumer confidence and certainty that they know what they are purchasing, particularly in this period of rapid transition.

The examples of trusted certification I mentioned earlier are far from unique. Various private certification and evaluation efforts exist, available by searching phrases such as "is 'product name' legit." Online retailers also address the problem by trying to reassure customers about their efforts to police fraud. But those efforts often fall short – not to mention on deaf ears – as consumers increasingly turn to third-party chat boards and evaluation services.

The proliferation of these sources merely increases consumer search costs and bewilderment: What types of standards does each evaluation service? Moreover, how can your average consumer know whether the certification group, or even the product review, is legitimate? What in today's world *can* be trusted or taken at face value? A standardized certification body – one that is focused on reassuring consumers in the rapidly changing environment of AI – could help stabilize value throughout the intellectual property regimes. Of course, the body could do other things as well, including serve to establish best practices for responsible use of AI. But my focus here is on reliability and trust.

Consider the ubiquitous Nutrition Facts label, which can be found on most packaged foods. From bread and milk to cereal and seaweed snacks, virtually all packaged foods display basic nutrition information in an easy-to-assimilate format. Wouldn't it be nice if people could similarly determine the extent to which products we consume from information-related industries are made of high-quality ingredients? For information industries such as news, search, generative AI, social media, and others, consumers should be able to tell whether and how much the material was created by AI, promoted by AI bots, sourced from AI-created materials, or simply produced as a deepfake.

The ability to obtain this information reliably and in a standard, easy-to-understand format could greatly enhance society's confidence in many of the types of products protected by intellectual property. Following the lead of Nutrition Facts, a certification body could develop a list of evaluators that could be easily reached for a given content area.

Such a label would answer questions more complex than whether AI played any role in creating the content. AI tools most likely already assist with color balancing, focusing, and other aspects of images in most news stories today, with the result the question of whether any AI is involved may not be helpful. Instead, a certification body could establish scales and measures for a given story, so that people know the "nutritional quality" of what they are consuming. Eventually, a small box, about the size of the Nutrition Facts label, could become instantly recognizable and universally trusted for evaluating information products.

This is not to suggest that the certification body would provide an analysis of whether the contents represent "The Truth." Rather, the goal would be to provide information on the sources and methods, letting consumers make their own choices in the marketplace of ideas.

In theory, the AI industry itself could establish its own certification, collaborating on certification criteria and on setting best practices. Given its expertise with its own products, that industry may be best suited to engage in a coordinated certification endeavor. Moreover, the AI industry, and particularly the more established players within it, has an incentive to police itself, along with any questionable uses of AI in the broader market. After all, major players fear the potential reputational damage that rogue actors and irresponsible elements could wreak. Perhaps, just perhaps, if the industry can get its own house in order, there will be less of a need for government to step in and write the rules itself.

However, the creative-content industry may object to allowing the AI industry to certify itself. From their perspective, it would be like inviting the fox to guard the henhouse. In addition, a private industry certification attempt would raise serious antitrust concerns. When a group of competitors get together to collaborate, antitrust lawyers – not to mention antitrust authorities – normally break out in hives. Key antitrust doctrines are designed to ensure that competitors fight each other fiercely for consumer attention, rather than shake hands and agree on a coordinated business approach that all must follow. The risk that such a gathering would be branded as collusion or oligopolistic behavior could deter the wise from participating. From that perspective, a private certification body from outside the AI industry could better withstand antitrust scrutiny, although it might lack the necessary cutting-edge information as the industry evolves.

Any private certification body, however, lacks the power to do anything but serve as a bully pulpit. The best a private body can do is encourage (or shame) industry participants into better behavior. Shaming and applauding are nice but carry little enforcing power. Consumers could ignore the certification body's message – opting perhaps for the allure of a lower price, quick access, or other shiny baubles. Similarly, the entire industry could ignore the certification body, and the message would disappear into the ether.

The key takeaway here is that a private industry certification body lacks the regulatory power to bind or restrict industry participants. For that, one needs government.

10.2 PUBLIC APPROACH

The private sector is not the only historic provider of certification services. A public sector certification effort for AI could be modeled after emblems such as the Department of Agriculture's USDA certifications or the strict Food and Drug Administration (FDA) regime in which prescription medication in interstate commerce must receive approval by the agency.

Either the federal government or individual states could establish certification bodies. In fact, California has already tried to dip its toes in these waters.[6] A federal body has the advantage, however, of avoiding a cacophony of individual state legislative approaches. The burden of different overlapping and conflicting regimes could hobble the development of artificial intelligence to the extent that it threatens the US lead over other international players in the industry. Thus, ideally, the federal government would be in the best position to establish an AI certification body, perhaps preempting state efforts.

10.3 A PUBLIC–PRIVATE CERTIFICATION MODEL

A public–private model would blend the best aspects of both types of certification bodies. Government, by itself, lacks the expertise to evaluate and keep abreast of this complex and rapidly evolving field. And as tempting as the FDA model may be, it would take far too long for the government to develop a similarly knowledgeable expert agency, even assuming Congress acted immediately to create and authorize one. On the other hand, industry lacks the ability to impose strictures or regulate in other ways – for example, by ensuring that relevant companies cooperate with the certification body. And, of course, industry players cannot even get into the same room, let alone coordinate, without having to tiptoe around antitrust constraints. Together, however, government and industry could power an efficient and effective certification process.

Models for certification organizations currently exist in the form of private organizations or as collaborations between industry and public bodies. These are less focused on comparative evaluation and certification than setting standards, however. In addition, the guidelines set by standards bodies may lack binding authority unless incorporated into voluntary contracts or government regulation.[7] In contrast, a public–private AI certification body would need, and could provide, greater authority.

10.4 PAYING FOR A PUBLIC–PRIVATE MODEL

And now for the toughest part: Where will we get the funding for a major certification endeavor? Any such enterprise will need extensive funding to remain constantly updated and stay ahead of the latest AI techniques. In the current economic environment, the federal government is seriously constrained in finding dollars to spend on anything new, and certainly for something as expensive as a public–private certification body. One could conceivably charge AI companies themselves for the certification, analogous to the user fees that produce significant income for the FDA. But while charging Google, Meta, Open AI, or Anthropic might be perfectly acceptable to many readers, the burden on startups and small enterprises proliferating the landscape could be crushing. The last thing the US needs is to discourage innovation in AI, given the importance of protecting our status as an international competitor, for both economic and national security reasons.

One can minimize the impact of a large cost by spreading that cost across a broad population. In that vein, one could spread some of the cost of the agency across all business and consumer internet connections. For example, one could establish small fees to be collected by internet service providers and/or by telecom services that offer access to broadband internet access.

To offer a back-of-the-envelope calculation, there were roughly 131 million broadband subscribers[8] and 386 million wireless phone subscriptions[9] in the United States in 2023. Together, that constitutes roughly 500 million accounts. If the government were to charge fifty cents a month the fee would generate $3 billion a year. The fee could be called a "Trust Fee," given that the certification body's goal is to enhance trust in anything related to information products. The money collected could fund – or at least help fund – a robust and effective AI certification body.

Of course, certification cannot solve all problems. Theft will always be a cat-and-mouse game, with enforcers needing to enhance their approaches as crafty thieves adapt. In a world without a coordinated and sanctioned certification body, individual rights holders could be left out in the cold in a Wild-West-style world of sophisticated AI tools, ones created and deployed both domestically and by foreign adversaries.

Nor can one find complete solace in the combination of both (1) limiting supply to enhance value and (2) a certification body. AI already has, and will continue to have, a profound impact on the intellectual property regimes. Nevertheless, the two pathways outlined could offer considerable progress toward mitigating the negative impact of AI.

CONCLUSION

Since generative AI models burst into the public consciousness a few, short years ago, scholars and commentators have pondered its impact on intellectual property. Of course, neither artificial intelligence nor generative models sprang from the earth fully formed in late 2022. Rather, AI technology has been seeping into numerous aspects of society for over a decade, gaining proficiency and sophistication at a breakneck pace. Developments in recent years, however, have launched AI into the next phase at quantum speed, and developments today are unfolding more rapidly than ever. The impact of AI on societal issues across the board will be legion, with intellectual property especially shaken.

Amidst this tumult, one aspect of AI has gone largely unnoticed. Specifically, as AI reaches its tendrils throughout our lives, it threatens to undermine the foundations of what we choose to protect with IP and how that work derives value, as well as how the IP system itself derives value. These shifting sands undermine the purpose and value of intellectual property, threatening, in turn, our conceptions of the value of human invention and creativity. AI threatens to substantially shrink the pool of inventions that can sustain patentability; elsewhere, AI threatens to shake confidence, dissolve the mystique, and undermine the value proposition of the various IP regimes themselves.

The intellectual property regimes, in many cases, do contain doctrines that can help measure the value of human contribution, although some are largely ignored or have lain dormant. By reshaping and reinvigorating these doctrines, intellectual property can evolve to manage the advent of AI while preserving respect for human contributions. In particular, AI can limit the pool of those things protectible to the more brilliant diamonds, helping to preserve value for all forms of creativity in the AI environment. This approach can be supported by the creation of a single, universally accepted, public–private certification body. Together, the strategies of trimming to save and enhancing confidence would help mitigate the looming problems in all four regimes of intellectual property, with some regimes benefitting from both.

An expert in the field of AI recently told me that they had always thought that we would know more about cognition by the time we reached this point with AI. And, indeed, the gap between the state of our technology and our understanding of it, as well as its impact, is vast. I return now to the opening sentiments of this book as a reminder that not only have we come very far, but also that we have very far to go. In that context, another of Alexander Pope's three-centuries-old observations remains remarkably prophetic: "Fools rush in where Angels fear to tread."[1] In truth, as AI continues to develop and society scrambles to adapt, we still have a lot of learning left to do[2] – about the technology, about its impact, and most important, about how society should best approach it.

NOTES

Introduction

1 U.S. CONST. art. I, § 8, cl. 7.
2 *Id.* cl. 9.
3 *Id.* cl. 8.
4 *See infra* Section 2.3 (discussing ways in which trademark is different from the other three intellectual property regimes).
5 *See generally* Mark A. Lemley, *Property, Intellectual Property, and Free Riding*, 83 TEX. L. REV. 1031, 1033 n. 4 (2005) (tracing the history of the term's modern use to the establishment of World Intellectual Property Organization); Justin Hughes, *Copyright and Incomplete Historiographies: Of Piracy, Propertization, and Thomas Jefferson*, 79 S. CAL. L. REV. 993, 1001 (2006).
6 *See, e.g.*, Jessica L. Gillotte, Note, *Copyright Infringement in AI-Generated Artwork*, 53 U.C. DAVIS L. REV. 2655 (2020) (discussing the increasingly popular use of AI to generate artwork and the accompanying copyright infringement issues); Eric Sunray, Note, *Train in Vain: A Theoretical Assessment of Intermediate Copying and Fair Use in Machine AI Music Generator Training*, 13 AM. U. INTELL. PROP. BRIEF 1 (2021) (arguing that "intermediate copying" of copyrighted works for the purposes of training an AI model should not be excused under the fair use doctrine); *cf.* Van Lindberg, *Building and Using Generative Models under US Copyright Law*, 18 RUTGERS BUS. L. REV. 1 (2023) (analyzing the question of copyright infringement by the training of generative deep learning AI models and arguing that such use should be exempted under fair use). *See also* Zeynep Ülkü Kahveci, *Attribution Problem of Generative AI: A View from US Copyright Law*, 18 J. INTELL. PROP. L. & PRAC. 796 (2023) (analyzing copyright infringement through an attribution lens and finding that authors whose intellectual property rights have been infringed and wish to bring a claim for attribution under US law will face many legal hurdles); Katherine B. Forrest, *Copyright Law and Artificial Intelligence: Emerging Issues*, 65 J. COPYRIGHT SOC'Y U.S.A. 355, 369–70 (2018) ("A lack of ability to control reproduction and display leads to a lack of control over essential aspects of

the bundle of rights conveyed by the copyright. There is ultimately at least a short-term economic issue of skewed incentives: a lack of ability to control reproduction or display could lead to lessened willingness to undertake the costs of creation. Reduced incentives to create lead to reduced innovation."); Matthew Sag, *The New Legal Landscape for Text Mining and Machine Learning*, 66 J. COPYRIGHT SOC'Y U.S.A. 291, 301 (2019) (discussing the potential copyright infringement from data mining text, an integral part of ML, and arguing that it amounts to a non-expressive use of expressive works and thus that it should be permitted without authorization); *cf.* Daryl Lim, *AI & IP: Innovation & Creativity in an Age of Accelerated Change*, 52 AKRON L. REV. 813, 853 (2018) ("The U.S. would be foolish not to use all that fair use has to offer to its advantage and supercharge the growth of AI-generated works."). *See also* recent cases *infra* note 8.

7 *See, e.g.*, CHRISTOPHER T. ZIRPOLI, CONGR. RSCH. SERV., LSB10922, GENERATIVE ARTIFICIAL INTELLIGENCE AND COPYRIGHT LAW (2023), https://crsreports.congress.gov/product/pdf/LSB/LSB10922 (discussing the potential for generative AI to infringe other people's intellectual property rights both through use of protected materials for training data and through generating outputs resembling protected works); Gil Appel, Juliana Neelbauer, & David A. Schweidel, *Generative AI Has an Intellectual Property Problem*, HARV. BUS. REV. (Apr. 7, 2023) (arguing that companies should be required to obtain creator-consent before using their work to train AI models and proposing that creators use their protected works to build their own datasets to train models which could then be licensed for use); THE ECONOMIST, *Schumpeter: Napster, Remixed*, London Vol. 446, Iss. 9338 (Mar. 18, 2023): 62 (describing the "legal minefield" of balancing creators' rights against technological advancement); *Data Colonialism and Data Sets*, HARV. L. REV. BLOG (June 22, 2023), https://harvardlawreview.org/blog/2023/06/data-colonialism-and-data-sets ("The colonization of data to generate training sets resembles a familiar plot in our world. Pioneers have once again sailed into the horizons, hoarding wealth and disregarding potential claims to property that don't fit within the dominant legal system. However, with data, society has an opportunity to not make the same mistakes of the past.... Even if copyright law might offer a judicial remedy against nonconsensual use of data, statutory oversight will likely be needed in order to protect parties without the resources to pursue litigation."). *See also* Alex Baldwin, *AI Can't Be Patent Inventor, Top UK Court Rules*, LAW360 (Dec. 20, 2023, 10:05 AM GMT), https://www.law360.com/articles/1777845/ai-can-t-be-patent-inventor-top-uk-court-rules (reporting on the U.K. Supreme Court's ruling in Thaler v. Comptroller-General of Patents, Designs and Trade Marks [2023] UKSC 49, which held that an artificial intelligence model cannot be an inventor under U.K. patent law).

8 There have been several lawsuits challenging the legality of artificial intelligence models using protected materials as training data. *See, e.g.*, Complaint, Andersen v. Stability AI Ltd., No. 3:23-cv-00201 (N.D. Cal. Jan. 13, 2023) (alleging on behalf of a class of artists that Stability AI and others have unlawfully used complainants' web-published copyrighted images to train the companies' image-generating artificial intelligence model); Complaint, Tremblay v. OpenAI, Inc., No. 3:23-cv-03223 (N.D. Cal. June 28, 2023) (alleging in a class action lawsuit on behalf of a class of authors that OpenAI has unlawfully duplicated and ingested authors' copyrighted materials as training material for its large language AI model, ChatGPT, without due compensation to the authors); Complaint, Thomson Reuters Enterprise Centre GmbH v. ROSS Intelligence Inc., No. 1:20-cv-00613 (D. Del. May 6, 2020) (alleging that ROSS Intelligence used the legal database of Westlaw, owned by the plaintiff Thomson Reuters, without permission to train its own AI-powered legal research software); Complaint, Getty Images (US), Inc. v. Stability AI, Inc., No. 1:23-cv-00135 (D. Del. Feb. 3, 2023) (alleging that Stability AI infringed upon Getty Images' registered copyrights and trademarks by unlawfully using copyrighted photographs to train Stability AI's image-generating model, Stable Diffusion, which then generated infringing derivative works as output); Complaint at 11, Silverman v. OpenAI, Inc., No. 3:23-cv-03416 (N.D. Cal. July 7, 2023) ("Because the output of the OpenAI Language Models is based on expressive information extracted from Plaintiffs' works (and others), every output of the OpenAI Language Models is an infringing derivative work, made without Plaintiffs' permission and in violation of their exclusive rights under the Copyright Act"); Complaint, J.L. v. Alphabet Inc., No. 3:23-cv-03440 (N.D. Cal. July 11, 2023) (alleging that Google's AI products relied on training data collected from the internet, including copyrighted texts, images, music, and other data).

9 *See, e.g.*, Mark A. Lemley & Bryan Casey, *Fair Learning*, 99 TEX. L. REV. 743, 748 (2021) (arguing that "ML systems should generally be able to use databases for training, whether or not the contents of that database are copyrighted"); Simon Chesterman, *Good Models Borrow, Great Models Steal: Intellectual Property Rights and Generative AI* (Nat'l Univ. of Sing. Law, Working Paper No. 2023/025, 2023) (arguing that while models should be trained, they should not be trained on "stolen" data, and that compensation should be paid to the original human creators whose work is used to train the models); Giorgio Franceschelli & Mirco Musolesi, *Copyright in Generative Deep Learning*, 4 DATA & POL'Y E17, 4–5 (2022) (analyzing the applicability of the fair use doctrine to generative deep learning models); Nicola Lucchi, *ChatGPT: A Case Study on Copyright Challenges for Generative Artificial Intelligence Systems*, EUR. J. OF RISK REGUL. 1 (2023) (discussing concerns over lawful collection and use of copyrighted materials

and arguing that training datasets should be considered shared resources available to all due to their need for collective participation); Benjamin L. W. Sobel, *Artificial Intelligence's Fair Use Crisis*, 41 COLUM. J.L. & ARTS 45, 74–75 (2017) ("Believing that machines differ fundamentally from human authors could imply that expressive machine learning always transforms the meaning of the works it appropriates. In a sense, this is true. The 'meaning' of a work does depend on its author and its reader. . . . In practice, however, the law disregards the idea, because it threatens to turn the doctrine to unenforceable mush. Every quotation reshapes meaning, but this does not turn every act of copying into transformative fair use; copying undertaken by artificial intelligence should be regarded with no less skepticism.").

10 *See, e.g.*, Ryan Abbott & Elizabeth Rothman, *Disrupting Creativity: Copyright Law in the Age of Generative Artificial Intelligence*, 75 FLA. L. REV. 1141, 1201 (2023) ("Encouraging the creation and dissemination of such content is the main purpose of the copyright system, and allowing copyright protection for AI-generated works will achieve this purpose. Once the desirability of protecting these works is acknowledged, acknowledging AI authorship then becomes nothing more than opting for reality instead of elaborate legal fictions."); Shlomit Yanisky-Ravid & Xiaoqiong (Jackie) Liu, *When Artificial Intelligence Systems Produce Inventions: An Alternative Model for Patent Law at the 3A Era*, 39 CARDOZO L. REV. 2215 (2018) (arguing against patent protection for AI inventions and instead proposing that society protect AI innovation by rewarding the creators of AI systems and proposing the use of tools that prevent digital counterfeiting, among other changes to the patent system). *See also* Cole G. Merritt, Note, *A Compulsory Solution to the Machine Problem: Recognizing Artificial Intelligence as Inventors in Patent Law*, 25 VAND. J. ENT. & TECH. L. 211, 223 (2023) ("AI is solely responsible for an invention in at least one known instance. . . This evidence alone, coupled with the profound likelihood that AI inventorship will become more pervasive, necessitates an update to US patent law to accommodate and embrace AI inventorship."); Faye F. Wang, *Copyright Protection for AI-Generated Works: Solutions to Further Challenges from Generative AI*, 5 AMICUS CURIAE (SERIES 2) 88, 97 (2023) (reviewing the status of AI-generated works in the U.K., including the debate over whether an AI system can legally be considered the author of such works); Lim, *supra* note 6 (discussing different approaches to protecting AI-generated work under copyright and patent laws); Gregory Hagen, *AI and Patents and Trade Secrets*, *in* ARTIFICIAL INTELLIGENCE AND THE LAW IN CANADA at ch. 2 (Florian Martin-Bariteau & Teresa Scassa eds., 2021) (exploring the extent to which AI can be considered an inventor under patent law); Ben Hattenbach & Gavin Snyder, *Rethinking the Mental Steps Doctrine and Other Barriers to Patentability of Artificial Intelligence*, 19 COLUM. SCI. & TECH. L. REV. 313, 327 (2018) (discussing the test for patentable subject matter as set out in

Alice Corp. v. CLS Bank Int'l and arguing that claims of the mental steps doctrine "if applied broadly in the artificial intelligence context, would make patenting in the area quite difficult").

11 *See* Martin Senftleben, *Generative AI and Author Remuneration*, 54 INT'L. REV. OF INTELL. PROP. & COMPETITION L. 1535, 1549 (proposing an AI levy system, under which "providers of generative AI systems would be obliged to pay remuneration for producing literary and artistic content that has the potential to replace human creations."). For a broad discussion on AI ethical concerns *see, e.g.*, Christina Pazzanese, *Ethical Concerns Mount as AI Takes Bigger Decision-Making Role in More Industries*, HARV. GAZETTE (Oct. 26, 2020), https://news.harvard.edu/gazette/story/2020/10/ethical-concerns-mount-as-ai-takes-bigger-decision-making-role (discussing three areas of ethical concern for AI use: privacy and surveillance, discrimination, and the role of human judgment); BRENT MITTELSTADT, COUNCIL OF EUR., THE IMPACT OF ARTIFICIAL INTELLIGENCE ON THE DOCTOR-PATIENT RELATIONSHIP 56–63 (2021) (discussing the variety of ethical risks arising from the use of AI in doctor-patient relationships and recommending that AI systems include contrastive explanation statements intelligible to patients, registration with a public body, and bias testing). For insight into how industry is considering AI ethics, *see* DELOITTE, STATE OF ETHICS AND TRUST IN TECHNOLOGY REPORT 46 (2d ed. 2023) (surveying a population of 1,716 "business and technical professionals who are actively involved in either developing, consuming, or managing emerging technologies" and found, *inter alia*, that 74 percent of survey respondents had begun testing generative AI technologies and that data privacy and transparency were primary ethical concerns with AI use). For discussion of the EU's approach to AI regulation, *see* Ulla-Maija Mylly, *Transparent AI? Navigating between Rules on Trade Secrets and Access to Information*, 54 INT'L REV. OF INTELL. PROP. & COMPETITION L. 1013 (2023) (discussing disclosure obligations under the EU's Artificial Intelligence Act imposed upon AI providers and analyzing how those obligations interfere with trade secret protections).

12 Kevin Aho, *Existentialism*, THE STANFORD ENCYCLOPEDIA OF PHILOSOPHY (Summer 2023 edition), Edward N. Zalta & Uri Nodelman (eds.) (Jan. 6, 2023), https://plato.stanford.edu/entries/existentialism/; JENNIFER A. GOSETTI-FERENCEI, ON BEING AND BECOMING: AN EXISTENTIALIST APPROACH TO LIFE 37–55 (2021); Jon Stewart, *Existentialism*, *in* ENCYCLOPEDIA OF APPLIED ETHICS 250–63 (Ruth Chadwick ed., 2d ed. 2012).

13 Sabotage, ONLINE ETYMOLOGY DICTIONARY, https://www.etymonline.com/word/sabotage (last visited Jan. 22, 2024).

14 Such images arise both in the fictional world and in current commentary. Joshua Rothman, *Why the Godfather of A.I. Fears What He's Built*, THE NEW YORKER (Nov. 13, 2023), https://www.newyorker.com/magazine/2023/11/

20/geoffrey-hinton-profile-ai (introducing Geoffrey Hinton, known as the "godfather of AI," who recently left his job at Google due to his perception of the "existential risk" of their AI products.); DANIEL H. WILSON, ROBOPOCALYPSE (2011) (writing of a fictional artificial intelligence technology which becomes humanity's deadly enemy); Kevin Roose, *Silicon Valley Confronts a Grim New A.I. Metric*, THE N. Y. TIMES (Dec. 6, 2023), https://www.nytimes.com/2023/12/06/business/dealbook/silicon-valley-artificial-intelligence.html (explaining "p(doom)," short for "probability of doom," which references how "some artificial intelligence researchers talk about how likely they believe it is that A.I. will kill us all . . . A high p(doom) means you think an A.I. apocalypse is likely, while a low one means you think we'll probably tough it out.").

15 *See infra* Chapter 2.

16 29 U.S.C. §§ 201–19 (2018) (Fair Labor Standards Act (FLSA), passed in 1938. The FLSA provides a national minimum hourly wage (§206), mandatory overtime compensation (§207), restricting employment of minors (§212), etc.).

17 CAL. PENAL CODE § 466 (West 2012) (amended 2018) (California statue for possession of burglarious tools); N.Y. PENAL LAW § 140.35 (New York statue for possession of burglarious tools).

18 Balanced Budget Downpayment Act, I of 1996, Pub L. No.104-99, § 128 (denying federal funding for germline gene-editing research on human embryos). *See also* Francis S. Collins, *Statement of NIH Funding of Research Using Gene-Editing Technologies in Human Embryos*, NATIONAL INSTITUTES OF HEALTH (Apr. 28, 2015), https://www.nih.gov/about-nih/who-we-are/nih-director/statements/statement-nih-funding-research-using-gene-editing-technologies-human-embryos (statement from then-current NIH director, Francis Collins, stating "NIH will not fund any use of gene editing technologies in human embryos").

19 ROBERT SOUTH, TWELVE SERMONS PREACHED UPON SEVERAL OCCASIONS 331 (1850).

20 *See, e.g.*, Lemley, *supra* note 5, 1033–46; Lester C. Thurow, *Needed: A New System of Intellectual Property Rights*, 75 HARV. BUS. REV. 95, 103 (1997) ("The world's current one-dimensional system must be overhauled to create a more differentiated one. Trying to squeeze today's developments into yesterday's system of intellectual property rights simply won't work.").

21 A common doctrinal expansion has been the "propertization" of intellectual property, which has drawn criticism for both its broad scope and its absolute nature of protection. *See, e.g.*, Michael A. Carrier, *Cabining Intellectual Property Through a Property Paradigm*, 54 DUKE L.J. 1, 12 (2004) ("In short, IP is quickly becoming property not only in the essentially unlimited scope and duration of its initial rights but also in the ubiquitous assertions that IP is absolute property."); Lemley, *supra* note 5, at 1032 (arguing that intellectual

property's goal of eliminating "free riding" is ill-suited to IP); Andrew Beckerman-Rodau, *The Problem with Intellectual Property Rights: Subject Matter Expansion*, 13 YALE J.L. & TECH. 35 (2010) (positing that the expansion of eligible subject matter has led to overprotection, in the form of overlapping protections from multiple bodies of intellectual property law); Robin C. Feldman, *Intellectual Property Wrongs*, 18 STAN. J.L., BUS. & FIN. 250 (2013) (describing questionable uses of intellectual property rights, such as harassing competitors and the establishing anti-competitive schemes); NEIL W. NETANEL, COPYRIGHT'S PARADOX (2008) (detailing the troublesome areas of copyright's expansion, including copyright duration, new media, etc.); LAWRENCE LESSIG, REMIX 18 (2008) (arguing that regulatory extremes in copyright law have made it unnecessarily difficult for creative work to proliferate); Chad J. Doellinger, *A New Theory of Trademarks*, 111 PENN ST. L. REV. 823 (2007) (critiquing the modern "economic perspective" of trademark); Mark P. McKenna, *A Consumer Decision-Making Theory of Trademark Law*, 98 VA. L REV. 67, 78–79 (2012) (summarizing critiques of consumer search costs, including reverse confusion, initial interest confusion, post-sale confusion, and dilution, among others); Robin Feldman & Charles Tait Graves, *Naked Price and Pharmaceutical Trade Secret Overreach*, 22 YALE J.L. & TECH. 61, 79–84 (2020) (explaining how increased trade secrecy claims, made outside of their commonplace civil litigation context, generate risks to the public interest); Charles T. Graves & Sonia K. Katyal, *From Trade Secrecy to Seclusion*, 109 GEO. L. J. 1337 (2021) (arguing that trade secret law has expanded beyond traditional use as a tool against intellectual property misappropriation, to a tool for concealment). Some scholars criticize the expansion of patent law stemming from the creation of the Federal Circuit Court of Appeals. *E.g.* Ian Ayres & Paul Klemperer, *Limiting Patentees' Market Power without Reducing Innovation Incentives: The Perverse Benefits of Uncertainty and Non-Injunctive Remedies*, 97 MICH. L. REV. 985, 986–89 (1999). Critics also take issue with what they deem ineligible subject matter, such as organic material, computer software, financial services, and business methods. *E.g.*, Michael A. Heller & Rebecca S. Eisenberg, *Can Patents Deter Innovation? The Anticommons in Biomedical Research*, 280 SCI. 698, 698–701 (1998) (describing the consequences to product development associated with patents on gene fragments and other biological materials); James Gleick, *Patently Absurd*, N.Y. TIMES (Mar. 12, 2000), https://archive.nytimes.com/www.nytimes.com/library/magazine/home/20000312mag-patents.html (documenting how the growing number of e-commerce patents at the turn of the century contributed to an influx in litigation); Seth Shulman, *Software Patents Tangle the Web*, MIT TECH. REV. (Mar. 1 2000), https://www.technologyreview.com/2000/03/01/236373/software-patents-tangle-the-web/ (describing the proliferation of software patents following a series of Supreme Court decisions in the

1990s). Some scholars believe existing eligible patent subject matter includes inventions that would have been generated otherwise, thereby producing a suboptimal amount of investment. *E.g.*, Ofer Tur-Sinai, *Beyond Incentives: Expanding the Theoretical Framework for Patent Law Analysis*, 45 AKRON L. REV. 243, 244–45 (2015).

22 *Cf.* the existentialists' concept of "absurdity," Douglas Burnham & George Papandreopoulos, *Existentialism*, INTERNET ENCYCLOPEDIA OF PHILOSOPHY, https://iep.utm.edu/existent/ ("Human beings can and should become profoundly aware of this lack of reason and the impossibility of an immanent understanding of it."); ALBERT CAMUS, THE MYTH OF SISYPHUS (1942) (credited with introduction of this concept, termed "existentialist absurdism") *with* theologians' conception of full knowledge belonging to a deity, and thus outside of human comprehension. *E.g., the New Living Translation of Isaiah* 55:8–9 ("'My thoughts are nothing like your thoughts,' says the LORD. 'And my ways are far beyond anything you could imagine. For just as the heavens are higher than the earth, so my ways are higher than your ways and my thoughts higher than your thoughts.'").

23 *See infra* Chapter 6.

Chapter 1

1 *See* John McCarthy et al., *A Proposal for the Dartmouth Summer Research Project on Artificial Intelligence*, 27 THE AI MAGAZINE 4 (2006) (reprinting the original 1955 research proposal).

2 John McCarthy, *What Is Artificial Intelligence?* JOHN MCCARTHY'S HOMEPAGE (Nov. 12, 2007, 2:05 AM), http://www-formal.stanford.edu/jmc/whatisai.pdf (arguing no widely accepted definition of AI exists, as definitions of human functions, like "intelligence," are difficult to classify); STUART J. RUSSELL & PETER NORVIG, ARTIFICIAL INTELLIGENCE: A MODERN APPROACH 2–14 (3rd ed. 2013) (including definitions for abstract ideas such as "thinking rationally" and "acting humanly"); MARCUS HUTTER, UNIVERSAL ARTIFICIAL INTELLIGENCE: SEQUENTIAL DECISIONS BASED ON ALGORITHMIC PROBABILITY 125–26, 231 (2010) (positing that AI systems are intelligent as they possess certain skills such as classification, language processing, and optimization, among others); Joshua A. Goland, *Algorithmic Disgorgement: Destruction of Artificial Intelligence Models as the FTC's Newest Enforcement Tool for Bad Data*, 29 RICH. J.L. & TECH. 1, 5 (2023) (differentiating "strong" and "weak" AI).

3 *See, e.g.*, DANIEL H. WILSON, ROBOPOCALYPSE (2011); ISAAC ASIMOV, I, ROBOT (1950); TERMINATOR (Orion Pictures 1984).

4 Daria Kim et al., *Ten Assumptions about Artificial Intelligence That Can Mislead Patent Law Analysis* (Aug. 1, 2021) (unpublished research paper, on file with author).

5 *See* Alicia Solow-Niederman, *Administering Artificial Intelligence*, 93 S. CAL. L. REV. 633, 635 (2020). *See also* Catalina Goanta et al., *Back to the Future: Waves of Legal Scholarship on Artificial Intelligence*, *in* TIME, LAW, AND CHANGE 1, 1 (Sofia Ranchordás & Yaniv Raznai eds., 2019); Dan L. Burk, *AI Patents and the Self-Assembling Machine*, 105 MINN. L. R. HEADNOTES 301, 302 (2021); Dan Robitzski, *You Have No Idea What Artificial Intelligence Really Does*, FUTURISM (Oct. 16, 2018, 11:25 AM), https://futurism.com/artificial-intelligence-hype [https://perma.cc/ZC36-FM2X] ("'People think AI is a smart robot that can do things a very smart person would – a robot that knows everything and can answer any question' . . . But this is not what experts really mean when they talk about AI. 'In general, AI refers to computer programs that can complete various analyses and use some pre-defined criteria to make decisions.'") (quoting Emad Mousavi).

6 Harry Surden, *Artificial Intelligence and Law: An Overview*, 35 GA. ST. U. L. REV. 1305, 1307 (2019); Clark D. Asay, *Artificial Stupidity*, 61 WM. & MARY L. REV. 1187, 1190 (2020); Matthew U. Scherer, *Regulating Artificial Intelligence Systems: Risks, Challenges, Competencies, and Strategies*, 29 HARV. J. L. & TECH. 353, 362 (2016); *What Is AI?: Learn About Artificial Intelligence*, ORACLE, https://www.oracle.com/artificial-intelligence/what-is-ai/ (May 13, 2021); Tiffany C. Li, *Algorithmic Destruction*, 75 SMU L. REV. 479, 484 (2022) ("AI refers to any form of intelligence that is man-made or artificial, generally relating to the idea of a constructed machine intelligence that could potentially equal the intelligence of a human being."); *see also* ARTIFICIAL INTELLIGENCE, OXFORD ENG. DICTIONARY, https://www.oed.com/view/Entry/271625 (last visited Apr. 3, 2023).

7 *See* Michael Wallace & George Dunlop, *ELIZA: A Very Basic Rogerian Psychotherapist Chatbot*, https://web.njit.edu/~ronkowit/eliza.html (last visited June 26, 2024).

8 Joseph Weizenbaum, *ELIZA – A Computer Program for the Study of Natural Language Communication between Man and Machine*, 9 COMPUTATIONAL LINGUISTICS 36, 37 (1966) (emphasis in original).

9 David Pierce, *From Eliza to ChatGPT: Why People Spent 60 Years Building Chatbots*, THE VERGE (Feb. 28, 2024, 7:00 AM PST), https://www.theverge.com/24054603/chatbot-chatgpt-eliza-history-ai-assistants-video. *See also* Robin Feldman and Caroline A. Yuen, *AI and Antitrust: "The Algorithm Made Me Do It*," 34 COMPETITION J. 1, 5–7 (2024).

10 *See* Marion Fourcade & Kieran Healy, *Seeing Like a Market*, 15 SOCIO-ECON. R. 1, 24 (2017) ("The new machines do not need to be able to think; they just need to be able to learn."); Burk, *supra* note 5, at 302 (citing Fourcade and Healy); *see also* THOMAS H. CORMEN ET AL., INTRODUCTION TO ALGORITHMS 5 (2d ed. 2002) ("[A]n algorithm is any well-defined computational procedure that takes some value, or set of values, as input and produces some value, or set of values, as output.").

11 Structured vs Unstructured Data, IBM (June 29, 2021), https://www.ibm.com/think/topics/structured-vs-unstructured-data.

12 MACHINE LEARNING: AN ARTIFICIAL INTELLIGENCE APPROACH 3–6 (Ryszard S. Michalski, Jaime G. Carbonell, & Tom M. Mitchell eds., 1983).

13 David Lehr & Paul Ohm, *Playing with the Data: What Legal Scholars Should Learn about Machine Learning*, 51 U.C. DAVIS L. REV. 653, 668–71 (2017); IAN H. WITTEN, EIBE FRANK, & MARK A. HALL, DATA MINING: PRACTICAL MACHINE LEARNING TOOLS AND TECHNIQUES 7–8 (3rd ed. 2011).

14 For example, in 1952, the computer scientist Arthur Samuel devised and demonstrated a machine-learning algorithm to learn how to play checkers at a high level. Here is the abstract from his famous 1959 publication on the subject:

Two machine-learning procedures have been investigated in some detail using the game of checkers. Enough work has been done to verify the fact that a computer can be programmed so that it will learn to play a better game of checkers than can be played by the person who wrote the program. Furthermore, it can learn to do this in a remarkably short period of time (8 or 10 hours of machine-playing time) when given only the rules of the game, a sense of direction, and a redundant and incomplete list of parameters which are thought to have something to do with the game, but whose correct signs and relative weights are unknown and unspecified. The principles of machine learning verified by these experiments are, of course, applicable to many other situations.

Arthur L. Samuel, *Some Studies in Machine Learning Using the Game of Checkers*, 3 IBM J. OF RSCH. AND DEV. 210 (1959).

15 IAN GOODFELLOW, YOSHUA BENGIO, & AARON COURVILLE, DEEP LEARNING 2–8 (2016).

16 Though this analogy aids understanding, it is important to not equate the two. For example, large differences in learning, creativity, generalization, and other areas persist between the human brain and modern AI products.

17 GOODFELLOW ET AL., *supra* note 15, at 104–5; Matt Crabtree, *Deep Learning (DL) vs Machine Learning (ML): A Comparative Guide*, DATACAMP (Feb. 29 2024), https://www.datacamp.com/tutorial/machine-deep-learning.

18 GOODFELLOW ET AL., *supra* note 15, at 6; Crabtree, *supra* note 17.

19 At the risk of oversimplifying, these models “learn” through an iterative process where each instance of data provided is: (1) first processed through the layers of the model in order to produce a prediction (known as “forward propagation”); (2) that prediction is then compared to an expected output in order to compute an error value (quantifying how well or poorly the model is preforming, also known as “loss/cost calculation”); (3) that error value is then used to calculate how much each parameter in the model contributed to the output error (“gradient calculation”); and finally (4) each parameter in the model is updated in order to minimize the error value when encountering

the next piece of training data ("gradient descent"). *See* GOODFELLOW ET AL., *supra* note 15, at 197–98.

20 The "deep" in "deep learning" is a nod to the many layers the training data passes through. GOODFELLOW ET AL., *supra* note 15, at 5–6.

21 Ernestas Naprys, *Scientists to Make Their Own Trillion Parameter GPTs with Ethics and Trust*, CYBERNEWS (Nov. 28, 2023, 10:24 AM), https://cybernews.com/tech/scientists-to-make-their-own-trillion-parameter-ai-models/ ("One of the most advanced private models, OpenAI's GPT-4, already, according to some sources, has 1.7 trillion parameters, more than the scientists' ambitious goal.").

22 Lauren Leffer, *Your Personal Information Is Probably Being Used to Train Generative AI Models*, SCI. AM. (Oct. 19, 2023) ("[D]evelopers amass their training sets through automated tools that catalog and extract data from the Internet. Web 'crawlers' travel from link to link indexing the location of information in a database, while Web 'scrapers' download and extract that same information.").

23 Crabtree, *supra* note 17.

24 *Id.*

25 Burk, *supra* note 5, at 303 ("It should be noted that the term intelligence in AI is something of a misnomer. What is now being touted as 'AI' is almost entirely, and perhaps altogether entirely, systems implementing machine learning routines. Such systems are not intelligent in any robust sense of the word.... There is at present no serious prospect of designing machines with such capabilities; as Fourcade and Healy have observed, computer science has given up on building machines that can think in favor of building machines that can learn."); Harry Surden, *Machine Learning and Law*, 89 WASH. L. REV. 87, 98 (2014) ("[R]esearchers have achieved success in automating complex tasks by focusing not upon the intelligence of the automated processes themselves, but upon the results that automated processes produce. Under this alternative view, if a computer system is able to produce outputs that people would consider to be accurate, appropriate, helpful, and useful, such results can be considered 'intelligent' – even if they did not come about through artificial versions of human cognitive processes.").

26 James B. Garvey, *Let's Get Real: Weak Artificial Intelligence Has Free Speech Rights*, 91 FORDHAM L. REV. 953, 955 (2022); NOAH WAISBERG & ALEXANDER HUDEK, AI FOR LAWYERS: HOW ARTIFICIAL INTELLIGENCE IS ADDING VALUE, AMPLIFYING EXPERTISE, AND TRANSFORMING CAREERS 5 (2021); JAN LIEDER, THE CAMBRIDGE HANDBOOK OF RESPONSIBLE ARTIFICIAL INTELLIGENCE: INTERDISCIPLINARY PERSPECTIVES 332 (Silja Voeneky et al. eds., Cambridge University Press 2022).

27 Yupeng Chang et al., *A Survey on Evaluation of Large Language Models*, 15 ACM TRANSACTIONS ON INTELL. SYS. AND TECH. 1, 4 ("Language

models (LMs) are computational models that have the capability to understand and generate human language. LMs have the transformative ability to predict the likelihood of word sequences or generate new text based on a given input.").

28 LIEDER, *supra* note 26; *What Is Strong AI?*, IBM, https://www.ibm.com/topics/strong-ai (last visited Jan. 30, 2024) ("Strong AI aims to create intelligent machines that are indistinguishable from the human mind. But just like a child, the AI machine would have to learn through input and experiences, constantly progressing and advancing its abilities over time.").

29 LIEDER, *supra* note 26; *See also* Max Roser, *AI Timelines: What Do Experts in Artificial Intelligence Export for the Future*, OUR WORLD IN DATA (Feb. 7, 2023), https://ourworldindata.org/ai-timelines (reporting the results of a survey of 352 AI experts, some of whom "believe that this level of technology will never be developed."). *See generally* NICK BOSTROM, SUPERINTELLIGENCE: PATHS, DANGERS, STRATEGIES (2014).

30 U.S. PAT. & TRADEMARK OFF., PUBLIC VIEWS ON ARTIFICIAL INTELLIGENCE AND INTELLECTUAL PROPERTY POLICY ii (2020) ("The majority of public commenters, while not offering definitions of AI, agreed that the current state of the art is limited to 'narrow' AI."); LIEDER, *supra* note 26; Jamal A. Dargham et al., *Artificial Intelligence and the Future of Mankind, in* 67–82 INTERNET OF THINGS AND ARTIFICIAL INTELLIGENCE FOR SMART ENVIRONMENTS (Hoe T. Yew et al. eds., Springer 2024).

31 *See* Cade Metz, *The Robot Surgeon Will See You Now*, N.Y. TIMES (Apr. 30, 2021), https://www.nytimes.com/2021/04/30/technology/robot-surgery-surgeon.html (discussing the use of artificial intelligence to automate surgical robots).

32 *See* The Waymo Team, *Waymo Significantly Outperforms Comparable Human Benchmarks over 7+ Million Miles of Rider-Only Driving*, WAYPOINT (Dec. 20, 2023), https://waymo.com/blog/2023/12/waymo-significantly-outperforms-comparable-human-benchmarks-over-7-million/ (suggesting in an autonomous car safety report a possible replacement for human drivers).

33 Bryce Hoffman, *Leaders Looking to Leverage AI Need to Think about Context*, FORBES (Mar. 31, 2023), https://www.forbes.com/sites/brycehoffman/2023/03/31/leaders-looking-to-leverage-ai-need-to-think-about-context/ (outlining some outstanding limitations of AI systems).

34 Garvey, *supra* note 26 ("[Weak AI] is described as a 'one-trick pony' and performs a particular task in a particular way, like a self-driving car or search engine . . . AGI is a type of AI that can do anything a human can do but is currently more of a concept or theory with less technological advancement.").

35 At the risk of creating confusion that may not exist, I note that some readers encountering various AI terms for the first time may confuse the term

"generative AI" with the term "artificial general intelligence." To the non-expert, the two sound frustratingly similar. Nevertheless, they are worlds apart. Artificial general intelligence refers to the strong AI systems described above – ones that exist only in the minds of theorists. *Generative* AI systems are the ones familiar to us today as ChatGPT and its fellow travelers. To remember the difference, one can think of artificial general intelligence as the general who dispatches the troops in any directions and to many different tasks. In contrast, think of generative AI as a system that generates responses to queries based on the output that most likely would come next.

36 *See* Saidul Islam et al., *A Comprehensive Survey in Applications of Transformers for Deep Learning Tasks*, ARXIV (June 11, 2023, 11:13 PM UTC), https://arxiv.org/abs/2306.07303 ("Transformer is a deep [learning] neural network that employs a self-attention mechanism to comprehend the contextual relationships within sequential data.").

37 Walter H. L. Pinaya et al., *Generative AI for Medical Imaging: Extending the MONAI Framework*, ARXIV (July 27, 2023, 9:58 PM UTC), https://arxiv.org/abs/2307.15208 ("Generative AI refers to a set of artificial intelligence techniques and models designed to learn the underlying patterns and structure of a dataset and generate new data points that plausibly could be part of the original dataset."); U.S. GOV'T ACCOUNTABILITY OFF., SCIENCE & TECH SPOTLIGHT: GENERATIVE A.I. 1 (2023) ("Generative artificial intelligence . . . is a technology that can create content, including text, images, audio, or video, when prompted by a user. Generative AI systems create responses using algorithms that are trained often on open-source information, such as text and images from the internet."). Importantly, the reader should not confuse the prompts a user inputs into an AI-based chatbot with the data used for an AI model's initial training. Depending on the company and product, user prompts may be collected and incorporated as training data, but only in later versions of existing models. Stated another way, AI chatbot user prompts are not used to the update the chatbot in real time. *See, e.g.*, OpenAI, *Privacy Policy* (Nov. 14, 2023), https://openai.com/policies/privacy-policy/; OpenAI, *How Your Data Is Used to Improve Model Performance*, https://help.openai.com/en/articles/5722486-how-your-data-is-used-to-improve-model-performance.

38 Jon Porter, *ChatGPT Continues to Be One of the Fastest Growing Services Ever*, THE VERGE (Nov. 6, 2023, 10:03 AM PST), https://www.theverge.com/2023/11/6/23948386/chatgpt-active-user-count-openai-developer-conference ("ChatGPT was widely seen as the fastest-growing consumer internet app of all time, . . . notching an estimated 100 million monthly users in just two months. Facebook, for example, took around four and a half years to hit 100 million users after its launch in 2004.").

39 Kevin Roose, *How ChatGPT Kicked Off an A.I. Arms Race*, N.Y. TIMES (Feb. 3, 2023), https://www.nytimes.com/2023/02/03/technology/chatgpt-openai-artificial-intelligence.html?smid=url-share; Gerrit De Vynck, *ChatGPT Loses Users for First Time, Shaking Faith in AI Revolution*, THE WASH. POST (July 7, 2023, 6:00 AM EDT), https://www.washingtonpost.com/technology/2023/07/07/chatgpt-users-decline-future-ai-openai/ (providing examples of large investments and popularity growth); Kevin Roose, *A Coming-Out Party for Generative A.I., Silicon Valley's New Craze*, N.Y. TIMES (Oct. 21, 2022), https://www.nytimes.com/2022/10/21/technology/generative-ai.html?smid=url-share.

40 *See, e.g.*, Ege Gurdeniz & Kartik Hosanagar, *Generative AI Won't Revolutionize Search – Yet*, HARVARD BUS. REV. (outlining "practical, technical, and legal challenges" of large language models replacing search engines). *But see* Ben Wodecki, *ChatGPT Can Now Give You Real-time Information*, AI BUS (Sep. 28, 2023) (reporting ChatGPT can now "access the internet and provide real time information to users, courtesy of Bing Search").

41 More specifically, Washington, D.C. in our analogy represents the human language as embodied in text.

42 Today's more sophisticated approaches might create chunks of "tokens" according to how important they are for navigating – that is, how often they are used. For example, the White House might have its own segment. Some street blocks might be grouped together, such as all of the streets that make up the National Mall area. And a rarely visited alleyway might be grouped with an adjacent street. The goal is to efficiently represent all the information about the city with as few segments as possible.

43 Think of these as not just north-south, but 300 different angles. In the AI model, this is like setting the dimensions of each token's vector – 300 numbers to capture its meaning. More directions mean more detail, but that's harder to manage.

44 ChatGPT 4 is reported to have approximately 120 attention heads per layer.

45 Prior machine-learning approaches would have structured the data. For example, a spam-detection software might have begun with examples of spam emails or information on the common characteristics of spam, including words or phrases commonly found in spam or the use of many explanation points and words in bold. The mind-boggling nature of modern generative AI models is that they will "find" the connections and pathways on their own, beginning with little more than the directive to find 100 million of them.

46 Rather than leaving out the last part of the sequence, some models omit one of the chunks (tokens) from the middle of the sequence. Models that try to predict a token from inside the sequence have the advantage of gaining more insight into contextual relationships of vocabulary in both directions.

47 The part of the training calculation that adjusts for errors is known as the gradient descent algorithm.

48 One should think of each map-making expedition as containing a fresh team of 100 tour guides. During the first expedition, these 100 guides develop their own specializations as they explore Washington, D.C. – some focusing on monuments, others on waterways, others on government institutions. At the end of this expedition, their individual maps are combined into a single, comprehensive "expedition 1 map." When the second expedition begins, a new set of 100 guides receives this combined map as their starting point. These guides don't inherit the specific specializations from the first expedition's guides. Instead, they're free to develop their own specializations based on the relationships they find to be important in the combined map they received. This process repeats for all twelve expeditions, with each layer building upon the combined knowledge of the previous layer but developing fresh perspectives and specializations.

The entire corpus of data training data could contain as much as billions of documents. These billions of documents could be divided into many thousands of batches of examples, with each batch containing hundreds of thousands of sequences.

49 The entire corpus of data training data could contain as much as billions of documents. These billions of documents could be divided into many thousands of batches of examples, with each batch containing hundreds of thousands of sequences.

50 Whether you call them pathways, connections, or bridges, the information developed by the model regarding the relationships among the chunks of data as analyzed in 300 dimensions can lead to insights not contained in any single piece of input data. To offer a purely fictional example, perhaps our model might find that the acoustics in different government buildings correlate with the typical tone of statements made within those building, thereby capturing how architecture subtly influences communication. The point is simply that the models can derive information beyond the four corners of the training documents. But of course, current models also are known to produce so-called hallucinations, in which the model provides a response that is downright inaccurate. Predicting the next chunk of data is not an exact science – at least not yet.

51 If a chunk were not on the map, the model would have to make its best guess from surrounding chunks in the prompt and connections that exist on the map related to those.

52 Nicholas Carlini et al., *Quantifying Memorization across Neural Language Models*, ARXIV 1 (Mar. 6, 2023, 6:28 AM UTC) https://arxiv.org/abs/2202.07646 (providing research overview on language models and memorization).

53

Chunks or Pieces	Tokens
300-dimensional coordinates	Vectors
Tour guides	Attention heads
Map expeditions	Layers
Importance dials	Weights and biases

54 Michalski et al., *supra* note 12, at 3–25.

55 *See, e.g.*, Zaheer Allam & Zaynah A. Dhunny, *On Big Data, Artificial Intelligence, and Smart Cities*, 89 CITIES 80 (2019).

56 Neil C. Thompson, Shuning Ge, & Gabriel F. Manso, *The Importance of (Exponentially More) Computing Power*, ARXIV (June 28, 2022, 1:50 PM UTC), https://arxiv.org/abs/2206.14007.

57 *See* Richard Sutton, *The Bitter Lesson*, INCOMPLETE IDEAS (Mar. 13, 2019), http://www.incompleteideas.net/IncIdeas/BitterLesson.html. Sutton wrote the essay three years prior to the release of ChatGPT, using the term natural language processing, rather than the more general term used in this book, "generative AI." *See, e.g.*, Thompson et al., *supra* note 57 (finding that "computational power explains 49%–94% of the performance improvements in [weather prediction, protein folding, and oil exploration] domains").

58 John O. McGinnis, *Accelerating AI*, 104 NW. L. REV. COLLOQUY 366 (2009–10) ("[A]lmost every aspect of the digital world – from computational calculation power to computer memory – is growing in density at a similarly exponential rate."). Dan L. Burk & Mark A. Lemley, *Policy Levers in Patent Law*, 89 VA. L. REV. 1575, 1620 n.147 (2003).

59 GPT-4 is the architecture that supports the popular chatbot ChatGPT.

60 Josh Achiam et al., *GPT-4 Technical Report*, ARXIV (Mar. 4, 2023, 6:01 AM UST). https://arxiv.org/abs/2303.08774.

61 *See* Geoffrey E. Hinton, Simon Osindero, & Yee-Whye Teh, *A Fast Learning Algorithm for Deep Belief Nets*, 18 NEURAL COMPUTATION 1527 (2006).

62 *See* Ian J. Goodfellow et al., *Generative Adversarial Nets*, *in* ADVANCES IN NEURAL INFORMATION PROCESSING SYSTEMS 27 (Z. Ghahramani et al. eds., 2014).

63 *See* Islam et al., *supra* note 36, and accompanying text.

64 STABILITY.AI, https://stability.ai/ (last visited Jan. 30, 2024).

65 Peng Zhang & Maged N. Kamel Boulos, *Generative AI in Medicine and Healthcare*, 15 FUTURE INTERNET 286 (Aug. 23, 2023).

66 Iain M. Cockburn, Rebecca Henderson, & Scott Stern, *The Impact of Artificial Intelligence on Innovation: An Exploratory Analysis*, *in* THE ECON. OF ARTIFICIAL INTELL. 115 (Ajay K. Agrawal, Joshua Gans, & Avi Goldfarb eds., 2019) (documenting empirically a "striking shift … towards deep learning based application-oriented research").

67 Julia Angwin et al., *Machine Bias*, PROPUBLICA (May 23, 2016), https://www.propublica.org/article/machine-bias-risk-assessments-in-criminal-sentencing.

68 Kalley Huang, *Alarmed by A.I. Chatbots, Universities Start Revamping How They Teach*, N.Y. TIMES (Jan. 16, 2023) https://www.nytimes.com/2023/01/16/technology/chatgpt-artificial-intelligence-universities.html?smid = url-share (classroom overhauls due to essay plagiarism); Jey Willmore, *AI Education and AI in Education*, U.S. NAT'L SCI. FOUND. (Dec. 4, 2023), https://new.nsf.gov/science-matters/ai-education-ai-education (NSF-funded educational projects related to AI).

69 Robin C. Feldman & Kara Stein, *AI Governance in the Financial Industry*, 27 STAN. J.L. BUS. & FIN. 94 (2022).

70 ANDREW A. TOOLE ET AL., OFF. OF THE CHIEF ECONOMIST AT THE U.S. PAT. AND TRADEMARK OFF., INVENTING AI: TRACING THE DIFFUSION OF ARTIFICIAL INTELLIGENCE WITH U.S. PATENTS 3 (2020), https://www.uspto.gov/sites/default/files/documents/OCE-DH-AI.pdf.

71 FRANK A. PASQUALE, THE BLACK BOX SOCIETY: THE SECRET ALGORITHMS THAT CONTROL MONEY AND INFORMATION (2015).

72 The degree to which a human observer can intrinsically understand the cause of a model's decision is described by the machine learning community as an AI system's "interpretability" or "explainability."

73 *See, e.g.*, Warren J. von Eschenbach, *Transparency and the Black Box Problem: Why We Do Not Trust AI*, 34 PHIL. & TECH. 1607 (2021).

74 *See* Mark Bovens, *Analysing and Assessing Accountability: A Conceptual Framework*, 13 EUR. L.J. 447, at 450 ("['Accountability'] is one of those evocative political words that can be used to patch up a rambling argument, to evoke an image of trustworthiness, fidelity and justice, or to hold critics at bay. For anyone reflecting on accountability, it is impossible to disregard these strong evocative overtones.").

75 *See, e.g.*, U.S. GOVERNMENT ACCOUNTABILITY OFFICE, WHO IS ACCOUNTABLE? TO WHOM? FOR WHAT? HOW?, https://gao.gov/products/111071#:~:text = In%20a%20democracy%2C%20accountability%20is, President%2C%20his%20cabinet%20and%20officers (Dec. 6, 1979) ("In a democracy, accountability is an implicit tenet in the idea of popular representation. Article II of the Constitution established the accountability of the President, his cabinet and officers."); U.S. GOVERNMENT ACCOUNTABILITY OFFICE, GAO AT A GLANCE, https://www.gao.gov/assets/2023-08/About-GAO_Brochure_2023.pdf (Aug. 2023) (Describing the origin of the GAO and its general responsibilities in the oversight of various government programs and policies); Rebecca L. Brown, Accountability, Liberty, and the Constitution, 98 COLUM. L. REV. 531, 535 (1998) ("[A]ccountability is best understood … as a structural feature of the constitutional architecture, the goal of which is to protect liberty. In this respect it is much like the other

structural constitutional features such as separation of powers, checks and balances, and federalism[.]"); Nicholas O. Stephanopoulos, *Accountability Claims in Constitutional Law*, NW. U. L. REV. 989, 999–1004 (2018) (defining "accountability" with special emphasis on its relationship to retrospective voting.).

76 *See, e.g.*, Claudio Novelli, Mariarosaria Taddeo, & Luciano Floridi, *Accountability in Artificial Intelligence: What It Is and How It Works*, AI & Soc. 1, 2 (2023) ("Accountability has many definitions but, at its core, is an obligation to inform about, and justify one's conduct to an authority.") (citations omitted); Bovens, *supra* note 75, at 447 ("'Accountability' is not just another political catchword; it also refers to concrete practices of account giving. The most concise description of accountability would be: 'the obligation to explain and justify conduct'. This implies a relationship between an actor, the accountor, and a forum, the accountholder or accountee."); Richard Mulgan, *'Accountability': An Ever-Expanding Concept?*, 78 PUB. ADMIN. 555, 561 ("External accountability seeks to investigate and assess actions taken (or not taken) by agents or subordinates and to impose sanctions.... It make [sic] sense to say that particular public servants are accountable to certain other people and bodies through certain mechanisms for the performance of certain tasks.").

77 *See id.*

78 *See, e.g.*, Jennifer Shkabatur, *Transparency With(out) Accountability: Open Government in the United States*, YALE L. & POL'Y REV. 79, 80 (2012) ("[R]egulatory transparency has traditionally been regarded as a means for improving agencies' public accountability.").

79 *See, e.g.*, Luca Collina et al., *Critical Issues about A.I. Accountability Answered*, CAL. REV. MGMT., https://cmr.berkeley.edu/2023/11/critical-issues-about-a-i-accountability-answered/ (Nov. 6, 2023) ("As A.I. becomes more widespread, who should be held responsible if these systems make poor choices is unclear. The traditional top-down accountability model from executives to managers faces challenges with A.I.'s black box nature.").

80 *See* Gerrit De Vynck, *Cruise Settles with Person Dragged under One of Its Robotaxis*, THE WASH. POST (May 15, 2024).

81 *See* Dana Hull & David Welch, *GM's Cruise Halts Robotaxi Fleet after California Suspension*, BLOOMBERG NEWS (Oct. 26, 2023).

82 Quinn Emanuel Urquhart & Sullivan, LLP, Report to the Board of Directors of Cruise LLC, GM Cruise Holdings LLC, and General Motors Holdings LLC Regarding the October 2, 2023 Accident in San Francisco (2024).

83 *Id.* at 81 (describing in detail Cruise's decision to let the video of the incident "speak for itself").

84 *Id.* at 95–96.

85 *See* WHITE HOUSE OFFICE OF SCIENCE AND TECHNOLOGY POLICY, BLUEPRINT FOR AN AI BILL OF RIGHTS: MAKING AUTOMATED SYSTEMS WORK FOR THE AMERICAN PEOPLE (2022).

86 *Id.* ("The Blueprint for an AI Bill of Rights is non-binding and does not constitute U.S. government policy. It does not supersede, modify, or direct an interpretation of any existing statute, regulation, policy, or international instrument. It does not constitute binding guidance for the public or Federal agencies and therefore does not require compliance with the principles described herein. It also is not determinative of what the U.S. government's position will be in any international negotiation.").

87 *Id.* ("It is intended to support the development of policies and practices that protect civil rights and promote democratic values in the building, deployment, and governance of automated systems.").

88 2024 O.J. (L)(EU) 2024/1689. The EU AI Act was first proposed in April 2021 and finally adopted in May 2024. *See* The Act Texts, EU Artificial Intelligence Act, https://artificialintelligenceact.eu/the-act/ (last visited July 25, 2024). Chapters of the Act will come into force on an incremental basis starting in August 2024. *See* Historic Timeline, EU Artificial Intelligence Act, https://artificialintelligenceact.eu/developments/ (last visited July 25, 2024). The EU AI Act's stated purpose is to "improve the functioning of the internal market and promote the uptake of human-centric and trustworthy artificial intelligence[.]" *Id.* at art. 1.

89 *See, e.g.*, Kim Mackrael & Sam Schechner, *European Lawmakers Pass AI Act, World's First Comprehensive AI Law*, WALL STREET J., https://www.wsj.com/tech/ai/ai-act-passes-european-union-law-regulation-e04ec251 (Mar. 13, 2024, 12:45 PM ET); Karen Gilchrist & Ruxandra Lordache, *World's First Major Act to Regulate AI Passed by European Lawmakers*, CNBC (Mar. 13, 2024, 12:14 PM EDT), https://www.cnbc.com/2024/03/13/european-lawmakers-endorse-worlds-first-major-act-to-regulate-ai.html; Brian Fung, *EU Approves Landmark AI Law, Leapfrogging US to Regulate Critical but Worrying New Technology*, CNN (Mar. 13, 2024, 8:04 AM EDT), https://www.cnn.com/2024/03/13/tech/ai-european-union/index.html.

90 The comprehensive legislation relies on enforcement at two levels: At the Union level via the European Commission and at the national member states level via national market surveillance authorities. *See id.* at preamble 148.

91 The relevant language specifies that based on plans to be set out by the European Commission, the provider "shall actively and systematically collect, document and analyse data which . . . allow the provider to evaluate the continuous compliance of AI systems with the requirements of [the relevant provisions of the Act]." *Id.* at art. 72(2).

92 *Id.* at art. 3(49).

93 *Id.* at art. 73(2).

94 Shengcheng shi ren gong zhineng fuwu guanli zanxing banfa (生成式人工智能服务管理暂行办法) at Section 4(5) (in Chinese only).

95 Robin C. Feldman, Oral Testimony from Robin C. Feldman to USPTO AI Inventorship Listening Session – East Coast (Feb. 12 2023) (unpublished comments on file with author).

96 *See* Scherer, *supra* note 6, at 355 nn. 8–10 (summarizing tech leaders' concerns and desire for regulation of AI); Kevin Roose, *A.I. Poses 'Risk of Extinction,' Industry Leaders Warn,* N.Y. TIMES (May 30, 2023), https://www.nytimes.com/2023/05/30/technology/ai-threat-warning.html (describing "open letter . . . signed by more than 350 executives, researchers and engineers working in A.I." on the "risk of extinction from A.I.").

97 *See, e.g.,* NICOLAS CARR, THE SHALLOWS: WHAT THE INTERNET IS DOING TO OUR BRAINS (2010) (questioning how use of internet might lead to sacrificing of human ability to read and think deeply); *Ledger of Harms,* CENTER FOR HUMANE TECHNOLOGY (June 2021), https://ledger.humanetech.com/ (compiling diverse harms related to AI-powered digital platform use, including those related to "Physical and Mental Health" and "Social Relationships").

98 *See, e.g.,* Angwin et al., *supra* note 68 (exemplifying embedded racial bias in risk assessment algorithm used to support courtroom sentencing); CODED BIAS (7th Empire Media 2020) (highlighting race and gender biases embedded in artificial intelligence technologies).

99 *See, e.g.,* DARON ACEMOGLU ET AL., AI AND JOBS: EVIDENCE FROM ONLINE VACANCIES (2020); James Bessen, *Artificial Intelligence and Jobs: The Role of Demand, in* THE ECONOMICS OF ARTIFICIAL INTELLIGENCE: AN AGENDA 291, 301 (Ajay Agrawal, Joshua Gans, & Avi Goldfarb eds., 2019) (emphasizing "importance of demand in mediating the impact of [AI] automation").

100 Joshua Rothman, *Why the Godfather of A.I. Fears What He's Built,* THE NEW YORKER (Nov. 13, 2023), https://www.newyorker.com/magazine/2023/11/20/geoffrey-hinton-profile-ai ("existential risk" of AI); Kevin Roose, *Silicon Valley Confronts a Grim New A.I. Metric,* THE N. Y. TIMES (Dec. 6, 2023), https://www.nytimes.com/2023/12/06/business/dealbook/silicon-valley-artificial-intelligence.html ("p(doom)").

101 Fiza Fatima, *The 5 Leading Small Language Models of 2024: Phi 3, Llama 3, and More,* DATA SCI. DOJO (May 5, 2024), https://datasciencedojo.com/blog/small-language-models-phi-3/.

102 Billy Perrigo, *No One Truly Knows How AI Systems Work. A New Discovery Could Change That,* TIME (May 21, 2024, 11:00 AM PDT), https://time.com/6980210/anthropic-interpretability-ai-safety-research/ (last visited July 29, 2024).

Chapter 2

1 SAMUEL SCHEFFLER, THE REJECTION OF CONSEQUENTIALISM 1 (OXFORD UNIVERSITY PRESS 1982); UTILITARIANISM AND BEYOND 3–5 (Amartya Sen & Bernard Williams, eds., Cambridge University Press 1982); For a

comprehensive analysis of the nuances within moral philosophy, including the intricacies of consequentialism and non-consequentialism, *see* Robin Feldman, *Consumption Taxes and the Theory of General and Individual Taxation*, 21 Va. Tax Rev. 293, 303–14, 304 n.16, 311 n.47 (2002) (exploring these concepts within the broader framework of modern tax theory and clarifying terms often misinterpreted in legal scholarship, such as teleological, deontological, and rights-based theories).

2 F. M. KAMM, INTRICATE ETHICS: RIGHTS, RESPONSIBILITIES, AND PERMISSIBLE HARM 11–12 (Oxford University Press 2007); SCHEFFLER, *supra* note 1, at 2–5.

3 This conclusion follows the logic of declining marginal utility. *See* Feldman, supra note 1, at 309–10.

4 *See id.*

5 *See* Daniel N. Shaviro, *Inequality, Wealth, and Endowment*, 53 TAX L. REV. 397, 413 (2000) ("From a welfarist perspective, where the desirability of a state of affairs depends purely on people's well-being in it, the tax rate is set to optimize the value of the progressive redistribution that can be accomplished relative to the cost of deterring work effort through the tax."); *see also* James A. Mirrlees, *The Economic Uses of Utilitarianism, in* UTILITARIANISM AND BEYOND, *supra* note 1, at 63 (noting that a utilitarian redistribution of wealth must ensure that productive individuals are not incentivized to diminish or dissemble their productivity); James A. Mirrlees, *An Exploration in the Theory of Optimum Income Taxation*, 38 REV. ECON. STUD. 175 (1971) (acknowledging the labor-discouraging effect of redistributive tax systems).

6 *See* Shaviro, *supra* note 5, at 417, 419 (discussing theorists who approach distributive justice from the standpoint that "rights matter independently of consequences" and contrasting them with utilitarians); Liam Murphy, *Liberty, Equality, Well-Being: Rakowski on Wealth Transfer Taxation*, 51 TAX L. REV. 473, 477 (1996) (framing this moral debate as a tradeoff central to liberalism generally: "If there is anything that can be identified as the core commitment of liberalism, it is surely the commitment to the moral importance of an individual's freedom to make her own choices about how to live her life. Of course, there is a limit to liberalism's respect for individual autonomy, and traditionally, it is drawn at the point where one person's exercise of her autonomy infringes the autonomy of others.").

7 The United States is a party to several international treaties that recognize moral rights within the realm of copyright and performance rights for artists, such as singers and actors. These include the Berne Convention, the WIPO Copyright Treaty, and the WIPO Performances and Phonograms Treaty. *See* Berne Convention for the Protection of Literary and Artistic Works art. 11bis(2), Sept. 28, 1979, S. Treaty Doc. No. 99-27, 1161 U.N.T.S. 3; WIPO Copyright Treaty, Dec. 20, 1996, 2186 U.N.T.S. 121; WIPO

Performances and Phonograms Treaty art. 5, Dec. 20, 1996, 2186 U.N.T.S. 203.

8 For a discussion on the utilitarian foundation of patent law, *see, e.g.*, Adam Mossoff, *Who Cares What Thomas Jefferson Thought about Patents? Reevaluating the Patent "Privilege" in Historical Context*, 92 CORNELL L. REV. 953, 962 & n.41, 963–65 (2007) ("Although scholars today identify many operative policies in patent law, these policies are only different applications of the same utilitarian, incentive-creating theory."); Alan J. Devlin & Neel U. Sukhatme, *Self-Realizing Inventions and the Utilitarian Foundation of Patent Law*, 51 WM. & MARY L. REV. 897, 913 (2009) ("[A]cademic commentators have resoundingly embraced the position that patent law exists to promote purely utilitarian concerns. More importantly, the U.S. Supreme Court has consistently reaffirmed the same view on several occasions."); FRITZ MACHLUP, STAFF OF S. SUBCOMM. ON PATENTS, TRADEMARKS, AND COPYRIGHTS, 85TH CONG., STUDY OF AN ECONOMIC REVIEW OF THE PATENT SYSTEM 33 (Comm. Print 1958) ("The thesis that the patent system may produce effective profit incentives for inventive activity and thereby promote progress in the technical arts is widely accepted."); *see also* Kewanee Oil Co. v. Bicron Corp., 416 U.S. 470, 480 ("The patent laws promote [the 'Progress of Science and useful Arts'] by offering a right of exclusion for a limited period as an incentive to inventors to risk the often enormous costs in terms of time, research, and development. The productive effort thereby fostered [by patent laws] will have a positive effect on society through the introduction of new products and processes of manufacture into the economy, and the emanations by way of increased employment and better lives for our citizens."). For the utilitarian basis of copyright law, *see, e.g.*,William W. Fisher III, *Reconstructing the Fair Use Doctrine*, 101 HARV. L. REV. 1659, 1703 (1988) (discussing copyright's fair use doctrine and noting that "to avoid underproduction of original works, it is necessary to empower the creators of such works to charge fees for the privilege of using them, but granting the creators that right causes monopoly losses, which vary between types of copyrighted works. The task of a lawmaker who wishes to maximize efficiency, therefore, is to determine, with respect to each type of intellectual product, the combination of entitlements that would result in economic gains that exceed by the maximum amount the attendant efficiency losses"); Jeanne C. Fromer, *Expressive Incentives in Intellectual Property*, 98 VA. L. REV. 1745, 1750–51 n.22, 24 (2012) ("The Supreme Court, Congress, and many legal scholars consider utilitarianism the dominant purpose of American copyright ... law."); Brief for Tyler T. Ochoa et al. as Amici Curiae Supporting Petitioners, Eldred v. Ashcroft, 537 U.S. 186 (2003) (No. 01-618), 2002 WL 1051765, at *28–29 (discussing *Wheaton v. Peters* and explaining that "[i]n rejecting Wheaton's claim of perpetual common-law copyright, the U.S. Supreme Court confirmed the utilitarian

view embodied in the Constitution that patents and copyrights are exclusive rights of limited duration, granted in order to serve the public interest in promoting the creation and dissemination of new works"). For those who challenge the dominant utilitarian perspective, *see, e.g.*, Tom G. Palmer, *Are Patents and Copyrights Morally Justified? The Philosophy of Property Rights and Ideal Objects*, 13 HARV. J. L. & PUB. POL'Y 817 (1990) (critiquing four common arguments in favor of intellectual property). Rights-based (deontological) theories also provide an alternative framework. Among the most prevalent is the natural rights theory, which asserts that creators should hold ownership over their creations, drawing from Lockean philosophy that ties labor to (intellectual) property rights. *See* Justin Hughes, *The Philosophy of Intellectual Property*, 77 GEO L. J. 287, 297 (1988) (discussing Locke's theory of property); HELEN NORMAN, INTELLECTUAL PROPERTY LAW DIRECTIONS 89 (2d ed. Oxford University Press 2014). Variations on this theory include the moral/desert theory, the personhood theory, the personal autonomy theory, and the human rights-based theory. The moral/desert theory argues that creators deserve control over their works due to the effort invested. *See* Lawrence C. Becker, *Deserving to Own Intellectual Property*, 68 CHI.-KENT L. REV. 609, 620 (1993). The personhood theory suggests that creation is an extension of the creator's personality, making control over the creation essential to maintaining the creator's identity. Margaret J. Radin, *Property and Personhood*, 34 STAN. L. REV. 957, 957, 959–61 (1982); Hughes, *id.* at 330. The personal autonomy theory posits that personal autonomy involves the right to control objects closely tied to one's identity. TANYA APLIN & JENNIFER DAVIS, INTELLECTUAL PROPERTY LAW: TEXTS, CASES AND MATERIALS 63 (3rd ed. Oxford University Press 2017). The human rights-based theory sees intellectual property as human rights, deserving protection for individual use and disposal, differing from natural rights theory by drawing on international human rights conventions rather than divine rights. *See* J. Janewa Osei-Tutu, *Humanizing Intellectual Property: Moving beyond the Natural Rights Property Focus*, 20 VAND. J. ENT. & TECH. L. 207, 223–26 (2017). These theories have been criticized. *See* F. Scott Kieff, *Property Rights and Property Rules for Commercializing Inventions*, 85 MINN. L. REV. 697, 698 n.2 (2001) ("Yet those natural rights theories tying invention to inventor leave many questions unanswered. Assuming inventions are the natural property of the inventor, what rights do simultaneous inventors have? Should independent origination be a complete defense to patent infringement as it is for copyright infringement? More fundamentally, should the patent right include some affirmative right to use?"); Clarissa Long, *Patent Signals*, 69 U. CHI. L. REV. 625, 626–27 (2002).

9 *See* Fisher III, *supra* note 8.

10 U.S. CONST. art. 1, § 8, cl. 8.

11 It is important to recognize here that the Constitution explicitly defines the "good" to be maximized, namely, the progress of science. *See id.*

12 383 U.S. 1, 9 (1966).

13 *See* Kenneth W. Dam, *The Economic Underpinnings of Patent Law*, 23 J. LEGAL STUD. 247, 247 (1994).

14 *Id.*; *see also* Kenneth J. Arrow, *Economic Welfare and the Allocation of Resources for Invention*, in THE RATE AND DIRECTION OF INVENTIVE ACTIVITY: ECONOMIC AND SOCIAL FACTORS 609, 614–15 (Princeton University Press 1962).

15 Mark A. Lemley, *Property, Intellectual Property, and Free Riding*, 83 TEX. L. REV. 1031, 1033–46 (2005) (analyzing and critiquing the concept of the free riding problem as a misguided concept).

16 *See* Fisher III, *supra* note 8, at 1700 (describing how the reproducibility of creative works contributes to the risk that, absent copyright protections, financial incentives will be inadequate for the production "of useful ideas and original forms of expression."); *see also* William M. Landes & Richard A. Posner, *An Economic Analysis of Copyright Law*, 18 J. LEGAL STUD. 325, 326 (1989) ("Copyright protection [. . .] trades off the costs of limiting access to a work against the benefits of providing incentives to create the work in the first place").

17 Landes & Posner, *supra* note 16, at 331–32.

18 *See generally* Mark P. McKenna, *The Normative Foundations of Trademark Law*, 82 NOTRE DAME L. REV. 1840, 1844–49 (2008) (discussing how commentators have framed the consumer search cost theory as foundational to trademark law); Sonia K. Katyal & Aniket Kesari, *Trademark Search, Artificial Intelligence, and the Role of the Private Sector*, 35 BERKELEY TECH. & L.J. 501, 509–14 (2020) (examining how trademarks function to reduce consumer search costs).

19 Mark P. McKenna, *A Consumer Decision-Making Theory of Trademark Law*, 98 VA. L. REV. 67, 73 (2012) ("[T]rademark law operates to enable consumers to rely on trademarks as repositories of information about the source and quality of products, thereby reducing the costs of searching for goods that satisfy their preferences."). *See* William M. Landes & Richard A. Posner, *Trademark Law: An Economic Perspective*, 30 J. L. & ECON. 265, 270, 275 (1987) (identifying the reduction of consumer search costs as the "essential economic function of trademarks" and arguing that a firm's incentive to invest in a strong mark hinges on its ability to maintain product quality); Mark A. Lemley, *The Modern Lanham Act and the Death of Common Sense*, 108 YALE L. J. 1687 (1999) (noting that trademarks also facilitate the complex, long-term distribution across broad geographies, such as in franchising).

20 *See* Union Nat'l Bank of Tex., Laredo, Tex. v. Union Nat'l Bank of Tex., Austin, Tex., 909 F.2d 839, 844 (5th Cir. 1990) ("The idea is that trademarks are 'distinguishing' features which lower consumer search costs and

encourage higher quality production by discouraging free-riders."); Qualitex Co. v. Jacobsen Prods. Co., 514 U.S. 159, 163–64 (1995) ("In principle, trademark law, by preventing others from copying a source-identifying mark, 'reduce[s] the customer's costs of shopping and making purchasing decisions,' ... [and] helps assure a producer that it (and not an imitating competitor) will reap the financial, reputation-related rewards associated with a desirable product.") (quoting 1 J. THOMAS MCCARTHY, MCCARTHY ON TRADEMARKS AND UNFAIR COMPETITION § 2.01[2], 2–3 (3d ed. 1994)).

21 This book focuses exclusively on the histories of American law. For discussions that also explore English law or delve further back in time, *see generally* Sidney A. Diamond, *The Historical Development of Trademarks*, 65 TRADEMARK REP. 265 (1975); FRANK I. SCHECHTER, THE HISTORICAL FOUNDATIONS OF THE LAW RELATING TO TRADE-MARKS (Columbia University Press 1925); Edward S. Rogers, *Some Historical Matter Concerning Trade-Marks*, 9 MICH. L. REV. 29 (1911); Benjamin G. Paster, *Trademarks – Their Early History*, 59 TRADEMARK REP. 551 (1969). *See also*, Daniel M. McClure, *Trademarks and Unfair Competition: A Critical History of Legal Thought*, 69 TRADEMARK REP. 305, 310–14 (1979); McKenna, *Normative Foundations*, *supra* note 18, at 1149–58.

22 *See, e.g.*, Coats v. Holbrook, 2 Sand. Ch. 586, 594 (N.Y. Ch. 1845) ("[A person] has no right, and he will not be allowed, to use the names, letters, marks, or other symbols by which he may palm off upon buyers as the manufactures of another, the article he is selling; and thereby attract to himself the patronage that without such deceptive use of such names ... would have inured to the benefit of that other person."). *See also* McKenna, *Normative Foundations*, *supra* note 18, at 1841 ("[T]rademark law, like all unfair competition law, sought to protect producers from illegitimate diversions of their trade by competitors.").

23 *See, e.g.*, McClure, *supra* note 21, at 315 ("The early development of trademark law in America was thus firmly based on notions of morality, focusing on the fraudulent activity of the defendant."); Amoskeag Mfg. Co. v. Spear, 2 Sand. 599, 605–06 (N.Y. Sup. Ct. 1849) ("He who affixes to his own goods an imitation of an original trademark, by which those of another are distinguished and known, seeks, by deceiving the public, to divert and appropriate to his own use, the profits to which the superior skill and enterprise of the other had given him a prior and exclusive title.").

24 JAMES L. HOPKINS, THE LAW OF TRADEMARKS, TRADENAMES AND UNFAIR COMPETITION § 1, at 1 (2d ed. 1905) ("Unfair competition consists in passing off one's goods as the goods of another, or in otherwise *securing patronage that should go to another*, by false representations that lead the patron to believe that he is patronizing the other person") (emphasis added). McKenna, *Normative Foundations*, *supra* note 18, at 1841, 1865 ("In fact,

courts denied relief in many early trademark cases despite clear evidence that consumers were likely to be confused by the defendant's use. Invariably they did so because the plaintiff could not show that the defendant's actions were likely to divert customers who otherwise would have gone to the plaintiff.") ("Importantly, this formulation did not depend on whether the case involved a claim of trademark infringement or unfair competition. In both types of cases, courts primarily focused on a producer's diverted trade, sometimes mentioning the public's interest as well.").

25 *See* McKenna, *Normative Foundations, supra* note 18, at 1860 ("Because the purpose of trademark protection traditionally was to prevent trade diversion by competitors, it has long been regarded as a species of the broader law of unfair competition, and even more broadly, as part of the law governing other fraudulent (and unfair) business practices."); HOPKINS, *supra* note 24.

26 McKenna, *Normative Foundations, supra* note 18, at 1841 (2007) ("American courts protected producers from illegitimately diverted trade by recognizing property rights. This property-based system of trademark protection was largely derived from the natural rights theory of property that predominately influenced courts during the time American trademark law developed in the nineteenth century.").

27 Daniel M. McClure, *Trademarks and Competition: The Recent History*, 59 L. & CONTEMP. PROBS. 13, 15 (1996). *See also*, McClure, *Trademarks and Unfair Competition, supra* note 21, at 317, 323 ("But it was the development of the 'property' concept as a unifying principle in trademark law that was the cornerstone of the rising structure of legal formalism in the late nineteenth century.") ("The furthest extension of the concept of 'protection of property' to expand protection of trademarks was proposed in 1927 by Frank I. Schechter in his famous article, 'The Rational Basis of Trade-Mark Protection.' Schechter argued against the traditional formulation of the function of a trademark as an indicator of source or origin of the goods"). *See also* McKenna, *Normative Foundations, supra* note 18, at 1860 n. 91 (referencing cases and scholarly commentary that endorse a property-based view of trademark law).

28 McClure, *Trademarks and Unfair Competition, supra* note 21, at 327 ("The lack of uniformity in decisions and the tenuousness of deriving rules from the 'property' conception became more and more apparent. The arbitrariness and inconsistency of the application of the rules became glaringly clear. '[T]he charge against conceptualism was that it was mystification: there simply was no deductive process, by which one could derive the 'right' legal answer from abstractions like freedom or property.'") (citing Duncan Kennedy, *Form and Substance in Private Law Adjudication*, 89 HARV. L. REV. 1685, 1748 (1976)). For a deeper exploration of the rationale behind realism, *see* McClure, *Trademarks and Unfair Competition, supra* note 21, at 327–29.

29 McClure, *Trademarks and Unfair Competition*, *supra* note 21, at 329 ("The result of the realist attack brought about changes in the rhetoric of judges and commentators, though the doctrinal changes were less dramatic. The property justification of protection was replaced by arguments in favor of protecting business good will or values resulting from use.").

30 *See* McKenna, *Normative Foundations*, *supra* note 18, at 1898 ("Significantly, as courts and commentators began to embrace the consumer protection theory as a justification for claims by producers, courts stopped referring to separate actions by consumers for fraud or deceit. Thus, while courts traditionally distinguished conceptually between trademark claims and claims aimed at protecting consumers, the latter needing to be pursued by consumers themselves, courts in the twentieth century began to conflate the two interests").

31 Many regard realist economist Edward Chamberlin as the leading proponent of this economic analysis of trademarks. *See* EDWARD H. CHAMBERLIN, THE THEORY OF MONOPOLISTIC COMPETITION (1st ed. 1933). *See, e.g.*, McClure, *Trademarks and Competition: The Recent History*, *supra* note 27, at 15 (attributing the "economic theory attack on trademark protection" to "a seminal book by economist Edward H. Chamberlin that presented a reasoned case against trademarks as reinforcing monopoly power."); HERBERT HOVERNKAMP, THE OPENING OF AMERICAN LAW: NEOCLASSICAL LEGAL THOUGHT 198 (Oxford University Press 2015) ("Edward Chamberlin's ground-shifting book on *Monopolistic Competition* pursued the relationship between IP rights and product differentiation.... Chamberlin's work was appealing to the Legal Realists, reinforcing their view that markets themselves are often instruments of coercion.").

32 The Chicago School of economic thought played a large role. McClure, *Trademarks and Competition: The Recent History*, *supra* note 27, at 28 ("Just as the Chicago School theorists have come to dominate thinking in antitrust law, so has the Chicago School influenced the development of basic trademark law."). *See id.* at 19–25 for an overview of the Chicago School's impact on trademark, unfair competition, and antitrust law.

33 Trademarks have long been intertwined with the broader domain of unfair competition law. Over time, scholars have fluctuated in their characterization of trademarks as either pro-competitive or anti-competitive. A key influence of the Chicago School on trademark law was its use of price theory to portray the expansion of trademark rights as ultimately serving consumer interests. *See* McClure, *Trademarks and Unfair Competition*, *supra* note 21, at 346–48.

34 McKenna, *A Consumer Decision-Making Theory of Trademark Law*, *supra* note 19, at 71 ("As a descriptive matter, courts did not elevate confusion to this central status because they had consumers' interests at heart; indeed, most of trademark law's expansive confusion doctrines were developed, often explicitly, for the purpose of protecting mark-owner interests. But courts

have had no trouble casting their decisions in consumer protection terms since their emphasis on confusion is so compatible with the dominant theoretical account of trademark law – namely, the search costs [sic] theory. Anything that can be characterized in confusion-based terms seems to raise search costs, and if search costs are the harm to be avoided, then anything that causes confusion ought to be at least prima facie actionable."). In fact, one of the significant influences of the Chicago School on trademark law was to use price theory to frame trademark expansion as benefiting consumers. *See* McClure, *Trademarks and Competition: The Recent History*, *supra* note 27, at 21 ("The Chicago School economists contended that trademarks (and advertising) were actually pro-competitive because they lower consumer search costs, facilitate entry by new competitors, and generate quality-control incentives.").

35 For an account of the development of trade secret law in the United States, *see* Sharon K. Sandeen, *The Evolution of Trade Secret Law and Why Courts Commit Error When They Do Not Follow the Uniform Trade Secrets Act*, 33 HAMLINE L. REV. 493 (2010). *See also* Mark A. Lemley, *The Surprising Virtues of Treating Trade Secrets as IP Rights*, 61 STAN. L. REV. 311, 312 n. 1 (2008); Suzana Nashkova, *Defining Trade Secrets in the United States: Past and Present Challenges – A Way Forward?*, 54 IIC 634 (2023).

36 *See, e.g.*, Vincent Chiappetta, *Myth, Chameleon or Intellectual Property Olympian? A Normative Framework Supporting Trade Secret Law*, 8 GEO. MASON L. REV. 69, 73 (1999) (contending that the "basic focus" of trade secret law is on the misappropriation of information); Lemley, *supra* note 35, at 312 ("While scholars periodically disagree over the purposes of the law . . . they seem to agree that misappropriation of trade secrets is a bad thing that the law should punish."); Michael Risch, *Why Do We Have Trade Secrets?*, 11 MARQ. INTELL. PROP. L. REV. 1, 43 (2007) ("[I]ronically, the law of trade secrets is necessary to cause less money to be spent on the protection of secrets, and as a result to cause less money to be spent by those trying to appropriate someone else's trade secrets, even if that means misappropriation is successful more often.").

37 *See* RESTATEMENT (FIRST) OF TORTS § 757 cls. b (1939) ("[A]n exact definition of trade secret is not possible.").

38 *See* Robert G. Bone, *A New Look at Trade Secret Law: Doctrine in Search of Justification*, 86 CAL. L. REV. 241, 304 (1999) ("Trade secret law is in a muddle today."); Chiappetta, *supra* note 36, at 69 ("United States trade secret law is in a state of disarray.").

39 *See* 18 U.S.C. § 1836.

40 *See supra* Section 2.3.

41 *See* Ruckelshaus v. Monsanto Co., 467 U.S. 986, 1002–03 (1984) ("This general perception of trade secrets as property is consonant with a notion of 'property' that extends beyond land and tangible goods and includes the

products of an individual's labor and invention.'"); Paula Samuelson, *Information as Property: Do* Ruckelshaus *and* Carpenter *Signal a Changing Direction in Intellectual Property Law?*, 38 CATH. U. L. REV. 365, 398 (1989) ("Clearly, the word property is a very powerful metaphor that radically changes the stakes in legal disputes.").

42 *See generally* Lemley, *supra* note 35 (laying out the various competing theories on trade secrets). *See also* David D. Freidman, William M. Landes, & Richard A. Posner, *Some Economics of Trade Secret Law*, 5 J. OF ECON. PERSP. 61, 71 (1991) ("The current structure of trade secret law may be the best compromise among the competing economic considerations. No stronger conclusion is possible.").

43 Kewanee Oil Co. v. Bicron Corp, 416 U.S. 470, 481 (1974) ("The maintenance of standards of commercial ethics and the encouragement of invention are the broadly stated policies behind trade secret law."). For discussions on the different theoretical bases underpinning trade secret law, *see* Risch, *supra* note 36, at 15–36; Lemley, *supra* note 35, at 319–29; Bone, *supra* note 38, at 251–303.

44 Peabody v. Norfolk, 98 Mass. 452, 457 (Mass. 1868). *See also* 1 MELVIN F. JAGER & BRAD LANE, TRADE SECRETS LAW § 2:3 (1996) (characterizing *Peabody* as "one of the most famous, and best-reasoned, early trade secret cases"); Michael J. Hutter, *Trade Secret Misappropriation: A Lawyer's Practical Approach to the Caselaw*, 1 W. NEW ENG. L. REV. 1, 7 (1978) ("*Peabody v. Norfolk* is frequently cited as the seminal case for much of the development of trade secrets law in the United States."); Bone, *supra* note 38, at 252 (describing the *Peabody* opinion as "crystallizing the law of trade secrets in the United States").

45 The earliest court decision involving trade secrets was Vickery v. Welch, 36 Mass. 523 (Mass. 1837), though the ruling did not provide a specific definition of what constitutes a trade secret.

46 Peabody v. Norfolk, 98 Mass. 452, 457 (Mass. 1868) ("It is the policy of the law, for the advantage of the public, to encourage and protect invention and commercial enterprise.").

47 Justice Gray argued that the value a business created through skill and effort, particularly in terms of business "good will," should be recognized as property by the law. *See id.* This combination of promoting societal progress and defending property rights illustrates the intertwining of different rationales for trade secret protection. *See, e.g.*, Risch, *supra* note 36, at 15–19 (comparing different paradigms for considering whether trade secrets qualify as property: "The middle ground is to treat trade secrets as . . . a collection of social rights and duties . . . A problem with the bundle of rights theory is that the word 'property' ceases to have any real meaning."); Bone, *supra* note 38, at 251–59 (examining the evolution of a general theory of trade secret law); Lemley, *supra* note 35, at 316 ("[C]ourts periodically spoke of trade secrets

as property rights, though it is not clear that they meant by that term what we mean today.").

48 Bone, *supra* note 38, at 259–60.

49 DuPont de Nemours Powder Co. v. Masland, 244 U.S. 100, 102 (1917).

50 *See* PETER S. MENELL ET AL., INTELLECTUAL PROPERTY IN THE NEW TECHNOLOGICAL AGE 48 (2023) (comparing a "property view" and "tort view" of trade secrets: "One significant difference, though, is that the tort view focuses first and foremost on the question of infringement – did the defendant do something wrong? The property and IP views, by contrast, first ask whether there is a property right at all to be protected."); JAGER & LANE, *supra* note 44, at § 1:3 ("The Anglo-American common law … began to develop protection for business secrets to enhance commercial morality and good-faith dealings in business."). *See also* RESTATEMENT (FIRST) OF TORTS § 757 cmt. f on cl. a (1939) ("A complete catalog of improper means is not possible. In general they are means which fall below the generally accepted standards of commercial morality and reasonable conduct.").

51 *See* Michael P. Simpson, *The Future of Innovation: Trade Secrets, Property Rights, and Protectionism – An Age-Old Tale*, 70 BROOK. L. REV. 1121, 1131 (2005) ("[The Restatement (Third) of Unfair Competition] recognizes that trade secret law has adopted the policy goals for copyright and patent law, explaining that trade secret protection is justified 'as a means to encourage investment in research by providing an opportunity to capture the returns from successful innovations.'") (quoting RESTATEMENT (THIRD) OF UNFAIR COMPETITION § 39 cmt. a (AM. BAR. ASS'N 1995)). For an overview of the Law and Economics movement's impact on intellectual property rights as a whole, and trade secret law in particular, *see* Amy Kapczynski, *The Public History of Trade Secrets*, 55 U.C. DAVIS L. REV., 1367, 1392–407 (2023). *See also* Kewanee Oil Co. v. Bicron Corp, 416 U.S. 470, 481 (1974); Ruckelshaus v. Monsanto Co., 467 U.S. 986 (1984); RESTATEMENT (THIRD) OF UNFAIR COMPETITION § 39 cmt. at b, d (AM. BAR. ASS'N 1995).

52 Charles Tait Graves & Sonia K. Katyal, *From Trade Secret to Seclusion*, 109 GEO. L.J. 1337, 1351 (2021) ("[T]rade secret law… consolidated around a nexus of marketplace competition… reflected in all [modern] official formulations of trade secret law.").

53 Bone, *supra* note 38, at 304 ("I have argued that this muddle is due to the absence of a convincing normative theory capable of making coherent sense of trade secret doctrine. Trade secret law took its current shape in the late nineteenth century when formalist reasoning prevailed, and its roots lie in a formalistic theory of property rights that equates property with factual exclusivity. Today we retain the doctrine even though we reject the theory that initially justified it.").

54 For instance, Justice Story's frequently cited 1817 opinion in *Lowell v. Lewis* laid the groundwork for the "moral utility doctrine," which has resurfaced

periodically over the past two centuries. 15 F. Cas. 1018, 1019 (C.C.D. Mass. 1817) (No. 8,568) ("All that the law requires is that the invention should not be frivolous or injurious to the well-being, good policy, or sound morals of society. The word 'useful,' therefore, is incorporated into the act in contradistinction to mischievous or immoral.").

55 *See, e.g.*, Brewer v. Lichtenstein, 278 F. 512 (7th Cir. 1922) ("lottery device"); Meyer v. Buckley Mfg. Co., 15 F. Supp. 640 (N.D. Ill. 1936) (novelty gambling vending machine); Schultze v. Holtz, 82 F. 448 (N.D. Cal. 1897) (coin-controlled apparatus used for gambling purposes); National Automatic Device Co. v. Lloyd, 40 F. 89 (N.D. Ill. 1889) ("toy automatic race-course" used for gambling purposes); Scott & Williams, Inc. v. Aristo Hosiery Co., 7 F.2d 1003 (2d Cir. 1925) (imitation of stockings); Mahler v. Animarium Co., 111 F. 530 (8th Cir. 1901) (incredible medical device); Rickard v. Du Bon, 103 F. 868 (2d Cir. 1900) (process for "spotting" tobacco leaves).

56 Margo A. Bagley, *Patent First, Ask Questions Later: Morality and Biotechnology In Patent Law*, 45 WM. & MARY L. REV. 469, 490 (2003) ("Eventually, however, courts began refusing to impose the [morality] requirement at all. The courts acknowledged that it was an area in which Congress could legislate, but that such determinations were not the proper purview of the judiciary or the USPTO."). The USPTO's policy stands in stark contrast to international patent offices, where patent law explicitly "prohibits the registration of immoral inventions." Christine Haight Farley, *A Research Framework on Intellectual Property and Morality, in* HANDBOOK OF INTELLECTUAL PROPERTY RESEARCH: LENSES, METHODS, AND PERSPECTIVES 791, 795 (Irene Calboli & Maria Lillà Montagnani eds., 2021).

57 Juicy Whip, Inc. v. Orange Bang, Inc., 185 F.3d 1364, 1367 (Fed. Cir. 1999); Bagley, *supra* note 56, at 493 ("*Juicy Whip v. Orange Bang* ... sounded the death-knell for the moral utility requirement.").

58 *See generally* Cynthia M. Ho, *Splicing Morality and Patent Law: Issues Arising from Mixing Mice and Men*, 2 WASH. U. J.L. & POL'Y 247, 284 (2000) ("Whether a new model can be crafted to adequately incorporate morality into the patent laws is questionable."); Benjamin D. Enerson, *Protecting Society from Patently Offensive Inventions: The Risk of Reviving the Moral Utility Doctrine*, 89 CORNELL L. REV. 685, 720 (2004) ("[T]he patent system should focus on whether society has a real-world use for a certain invention and not whether society should use this invention ... Laws outside the patent system — and not patent law itself — should shape national policy regarding the morality of controversial inventions.").

59 HANDBOOK OF INTELLECTUAL PROPERTY RESEARCH: LENSES, METHODS, AND PERSPECTIVES 797 (Irene Calboli & Maria Lillà Montagnani eds., 2021). *But see* David Saunders, *Copyright, Obscenity and Literary History*,

57 ENG. LITERARY HIST. 431 (1990) (historical overview of Anglo-American copyright law and morality).

60 Section 2(a) of the 1946 Lanham Act, 15 U.S.C. § 1052.

61 Matal v. Tam, 582 U.S. 218 (2017). In 2019, the Supreme Court extended this reasoning in *Iancu v. Brunetti*, striking down the "immoral" and "scandalous" provisions as unconstitutional. Iancu v. Brunetti, 588 U.S. 388 (2019). For a broader perspective on trademark's complex relationship with the First Amendment, *see* Pamela Samuelson, *Copyright and Freedom of Expression in Historical Perspective*, 10 J. INTELL. PROP. L. 319 (2003).

62 Matal v. Tam, 582 U.S. 218 (2017).

63 *Supra* notes 55–57 and accompanying text.

Chapter 3

1 *Introducing ChatGPT*, OpenAI (Nov. 30, 2022), https://openai.com/index/chatgpt/.

2 There are *many* large language models. For instance, as of this writing, the website llmmodels.org lists 130 models – and this is far from a complete list. *See All Large Language Models*, Llmmodels.com, https://llmmodels.org/ (last visited Aug. 21, 2024).

3 *See, e.g.*, Mark Lemley, *How Generative AI Turns Copyright Upside Down*, 25 COLUM. SCI. & TECH L. REV. 190 (2023); Jacob Alhadeff, Cooper Cuene, & Max Del Real, *Limits of Algorithmic Fair Use*, 19 WASH. J. L. TECH. & ARTS 1 (2024).

4 *See, e.g.*, Jeffrey Wu, *Bridging the AI Inventorship Gap*, 91 FORDHAM L. REV. 2515 (2023) (discussing whether and to what extent a natural person can be the legal inventor of AI-generated inventions); Raina Haque, Simone Rose, & Nick DeSetto, *The Non-Obvious Razor & Generative AI*, 25 N.C. J.L. & TECH. 399 (2024)(addressing the tension between patent law's obviousness doctrine, the person having ordinary skill in the art (PHOSITA), and artificial intelligence systems); *OpenAI v. Scarlett Johansson? Georgetown Law Professor Answers Legal Questions on AI-Generated Content*, GEORGETOWN UNIV. (June 4, 2024), https://www.georgetown.edu/news/ask-a-professor-openai-v-scarlett-johansson/ (Professor Kristelia García describes the right-of-publicity issues that arose in the context of OpenAI's use of a voiced chatbot that, to many listeners, sounded like Scarlett Johansson).

5 *See Getting Started with Prompts for Text-Based Generative AI Tools*, HARVARD UNIV. INFO. TECH. (Aug. 30, 2023), https://huit.harvard.edu/news/ai-prompts ("The information, sentences, or questions that you enter into a Generative AI tool ('prompts') are a big influence on the quality of outputs you receive. After you enter a prompt, the AI model analyzes your input and generates a response based on the patterns it has learned through its training. More descriptive prompts can improve the quality of the outputs.").

6 *See, e.g.*, Complaint, The New York Times Co. v. Microsoft Corp. et al., Docket No. 1:23-cv-11195, 24–37 (S.D.N.Y. Dec. 27, 2023).

7 *Id.*; *see also* Cecilia Ziniti, *The New York Times vs. OpenAI: A Historic Copyright Battle Begins*, LINKEDIN PULSE (Dec. 27, 2023), https://www.linkedin.com/pulse/new-york-times-vs-openai-historic-copyright-battle-begins-ziniti-12pwc/; Michael D. Murray, *Generative AI Art: Copyright Infringement and Fair Use*, 26 SMU SCI. & TECH. L. REV. 259, 280–81 (2023).

8 Feist Publications, Inc. v. Rural Tel. Serv. Co., 499 U.S. 340, 345 (1991) ("The *sine qua non* of copyright is originality. To qualify for copyright protection, a work must be original to the author. Original, as the term is used in copyright, means only that the work was independently created by the author (as opposed to copied from other works), and that it possesses at least some minimal degree of creativity. To be sure, the requisite level of creativity is extremely low; even a slight amount will suffice. The vast majority of works make the grade quite easily, as they possess some creative spark, 'no matter how crude, humble or obvious' it might be. Originality does not signify novelty; a work may be original even though it closely resembles other works so long as the similarity is fortuitous, not the result of copying." (citations omitted)).

9 *Id.* at 359–60 ("In summary, the 1976 revisions to the Copyright Act leave no doubt that originality, not 'sweat of the brow,' is the touchstone of copyright protection in directories and other fact-based works.").

10 *Id.* at 347–48 (On the one hand, "[t]he first person to find and report a particular fact has not created the fact; he or she has merely discovered its existence." But "[f]actual compilations, on the other hand, may possess the requisite originality. The compilation author typically chooses which facts to include, in what order to place them, and how to arrange the collected data so that they may be used effectively by readers. These choices as to selection and arrangement, so long as they are made independently by the compiler and entail a minimal degree of creativity, are sufficiently original that Congress may protect such compilations through the copyright laws.").

11 *See* Sony Corp. of Am. v. Universal City Studios, Inc., 464 U.S. 417, 451 (1984) ("Thus, although every commercial use of copyrighted material is presumptively an unfair exploitation of the monopoly privilege that belongs to the owner of the copyright, noncommercial uses are a different matter.").

12 See the below snippet from The Copyright Act of 1976, 17 U.S.C. § 107:

In determining whether the use made of a work in any particular case is a fair use the factors to be considered shall include –

(1) the purpose and character of the use, including whether such use is of a commercial nature or is for nonprofit educational purposes;
(2) the nature of the copyrighted work;

(3) the amount and substantiality of the portion used in relation to the copyrighted work as a whole; and
(4) the effect of the use upon the potential market for or value of the copyrighted work.

The fact that a work is unpublished shall not itself bar a finding of fair use if such finding is made upon consideration of all the above factors.

13 *See* Statute of Anne, 8 Ann., c. 21 (1710) (Eng.).

14 *See* The Copyright Act of 1976, 17 U.S.C. § 107 (listing the first factor as, "the purpose and character of the use, including whether such use is of a commercial nature or is for nonprofit educational purposes").

15 *See* Campbell v. Acuff-Rose Music, Inc., 510 U.S. 569, 578–579 (1994) ("The enquiry here may be guided by the examples given in the preamble to § 107, looking to whether the use is for criticism, or comment, or news reporting, and the like." (citations omitted)).

16 *See id.* at 579 ("The central purpose of this investigation is to see, in Justice Story's words, whether the new work merely 'supersede[s] the objects' of the original creation, or instead adds something new, with a further purpose or different character, altering the first with new expression, meaning, or message; it asks, in other words, whether and to what extent the new work is 'transformative.'" (citations omitted)); *see also* Sega v. Accolade, 977 F.2d 1510, 1527 (9th Cir. 1992) ("In determining whether a challenged use of copyrighted material is fair, a court must keep in mind the public policy underlying the Copyright Act. 'The immediate effect of our copyright law is to secure a fair return for an 'author's' creative labor. But the ultimate aim is, by this incentive, to stimulate artistic creativity for the general public good.'" Thus, "where disassembly is the only way to gain access to the ideas and functional elements embodied in a copyrighted computer program and where there is a legitimate reason for seeking such access, disassembly is a fair use of the copyrighted work, as a matter of law."); *See also* DSC Comm. v. DGI Tech., 81 F.3d 597 (5th Cir. 1996).

17 *See* Authors Guild v. Google, Inc., 804 F.3d 202, 221–22 (2d Cir. 2015) ("The Supreme Court said in *Campbell* that 'the extent of permissible copying varies with the purpose and character of the use' and characterized the relevant questions as whether 'the amount and substantiality of the portion used … are reasonable in relation to the purpose of the copying,' … Without doubt, enabling searchers to see portions of the copied texts could have determinative effect on the fair use analysis. The larger the quantity of the copyrighted text the searcher can see and the more control the searcher can exercise over what part of the text she sees, the greater the likelihood that those revelations could serve her as an effective, free substitute for the purchase of the plaintiff's book.").

18 *See* Andy Warhol Found. for the Visual Arts, Inc. v. Goldsmith, 598 U.S. 508, 536 (2023) (reversing the appellate court's finding of fair use and concluding that a work by the artist Andy Warhol that incorporated an earlier photographic work by Lynn Goldsmith "shared the objectives[] of Goldsmith's photograph, even if the two were not perfect substitutes").

19 *See, e.g.*, Sega v. Accolade, 977 F.2d 1510, 1518 (9th Cir. 1992) (in which a "computer file generated by [a] disassembly program, ... printouts of the disassembled code, and the computer files containing [a company's] modifications of the code that were generated during the reverse engineering process" all constituted intermediate copying).

20 *See id.* at 1518 (in which a "computer file generated by [a] disassembly program, ... printouts of the disassembled code, and the computer files containing [a company's] modifications of the code that were generated during the reverse engineering process" all constituted intermediate copying that fell "squarely within the category of acts that are prohibited by the [Copyright Act]").

21 Sony Comput. Ent., Inc. v. Connectix Corp., 203 F.3d 596, 609 (9th Cir. 2000) (concluding that Connectix's reverse engineering and related intermediate copying of Sony's firmware was fair use).

22 Atari Games Corp. v. Nintendo of Am. Inc., 975 F.2d 832, 847 (Fed. Cir. 1992) (affirming the lower court's preliminary injunction against Atari on grounds Nintendo had shown a likelihood of success on the merits with respect to its copyright infringement claim relating to Atari's intermediate copying).

23 *Id.* at 843 ("When the nature of a work requires intermediate copying to understand the ideas and processes in a copyrighted work, that nature supports a fair use for intermediate copying.").

24 *Id.* ("Fair use to discern a work's ideas, however, does not justify extensive efforts to profit from replicating protected expression.").

25 *What Is Data Scraping? Definition & Usage*, OKTA (Feb. 14, 2023, 11:26 AM), https://www.okta.com/identity-101/data-scraping/ ("Data scraping involves pulling information out of a website and into a spreadsheet. To a dedicated data scraper, the method is an efficient way to grab a great deal of information for analysis, processing, or presentation. For example: Imagine that you work for a local shoe company, and your manager asked you to find people who might be willing to promote your work on Instagram. You could run thousands of searches for people who could help. Or you could set up a scraping tool to populate a spreadsheet you can study. Guess which method is faster?").

26 *See supra* Chapter 1.

27 *See* IAN GOODFELLOW, YOSHUA BENGIO, & AARON COURVILLE, DEEP LEARNING 2–8 (2016).

28 U.S. CONST. art. I, § 8, cl. 8.

29 *See, e.g.*, Kamal Nahas, *Now AI Can Be Used to Design New Proteins*, SCIENTIST MAG. (Mar. 3, 2023), https://www.the-scientist.com/now-ai-can-be-used-to-design-new-proteins-70997 ("Artificial intelligence algorithms have had a meteoric impact on protein structure, such as when DeepMind's AlphaFold2 predicted the structures of 200 million proteins. Now, David Baker and his team of biochemists at the University of Washington have taken protein-folding AI a step further. In a *Nature* publication from February 22, they outlined how they used AI to design tailor-made, functional proteins that they could synthesize and produce in live cells, creating new opportunities for protein engineering. Ali Madani, founder and CEO of Profluent, a company that uses other AI technology to design proteins, says this study 'went the distance' in protein design and remarks that we're now witnessing 'the burgeoning of a new field.'").

30 Beth Stackpole, *The Impact of Generative AI as a General-Purpose Technology*, MIT SLOAN (Aug. 6, 2024), https://mitsloan.mit.edu/ideas-made-to-matter/impact-generative-ai-a-general-purpose-technology ("In a recent report about the economic impact of generative AI, Google visiting fellow and MIT Sloan principal research scientist Andrew McAfee makes the case that generative AI is not only a game-changing general-purpose technology but could also spur change far more quickly than preceding innovations due to its accessibility and ease of diffusion.").

31 *See* U.S. CONST., *supra* note 28.

32 For example, Common Crawl is a "corpus" that "contains petabytes of data." *See Common Crawl – Overview*, COMMON CRAWL, https://commoncrawl.org/overview (last visited Aug. 22, 2024) ("The corpus contains raw web page data, metadata extracts, and text extracts.").

33 *Id.*

34 Xinyin Ma, Gongfan Fang, & Xinchao Wang, *LLM-Pruner: On the Structural Pruning of Large Language Models*, ARXIV (Sept. 28, 2023).

35 *See* Brian Uzzi, *Will AI Kill Human Creativity?*, KELLOGG INSIGHT (May 26, 2023), https://insight.kellogg.northwestern.edu/article/will-ai-kill-human-creativity ("[T]he long game in understanding AI's impact on jobs and innovation shouldn't be just about money and power, but the potential death of human creativity, one AI neural network at a time. If consumers just want immediate gratification, and businesspeople want profits, Fake Drake and its ilk are the logical future across creative fields. And if that's the case, what will be the motivation for the next Mozart, Faulkner, or Curie to step forward? If innovators and artists come to realize that their future exists only as long as it take[s] to copy them, why bother trying at all? Ironically, the faster AI changes things, the faster we will be coming to a creativity halt.").

36 Sheena Iyengar, *AI Could Help Free Human Creativity*, TIME (June 23, 2023, 6:00 AM EDT), https://time.com/6289278/ai-affect-human-creativity/

("AI will not necessarily come up with our best ideas for us. But it will greatly reduce the cost – in time, money, and effort – of generating new ideas by instantaneously revealing untold options. It will enable us to efficiently discard the 'useless contraptions' that cloud our vision and identify useful combinations previously unseen. It will empower us to broadly and efficiently canvas an incredibly vast range of domains to pull relevant knowledge from unexpected places. If used properly, AI will ultimately help us seed far greater innovation throughout our society.").

37 *See, e.g.*, Geoff Brumfiel, *Research Shows AI Can Boost Creativity for Some, But at a Cost*, NPR (July 12, 2024, 2:00 PM ET), https://www.npr.org/2024/07/12/nx-s1-5033988/research-ai-chatbots-creativity-writing ("Hauser describes the divergent result as a 'classic social dilemma' – a situation where people benefit individually, but the group suffers. 'We do worry that, at large scale, if many people are using this . . . overall the diversity and creativity in the population will go down[.]'").

38 *See* Ilia Shumailov et al., *AI Models Collapse When Trained on Recursively Generated Data*, 631 NATURE 755 (2024).

39 *See* Sony Corp. of Am. v. Universal City Studios, Inc., 464 U.S. at 417.

40 *Id.*

41 *Id.* at 431.

42 *Id.*

43 *See* Perfect 10, Inc. v. Amazon.com, Inc., 508 F.3d 1146, 1165–68 (9th Cir. 2007).

44 *Id.* at 1165.

45 *Id.* at 1166.

46 *See* Authors Guild v. Google, Inc., 804 F.3d at 202.

47 *Id.* at 221.

48 *Id.* at 212 ("[W]hile authors are undoubtedly important intended beneficiaries of copyright, the ultimate, primary intended beneficiary is the public, whose access to knowledge copyright seeks to advance by providing rewards for authorship.").

49 Metro-Goldwyn-Mayer Studios Inc. v. Grokster, Ltd., 545 U.S. 913, 936–37 (2005).

50 *See id.* at 913 ("Discovery revealed that billions of files are shared across peer-to-peer networks each month. Respondents are aware that users employ their software primarily to download copyrighted files, although the decentralized networks do not reveal which files are copied, and when.").

51 *See id.*

52 *Id.* at 919 ("We hold that one who distributes a device with the object of promoting its use to infringe copyright, as shown by clear expression or other affirmative steps taken to foster infringement, is liable for the resulting acts of infringement by third parties.").

53 *Id.*

54 *See supra* note 6, at 30 ("[I]n 2019, The Times published a Pulitzer-prize winning, five-part series on predatory lending in New York City's taxi industry. The eighteen-month investigation included 600 interviews, more than 100 records requests, large-scale data analysis, and the review of thousands of pages of internal bank records and other documents, and ultimately led to criminal probes and the enactment of new laws to prevent future abuse. OpenAI had no role in the creation of this content, yet with minimal prompting, will recite large portions of it verbatim.")

55 Memorandum of Law in Support of OpenAI Defendants' Motion to Dismiss at 2, The New York Times Co. v. Microsoft Corp., No. 1:23-cv-11195 (S.D.N.Y. Feb. 26, 2024).

56 Consolidating three separate cases: Authors Guild v. OpenAI, Inc., No. 1:23-cv-08292 (S.D.N.Y. 2023); Alter v. OpenAI, Inc., No. 1:23-cv-10211 (S.D.N.Y. 2023); and Basbanes v. Microsoft Corp., No. 1:24-cv-00084 (S.D.N.Y. 2024), *see Case Tracker: Artificial Intelligence, Copyrights and Class Actions*, BAKERHOSTETLER, https://www.bakerlaw.com/services/artificial-intelligence-ai/case-tracker-artificial-intelligence-copyrights-and-class-actions/ (last visited July 3, 2024).

57 Complaint at 1–3, Doe v. Github, Inc., No. 3:22-cv-06823-KAW (N.D. Cal. Nov. 3, 2022).

58 Complaint at 1–2, Leovy v. Google, No. 3:23-cv-03440-LB (N.D. Cal. July 11, 2023).

59 *See Case Tracker, supra* note 56.

60 *See Comparing Timelines: What Do Statistics Reveal about the Length of International Commercial Arbitration vs. U.S. Federal Litigation?*, HUGHES HUBBARD & REED (Nov. 21, 2023), https://www.hugheshubbard.com/news/comparing-timelines ("The data shows that, where a case is not resolved before trial, the median time between filing and resolution at trial is 29.8 months. This does not include time between trial and issuance of a decision, which can add several months. Nor does it include any appeals procedures. It is also of note that this median duration of American federal court litigation includes federal courts in jurisdictions which do not typically handle a high volume of complex and cross-border commercial disputes (such as Idaho) – which helps lower the median. The median durations for District Courts known for handling such disputes is much longer: 35 months for SDNY, 40.6 months for Delaware, and 38.5 months for DC.").

61 Alhadeff et al., *supra* note 3, at 1 ("Ultimately, we argue that fair use's first factor, the purpose of the use, and its fourth factor, the impact on the market for the copyrighted work, both weigh against a finding of fair use in generative AI use cases. However, even if text-to-image models aren't found to be transformative, we argue that the potential for market usurpation alone sufficiently negates fair use.").

62 Matthew Sag, *Fairness and Fair Use in Generative AI*, 92 FORDHAM L. REV. 1887, 1921 (2024) ("When Generative AI models are pretrained, fine-tuned, and operated with care, they will likely qualify as non-expressive use and thus are strong candidates for fair use protection. This is not to say that whether or not a Generative AI model amounts to a non-expressive use is the be-all and end-all of fair use analysis – courts may consider additional considerations of fairness under the fourth fair use factor when the challenged use undermines the economic incentives that copyright is designed to create.").

63 Oren Bracha, *The Work of Copyright in the Age of Machine Production* (Sept. 24, 2023) (unpublished U. Texas Law, Legal Studies Research Paper) (available at SSRN), https://ssrn.com/abstract=4581738 or http://dx.doi.org/10.2139/ssrn.4581738.

64 *See id.* at 24 ("The merger doctrine, that operates as a crucial adjunct to subject matter rules provides that in cases where using expression is indispensable for accessing and using non-protectable elements of a work, the expression and the unprotectable element merge and the use is allowed, but only to the extent necessary for accessing the unprotectable material. In the case of completely incidental training copies, accessing the unprotectable meta-knowledge necessitates (at least in a narrow physicalist sense) reproducing the expression. The latter therefore merges with the former and its copying is outside the domain of copyright. In plain words: the reproduction of the physical patterns representing the work in the belly of the machine is a mere physical incident that inevitably attaches to the learning process, when done in digital rather than analog.").

65 Lemley, *supra* note 3, at 202.

66 Katrina Geddes, *Generative AI's Public Benefit* (June 14, 2024) (unpublished article) (available at SSRN), https://ssrn.com/abstract=4865510, at 57.

67 See Sega v. Accolade, 977 F.2d 1510 (9th Cir. 1992); Atari Games Corp. v. Nintendo of Am. Inc., 975 F.2d 832 (Fed. Cir. 1992).

68 *Cf.* Sony Comput. Ent., Inc. v. Connectix Corp., 203 F.3d 596, 609 (9th Cir. 2000) (concluding that Connectix's reverse engineering and related intermediate copying of Sony's firmware was fair use) *with* Atari Games Corp. v. Nintendo of Am. Inc., 975 F.2d 832, 843 (Fed. Cir. 1992) (agreeing that "[w]hen the nature of a work requires intermediate copying to understand the ideas and processes in a copyrighted work, that nature supports a fair use for intermediate copying" but declining to find fair use under the circumstances because "[f]air use to discern a work's ideas [] does not justify extensive efforts to profit from replicating protected expression").

69 Campbell v. Acuff-Rose Music, Inc., 510 U.S. 569, 579 (1994).

70 *See* Andy Warhol Found. for the Visual Arts, 598 U.S. at 531–32 ("A use that shares the purpose of a copyrighted work, by contrast, is more likely to provide 'the public with a substantial substitute for matter protected by the

[copyright owner's] interests in the original wor[k] or derivatives of [it],' [. . .] which undermines the goal of copyright" (*citing* Author's Guild v. Google, 804 F.3d at 214).).

71 Take, for example, parody. *See, e.g.*, Campbell, 510 U.S. at 591–92 ("We do not, of course, suggest that a parody may not harm the market at all, but when a lethal parody, like a scathing theater review, kills demand for the original, it does not produce a harm cognizable under the Copyright Act.").

72 "In part" is important: remember that the model is trained on *mountains* of data. So, while the previous logos probably play a role in the model's ability to reproduce new logos, those previous logos are far from solely responsible for the model's logo-making capabilities.

73 *See* Complaint, The New York Times Co. v. Microsoft Corp. et al., *supra* note 6, at 14–15.

74 *See, e.g.*, Sega v. Accolade, 977 F.2d 1510 (9th Cir. 1992); Authors Guild v. Google, Inc., 804 F.3d 202 (2d Cir. 2015).

75 Nicholas Carlini et al., *Quantifying Memorization across Neural Language Models*, ARXIV 1 (Mar. 6, 2023, 6:28 AM UTC). https://arxiv.org/abs/2202.07646.

76 *See* Complaint, The New York Times Co. v. Microsoft Corp. et al., *supra* note 6, at 23.

77 *Id.*

78 *Id.* at 31.

79 *See supra* Chapter 1.

80 *See* Steve Engelbrecht, *Output from AI LLMs Is Non-Deterministic. What That Means and Why You Should Care.*, SITATION (May 12, 2023), https://www.sitation.com/non-determinism-in-ai-llm-output/.

81 This is not to say the questions of infringement will always be easy: whether actual copying has occurred would likely remain dispositive. *See* Ryan Abbott & Elizabeth Rothman, *Disrupting Creativity: Copyright Law in the Age of Generative Artificial Intelligence*, 75 FLA. L. REV. 1141, 1192–93 (2023) ("AI-generated works may alter the infringement analysis with respect to proving copying and independent creation. Proving copying may no longer be an issue if an AI's training data can be accessed (although this depends on the AI system). If the allegedly infringed work is not in the training data, that proves there was no copying because the work was never accessed. Also, even if an AI were trained on a protected work, the AI could be queried for the specific works that contributed to a particular output and answer the question of whether the AI-generated work involved actual copying in addition to access. Thus, in the scenario where a troll posts a billion works to the internet, if it can be proven that an allegedly infringing AI-generated work came from a generative AI that was not trained on any of the troll's works, or that the troll's works were not directly used to generate the new work, there is no infringement.").

82 Complaint, The New York Times Co. v. Microsoft Corp. et al., *supra* note 6, at 30.

83 *Cf.* Conclusion of *MGM Studios v. Grokster*, OYEZ, https://www.oyez.org/cases/2004/04-480 (last visited Oct. 29, 2024) *with* Conclusion of *Andy Warhol Foundation for the Visual Arts, Inc. v. Goldsmith*, OYEZ, https://www.oyez.org/cases/2022/21-869 (last visited Oct. 29, 2024).

84 *See* Sony Corp. of Am., 464 U.S. at 417 (Justices Stevens (author), Burger, Brennan, White, and O'Connor in the majority; Justices Blackmun (dissenting author), Marshall, Powell, and Rehnquist in the dissent).

85 *See supra* Chapter 1.

86 *See* History.com Editors, *The Death Spiral of Napster Begins*, HISTORY, https://www.history.com/this-day-in-history/the-death-spiral-of-napster-begins (last visited July 15, 2024) ("The decision by the United States Court of Appeals for the Ninth Circuit rejected Napster's claims of fair use, as well as its call for the court to institute a payment system that would have compensated the record labels while allowing Napster to stay in business. Then, on March 5, 2001, District Court Judge Marilyn Patel issued a preliminary injunction ordering Napster to remove, within 72 hours, any songs named by the plaintiffs in a list of their copyrighted material on the Napster network. The following day, March 6, 2001, Napster, Inc. began the process of complying with Judge Patel's order. Though the company would attempt to stay afloat, it shut down its service just three months later, having begun the process of dismantling itself on this day in 2001.").

87 *See, e.g.*, Benjamin Mullin & Tripp Mickle, *Apple Explores A.I. Deals with News Publishers*, N.Y. TIMES (Dec. 22, 2023), https://www.nytimes.com/2023/12/22/technology/apple-ai-news-publishers.html.

88 *ASCAP Payment System*, ASCAP, https://www.ascap.com/help/royalties-and-payment/payment (last visited Mar. 13, 2024); *About What We Do*, BMI, https://www.bmi.com/about (last visited Mar. 13, 2024).

89 *See* WHITE HOUSE OFFICE OF SCIENCE AND TECHNOLOGY POLICY, BLUEPRINT FOR AN AI BILL OF RIGHTS: MAKING AUTOMATED SYSTEMS WORK FOR THE AMERICAN PEOPLE (2022); Bracha, *supra* note 63; *see also* Geddes, *supra* note 66.

90 *See* KIN HUBBARD, NEW SAYINGS BY ABE MARTIN AND VELMA'S VOW: A GRIPPING LOVE TALE BY MISS FAWN LIPPINCUT, Unnumbered Page (10th Page) (Abe Martin Publishing Company 1916). For an online image of the quote, *see When They Say It's Not About Money, It's About Money*, QUOTE INVESTIGATORS (Aug. 29, 2020), https://quoteinvestigator.com/2020/08/29/about-money/#r+438293+1+2.

91 Kate Knibbs, *Publishers Target Common Crawl in Fight over AI Training Data*, WIRED (June 13, 2024, 11:21 AM), https://www.wired.com/story/the-fight-against-ai-comes-to-a-foundational-data-set/.

92 Mighty Team, *What Is a Paywall? Everything You Need to Know for 2024*, Mighty Networks (Apr. 12, 2024), https://www.mightynetworks.com/resources/paywall ("A paywall is a digital gate that is used to monetize content, either completely or partially restricting users from accessing it until payment is made.").

93 Melissa Heikkilä, *This New Data Poisoning Tool Lets Artists Fight Back against Generative AI*, MIT TECH. REV. (Oct. 23, 2023), https://www.technologyreview.com/2023/10/23/1082189/data-poisoning-artists-fight-generative-ai/.

94 *See* Grokster, 545 U.S. at 913.

95 *See* Authors Guild v. Google, 804 F.3d at 202.

96 *See* Campbell, 510 U.S. at 569.

97 The Copyright Act of 1976, 17 U.S.C. § 107.

98 *See* Perfect 10, 508 F.3d at 1160–61 ("Google does not, however, display a copy of full-size infringing photographic images for purposes of the Copyright Act when Google frames in-line linked images that appear on a user's computer screen. Because Google's computers do not store the photographic images, Google does not have a copy of the images for purposes of the Copyright Act. In other words, Google does not have any 'material objects … in which a work is fixed … and from which the work can be perceived, reproduced, or otherwise communicated' and thus cannot communicate a copy.").

Chapter 4

1 In contrast, trademark law turns on ownership irrespective of who (or what) designed the mark, and trade secret law focuses on ownership, who holds the secret information, and whether the information is *truly* a secret as opposed to being readily ascertainable.

2 *See* 17 U.S.C. § 102 (2018), which contemplates the creation of copyrighted works using a "machine or device." *See also* U.S. Copyright Off., Copyright Rev. Bd., *Opinion Letter on Second Request for Reconsideration for Refusal to Register Théâtre D'opéra Spatial (SR #1-11743923581; Correspondence ID: 1-5T5320R)* 4 (Sep. 5, 2023) ("When analyzing AI-generated material, the Office must determine when a human user can be considered the 'creator' of AI-generated output. In March 2023, the Office provided public guidance on registration of works created by a generative-AI system. The guidance explained that, in considering an application for registration, the Office will ask 'whether the "work" is basically one of human authorship, with the computer [or other device] merely being an assisting instrument, or whether the traditional elements of authorship in the work (literary, artistic, or musical expression or elements of selection, arrangement, etc.) were actually conceived and executed not by man but by a machine.'"); *see also* Thaler

v. Perlmutter, 687 F. Supp. 3d 140, 146 (D.D.C. 2023) ("Copyright is designed to adapt with the times. Underlying that adaptability, however, has been a consistent understanding that human creativity is the *sine qua non* at the core of copyrightability, even as that human creativity is channeled through new tools or into new media.... Human involvement in, and ultimate creative control over, the work at issue was key to the conclusion that the new type of work fell within the bounds of copyright.").

3 *See* 35 U.S.C. § 101 (2018) (implicitly stating that an inventor must be a person, through use of the word "[w]hoever"); *see also* Inventorship Guidance for AI-Assisted Inventions, 89 FR 10043-01, USPTO (Mar. 5, 2024).

4 *See* James B. Garvey, *Let's Get Real: Weak Artificial Intelligence Has Free Speech Rights*, 91 FORDHAM L. REV. 953, 955 (2022).

5 *See* U.S. COPYRIGHT OFF., COMPENDIUM OF THE U.S. COPYRIGHT OFFICE PRACTICES (3d ed. 2021), Chapter 300 § 313.2 ("Similarly, the Office will not register works produced by a machine or mere mechanical process that operates randomly or automatically without any creative input or intervention from a human author. The crucial question is 'whether the "work" is basically one of human authorship, with the computer [or other device] merely being an assisting instrument, or whether the traditional elements of authorship in the work (literary, artistic, or musical expression or elements of selection, arrangement, etc.) were actually conceived and executed not by man but by a machine.'" (citations omitted)).

6 *See* Naruto v. Slater, 888 F.3d 418, 425–26 (9th Cir. 2018) ("The court in *Cetacean* did not rely on the fact that the statutes at issue in that case referred to 'persons' or 'individuals.' Instead, the court crafted a simple rule of statutory interpretation: if an Act of Congress plainly states that animals have statutory standing, then animals have statutory standing. If the statute does not so plainly state, then animals do not have statutory standing. The Copyright Act does not expressly authorize animals to file copyright infringement suits under the statute. Therefore, based on this court's precedent in *Cetacean*, Naruto lacks statutory standing to sue under the Copyright Act." (citation omitted)).

7 Inventorship Guidance for AI-Assisted Inventions, 89 FR 10043-01, 10045 (2024).

8 Thaler v. Vidal, 43 F.4th 1207, 1213 (Fed. Cir. 2022).

9 Robin Feldman, *Comments for Record at the USPTO Request for Comments on Artificial Intelligence and Inventorship* (May 13, 2023) (on file with author).

10 *Id.* at 3.

11 Ryan Abbott & Elizabeth Rothman, *Disrupting Creativity: Copyright Law in the Age of Generative Artificial Intelligence*, 75 FLA. L. REV. 1141, 1183 (2023) ("With AI-generated works, allowing protection will encourage people to develop and use creative AI to generate and disseminate socially valuable works, thereby achieving the goal of copyright law.").

12 *See DABUS Gets Its First Patent in South Africa under Formalities Examination*, IPWATCHDOG (July 29, 2021, 8:13 AM), https://ipwatchdog.com/2021/07/29/dabus-gets-first-patent-south-africa-formalities-examination/id = 136116/.

13 *See* Nicholas Tyacke et al., *Thaler Shut Down: High Court of Australia Confirms AI Incapable of Being an "Inventor,"* TECHNOLOGY'S LEGAL EDGE (Nov. 16, 2022), https://www.technologyslegaledge.com/2022/11/thaler-shut-down-high-court-of-australia-confirms-ai-incapable-of-being-an-inventor/.

14 *See* Jordana Goodman, *Homography of Inventorship: DABUS and Valuing Inventions*, 20 DUKE L. & TECH. REV. 1–47 (2022); *see also* Rita Matulionyte, *AI as an Inventor: Has the Federal Court of Australia Erred in DABUS?*, 13 JIPITEC 99 (2022); Desmond Oriakhogba, *Dabus Gains Territory in South Africa and Australia: Revisiting the AI-Inventorship Question*, 9 S. AFR. J. INTELL. PROP. L. 99 (2021).

15 Copyright Registration Guidance: Works Containing Material Generated by Artificial Intelligence, 88 FR 16190-01 (2023).

16 *Id.*

17 *Id.* at 16191 ("In the Office's view, it is well-established that copyright can protect only material that is the product of human creativity.").

18 *Id.* at 16192.

19 *Id.* ("[T]hese prompts function more like instructions to a commissioner artist – they identify what the prompter wishes to have depicted, but the machine determines how those instructions are implemented in its output.")

20 *Id.*

21 *See, e.g.*, U.S. Copyright Off., Copyright Rev. Bd., *Opinion Letter on Second Request for Reconsideration for Refusal to Register Théâtre D'opéra Spatial (SR #1-11743923581; Correspondence ID: 1-5T5320R)*; U.S. Copyright Off., Copyright Rev. Bd., *Opinion Letter on Second Request for Reconsideration for Refusal to Register A Recent Entrance to Paradise (SR 1-7100387071; Correspondence ID: 1-3ZPC6C3)*.

22 88 FR 16190-01, *supra* note 15, at 16193.

23 *Id.*

24 Katelyn Chedraoui, *This Company Got a Copyright for an Image Made Entirely With AI. Here's How*, CNET (Feb. 10, 2025), https://www.cnet.com/tech/services-and-software/this-company-got-a-copyright-for-an-image-made-entirely-with-ai-heres-how/.

25 This documentation process appears to jibe with The Copyright Office's guidance. See 88 FR 16190-01, *supra* note 15, at 16193 ("Individuals who use AI technology in creating a work may claim copyright protection for their own contributions to that work. They must [...] describe[] the authorship that was contributed by a human.").

26 Mark Lemley, *How Generative AI Turns Copyright Upside Down*, 25 COLUM. SCI. & TECH L. REV. 190, 200 (2024).

27 *Id.*

28 *Id.* at 201.

29 *See* Robert C. Denicola, *Ex Machina: Copyright Protection for Computer-Generated Works*, 69 RUTGERS UNIV. L. REV. 251, 267 (2016) ("The necessity of evaluating the respective contributions of computer and human in determining copyrightability requires an investigation into the creative process far beyond the modest inquiry undertaken by the Copyright Office in evaluating an application for copyright registration, which relies simply on a visual examination of the deposited work and registration materials.").

30 *See* Annemarie Bridy, *Coding Creativity: Copyright and the Artificially Intelligent Author*, 2012 STAN. TECH. L. REV. 5, 21 (2011). Professor Bridy traces the ultimate work all the way back to the author of the AI model itself: "The author of a procedurally generated artwork is, for all intents and purposes, *another copyrighted work* – a literary work in the form of a computer program. Human creativity is necessary for the production of the work, but the human creative agent is not the author of the work in the traditional sense. Nor is generative software an author's tool in the traditional sense; unlike a pen or a paintbrush, or even a camera, generative software has a verbal or visual vocabulary of its own and the ability to compose a range of distinct works from that vocabulary by independently applying a system of rules."

31 *See, e.g.*, U.S. Copyright Off., *supra* note 21.

32 *See* Nick Jain, *Embracing Uncertainty: The Role of Randomness in Generative AI Neural Networks*, LINKEDIN Pulse (Aug. 7, 2023), https://www.linkedin.com/pulse/embracing-uncertainty-role-randomness-generative-ai-neural-jain-cfa/ ("Neural networks are, by design, 'unstable', where the same input will sometimes give wildly different answers.").

33 89 Fed. Reg. 10043, 10046 (Feb. 13, 2024); Diamond v. Chakrabarty, 447 U.S. 303, 309–10 (1980) (Under the Patent Act, a claim is considered patentable subject matter if it is to "a nonnaturally occurring manufacture or composition of matter – *a product of human ingenuity* having a distinctive name, character and use." (emphasis added)).

34 *See* 89 FR 10043, 10047.

35 *Id.*

36 USPTO, *July 2024 Subject Matter Eligibility Examples*, USPTO, https://www.uspto.gov/sites/default/files/documents/2024-AI-SMEUpdateExamples47-49.pdf (last visited Oct. 22, 2024).

37 *Id.*

38 *Id.*

39 *Id.*

40 *See* Gaétan de Rassenfosse et al., *AI-Generated Inventions: Implications for the Patent System*, 96 S. CAL. L. REV. 1453 (2024) ("Finally, even if the flood of inventions from AI is not all patented, the democratization of invention machines could still have systemic consequences for the patent system.

Owners of such machines might not patent their inventions but generate a vast amount of prior art.").

41 The USPTO is certainly contemplating the problem of under-disclosure. *See, e.g.*, Yang (Alex) Li, *AI-Assisted Inventions: Is There a Duty to Disclose the Use of AI?*, SHEPPARD MULLIN RICHTER & HAMPTON LLP (Feb. 21, 2024), https://www.lexology.com/library/detail.aspx?g=a4ab7146-db64-4021-b922-62ee81d0f1b9 ("Importantly, this Guidance also discusses the duty of disclosure. The Guidance reminds patent applicants and practitioners that the duty of disclosure encompasses 'information that raises a prima facie case of unpatentability due to improper inventorship,' which 'could include evidence that demonstrates a named inventor did not significantly contribute to the invention because the person's purported contribution(s) was made by an AI system.'").

42 *See generally* Chapter 1.

43 Robin Feldman, *Whose Body Is It Anyway? Human Cells and the Strange Effects of Property and Intellectual Property Law*, 63 STAN. L. REV. 1377, 1386 (2011) (noting that, in the context of the law's separation of product and process, it would take a certain amount of "mental gymnastics" to fit genes and software into the then-current legal categories); *see also* Brief of Professor Robin Feldman and the U.C. Hastings Institute for Innovation Law as Amici Curiae Supporting Neither Party, Alice Corp. v. CLS Bank Int'l, 573 U.S. 208 (2014) (No. 13-298) (expanding on the concept to demonstrate the importance of developing rules of general applicability that can be used regardless of the type of invention).

44 *Id.* at 1386.

45 Robin Feldman, Comments for Record, USPTO (May 13, 2023) (on file with author).

Chapter 5

1 WESTON ANSON, RIGHT OF PUBLICITY: ANALYSIS, VALUATION, AND THE LAW 5 (ABA Book Publishing 2015). *See also* RESTATEMENT (THIRD) OF UNFAIR COMPETITION § 46 (American Law Institute 1995) ("[I]mposing liability on those who 'appropriate[] the commercial value of a person's identity by using without consent the person's name, likeness, or other indicia of identity for purposes of trade.'").

2 Haelan Labs., Inc. v. Topps Chewing Gum, Inc., 202 F.2d 866, 868 (2d Cir. 1953) ("We think that, in addition to and independent of that right of privacy (which in New York derives from statute), a man has a right in the publicity value of his photograph, i.e., the right to grant the exclusive privilege of publishing his picture, and that such a grant may be validly made 'in gross' i.e., without any accompanying transfer of a business or anything

else ... This right may be called a 'right of publicity.' For it is common knowledge that many prominent persons (especially actors and ball-players), far from having their feelings bruised through public exposure of their likenesses, would feel sorely deprived if they no longer received money for authorizing advertisements, popularizing their countenances ... This right of publicity would usually yield no money unless it could be made the subject of an exclusive grant which barred any other advertiser from using their pictures.").

3 Other early cases recognizing the value, if not the right, of publicity, include: Paramount Pictures, Inc. v. Leader Pres, 106 F.2d 229, 230 (10th Cir. 1939); Gautier v. Pro-Football Inc., 304 N.Y. 354 (1952); Uproar Co. v. N.B.C., 8 F. Supp. 358, 361 (D. Mass. 1934); Pittsburgh Athletic Co. v. KQV Broadcasting Co., 24 F. Supp. 490 (W.D. Pa. 1938); O'Brien v. Pabst Sales Co., 124 F.2d 167 (5th Cir. 1941); Lawrence v. Ylla, 184 Misc. 807, 55 N.Y.S. 2d 343 (Sup. Ct. 1945).

4 Melville B. Nimmer, *The Right of Publicity*, 19 L. & CONTEMP. PROBS. 203 (1954). This conventional history is also largely laid out in comment b of the Third Restatement of Unfair Competition. RESTATEMENT (THIRD) OF UNFAIR COMPETITION § 46 cmt. b.

5 JENNIFER E. ROTHMAN, THE RIGHT OF PUBLICITY: PRIVACY REIMAGINED FOR A PUBLIC WORLD 48 (Harvard University Press 2018).

6 MICHAEL D. MURRAY, RIGHT OF PUBLICITY IN A NUTSHELL 59 (West Academic Publishing 2018) ("[O]ver the decades [after *Zacchini*], the majority of the theoretical justifications for the protection of personality rights have come to parallel the justification of the protection of intellectual property."). For more on right of publicity as an IP right, *see* ANSON, *supra* note 1, at 34–36.

7 Zacchini v. Scripps-Howard Broad. Co., 433 U.S. 562, 576 (1977).

8 *Id.* at 576–77.

9 *See* ANSON, *supra* note 1, at 22. For more information on state-specific statues, *see generally id.* at 65–85.

10 Eileen McDermott et al., *Senators Introduce NO FAKES Act to Create a Universal Right to Control Digital Replicas*, IPWATCHDOG (July 31, 2024, 6:05 PM), https://ipwatchdog.com/2024/07/31/senators-introduce-no-fakes-act-create-universal-right-control-digital-replicas/id = 179705/.

11 *OpenAI v. Scarlett Johansson? Law Professor Answers Legal Questions on AI-Generated Content*, Geo. U. (June 4, 2024), https://www.georgetown.edu/news/ask-a-professor-openai-v-scarlett-johansson/.

12 OpenAI, *How the Voices for ChatGPT Were Chosen*, OPENAI, https://openai.com/index/how-the-voices-for-chatgpt-were-chosen/ (last visited Aug. 12, 2024) ("A statement from our CEO, Sam Altman, on May 20, 2024: 'The voice of Sky is not Scarlett Johansson's, and it was never intended to resemble

hers. We cast the voice actor behind Sky's voice before any outreach to Ms. Johansson. Out of respect for Ms. Johansson, we have paused using Sky's voice in our products. We are sorry to Ms. Johansson that we didn't communicate better.'").

13 *Id. See also* Bobby Allyn, *Voice Analysis Shows Striking Similarity between Scarlett Johansson and ChatGPT*, NPR (May 31, 2024, 8:35 PM ET), https://www.npr.org/2024/05/31/g-s1-2263/voice-lab-analysis-striking-similarity-scarlett-johansson-chatgpt-sky-openai.

14 Midler v. Ford Motor Co., 849 F.2d 460, 463 (9th Cir. 1988).

15 Sara H. Jodka, *Manipulating Reality: The Intersection of Deepfakes and the Law*, REUTERS (Feb. 1, 2024, 9:01 AM PST), https://www.reuters.com/legal/legalindustry/manipulating-reality-intersection-deepfakes-law-2024-02-01/.

16 *Id.*

17 *Id.*

18 Bobby Allyn, *Deepfake Video of Zelenskyy Could Be 'Tip of the Iceberg' in Info War, Experts Warn*, NPR (Mar. 16, 2022), https://www.npr.org/2022/03/16/1087062648/deepfake-video-zelenskyy-experts-war-manipulation-ukraine-russia.

19 *Id.*

20 Ajder Henry et al., *The State of Deepfakes: Landscape, Threats, and Impacts*, DEEPTRACE (September 2019).

21 Brian Contreras, *Tougher AI Policies Could Protect Taylor Swift – And Everyone Else – From Deepfakes*, SCI. AM. (Feb. 8, 2024), https://www.scientificamerican.com/article/tougher-ai-policies-could-protect-taylor-swift-and-everyone-else-from-deepfakes/.

22 Angus Watson, *Teenager Questioned after Explicit AI Deepfakes of Dozens of Schoolgirls Shared Online*, CNN (June 13, 2024, 10:54 PM EDT), https://www.cnn.com/2024/06/13/australia/australia-boy-arrested-deepfakes-schoolgirls-intl-hnk/index.html.

23 *See* McDermott et al., *supra* note 10; *see also* Miranda Perez, *How Gen Z Could Benefit from Proposed AI Regulation*, YR MEDIA (Aug. 6, 2024), https://yr.media/tech/gen-z-benefit-proposed-ai-regulation-miranda-perez/ ("The Senate's recent consideration of the NO FAKES Act also targets the creation of sexually explicit deepfakes is a crucial step in this direction. It would empower victims of non-consensual AI-generated content to seek damages from the perpetrators, providing a legal framework to combat such violations.").

24 Don Fallis, *The Epistemic Threat of Deepfakes*, 34 PHILOS. TECHNOL 623 (AUG. 6, 2020).

25 Charlie Warzel, *Believable: The Terrifying Future of Fake News*, BUZZFEED NEWS (Feb. 11, 2018, 5:45 PM), https://www.buzzfeednews.com/article/charliewarzel/the-terrifying-future-of-fake-news.

26 McDermott et al., *supra* note 10; *see also* Perez, *supra* note 23.

Chapter 6

1 LAWRENCE LESSIG, CODE AND OTHER LAWS OF CYBERSPACE (1999) [hereinafter LESSIG, CODE].
2 From a corresponding essay, Lawrence Lessig, *Code Is Law*, HARV. MAGAZINE (Jan. 1, 2000), https://www.harvardmagazine.com/2000/01/code-is-law-html [hereinafter Lessig, *Code Is Law*].
3 *Id.*; LAWRENCE LESSIG, CODE: VERSION 2.0, at 5 (2006) [hereinafter LESSIG, CODE VERSION 2.0] ("In real space we recognize how laws regulate – through constitutions, statutes, and other legal codes. In cyberspace we must understand how different 'code' regulates – how the software and hardware ... that make cyberspace what it is also regulate cyberspace as it is. As William Mitchell puts it, this code is cyberspace's 'law.' ... '[C]ode is law.' ").
4 Lessig, *Code Is Law*, *supra* note 2; LESSIG, CODE VERSION 2.0, *supra* note 3, at 18 ("One important difference is this: Unlike the victims of the general searches that the Framers of our Constitution were concerned about, the computer user never knows that his or her disk is being searched by the worm.").
5 Lessig, *Code Is Law*, *supra* note 2.
6 35 U.S.C. §§ 101–03, 112(a); DONALD S. CHISUM ET AL., PRINCIPLES OF PATENT LAW 72–73 (3d ed. 2004) ("Examination is conducted to ensure that the claimed invention is adequately disclosed ... new, ... non-nonobvious, ... useful, ... and within at least one of the statutory classes of patent subject matter...."). The Telephone Cases, 126 U.S. 1, 536; 8 S. Ct. 778, 783 (1888) ("The law does not require that a[n] ... inventor, in order to get a patent for a process, must have succeeded in bringing his art to the highest degree of perfection; it is enough if he describes his method with sufficient clearness and precision to enable those skilled in the matter to understand what the process is, and if he points out some practicable way of putting it into operation."); Graham v. John Deere Co., 383 U.S. 1, 17–18 (1966) (explaining that a determination of non-obviousness is to be made after establishing "the scope and content of prior art," the "differences between the prior art and the claims at issue," and "the level of ordinary skill in the pertinent art."); Brenner v. Manson, 383 U.S. 519, 528–29, 532 (1966) (stating that "one may patent only that which is useful[,]" and holding that the requirement that a chemical process be useful is not satisfied by showing that a "compound yielded belongs to a class of compounds now the subject of serious scientific investigation"); CHISUM ET AL., *supra* note 6, at 324 ("[The novelty requirement] requires a patent applicant to contribute something *new* to society."); *id.* at 772 ("[T]o be patentable, the invention must fall within one of four classes...: processes, machines, manufactures, or compositions of matter.").
7 John R. Allison, Mark A. Lemley, & David L. Schwartz, *Understanding the Realities of Modern Patent Litigation*, 92 TEX. L. REV. 1769, 1769–70, 1785

(2014) (expanding on the authors' prior article from 1998, which had found obviousness the single most commonly litigated element of patentability).

8 *See* John R. Thomas, *Formalism at the Federal Circuit*, 52 AM. U. L. REV. 771, 789 (2003) (using the phrase).

9 *See* Dmitry Karshtedt, *Nonobviousness: Before and After*, 106 IOWA L. REV. 1609, 1611 (2021) (using the phrase and citing to NONOBVIOUSNESS – THE ULTIMATE CONDITION OF PATENTABILITY (John F. Witherspoon ed., 1980) and Michael Abramowicz & John F. Duffy, *The Inducement Standard of Patentability*, 120 YALE L.J. 1590, 1593 (2011) (including list of references to those using the term)).

10 *See, e.g., In re* Schreiber, 128 F.3d 1473, 1477 (Fed. Cir. 1997) ("To anticipate a claim, a prior art reference must disclose every limitation of the claimed invention, either explicitly or inherently."); *see* 35 U.S.C. § 103 ("A patent for a claimed invention may not be obtained . . . if the differences between the claimed invention and the prior art are such that the claimed invention as a whole would have been obvious before the effective filing date of the claimed invention to a person having ordinary skill in the art to which the claimed invention pertains.").

11 *See, e.g.*, Robert P. Merges, *Uncertainty and the Standard of Patentability*, 7 HIGH TECH. L.J. 1, 13–14 (1992) ("Without [obviousness], anything differing only slightly from the prior art would be patentable. . . . [N]onobviousness is designed to maintain a penumbra around the stock of known devices, techniques, etc., insuring that trivial extensions from what is known will not be granted property rights."); *see also* Jeanne C. Fromer, *The Layers of Obviousness in Patent Law*, 22 HARV. J.L. & TECH. 75, 79 (2008) ("The nonobviousness doctrine seeks to ensure that patents are granted only for technologically significant advances to foster the patent system's goal of stimulating useful innovation.").

12 35 U.S.C. § 103 provides that "[a] patent for a claimed invention may not be obtained, notwithstanding that the claimed invention is not identically disclosed as set forth in section 102, if the differences between the claimed invention and the prior art are such that the claimed invention as a whole would have been obviousness before the effective filing date of the claimed invention to a *person having ordinary skill in the art* to which the claimed invention pertains" (emphasis added). In *KSR Int'l Co. v. Teleflex Inc.*, the Supreme Court summarized the position as follows: "When a work is available in one field, design incentives and other market forces can prompt variations of it, either in the same field or in another. If a person of ordinary skill can implement a predictable variation, . . . § 103 likely bars its patentability." 550 U.S. 398, 401 (2007); *see also Graham*, 383 U.S. at 17–18 (1966) ("Under section 103, the scope and content of the prior art are to be determined; differences between the prior art and the claims at issue are to be ascertained; and the level of ordinary skill in the pertinent art resolved.

Against this background, the obviousness or nonobviousness of the subject matter is determined.").

13 A full text of the play is available at the site *Everyman and Other Old Religious Plays, with an Introduction*, PROJECT GUTENBERG (Oct. 6, 2006), https://www.gutenberg.org/cache/epub/19481/pg19481-images.html.

14 *See, e.g.*, Custom Accessories, Inc. v. Jeffrey-Allan Indus., Inc., 807 F.2d 955, 962 (Fed. Cir. 1986) (referring to the PHOSITA as a "hypothetical person"); *In re* GPAC Inc., 57 F.3d 1573, 1579 (Fed. Cir. 1995) (citing to *Custom Accessories* and its use of the PHOSITA as a hypothetical person).

15 *See, e.g.*, Mayo Moran, *The Reasonable Person: A Conceptual Biography in Comparative Perspective*, 14 LEWIS & CLARK L. REV. 1233, 1245–47 (2010) (contrasting an Australian court's application of the reasonable person standard in *McHale v. Watson*, which resulted in the exoneration of a twelve-year-old boy who threw a dart at another child – the court stated "boys will be boys" – with a Michigan state court's application of the reasonable person standard in *Michigan Central Railroad Co. v. Hasseneyer*, which found a thirteen-year-old girl contributorily negligent for her own death by standing behind a reversing train, reasoning that "she would be more cautious to avoid unknown dangers … more particular to keep within the limits of absolute safety when the dangers which threatened were such as only great strength and courage could venture to encounter."); *see also* Wendy Parker, *The Reasonable Person: A Gendered Concept*, 23 VICTORIA U. WELLINGTON L. REV. 105, 108 (1993) ("Since its inception, the reasonable man standard has been endowed with attributes that are stereotypically and exclusively male. … This stereotypical maleness did not seem inappropriate in the typical negligence case involving activities and situations that were overwhelmingly male. … The problem, however, is that the standard was never considered to be anything other than universal and women have subsequently been required to meet the same standard without any attempt being made to include a woman's perspective based on her differing experiences.").

16 *See, e.g.*, Scott Astrada & Marvin L. Astrada, *The Enduring Problem of the Race-Blind Reasonable Person*, AMERICAN CONST. SOC'Y: EXPERT FORUM (May 11, 2020), https://www.acslaw.org/expertforum/the-enduring-problem-of-the-race-blind-reasonable-person (arguing, in the context of Fourth Amendment searches and seizures, that "the historical conception of a 'reasonable person' employed by the law becomes a means of perpetuating a politics of racial/ethnic exclusion of the 'Other,' i.e., a non-white racial/ethnic subject. The Other is required to comport themselves as a reasonable person that bears very little resemblance to their lived reality. This results in the 'Other' being constrained within a concept that excludes them by imposing the worldview, norms, values, etc., of a rendition of the reasonable person that is not reflective of their world."); Robert V. Ward, *Consenting to a Search and Seizure in Poor and Minority Neighborhoods: No Place for a "Reasonable*

Person," 36 HOWARD L.J. 239, 254 (1993) ("The objective, reasonable person test has been upheld by the Court because it believes the standard to be a method for police officers to readily understand when they are engaging in a search and seizure. Reliance is placed upon what are perceived to be objective observations. Some members of minority and poor inner city communities, however, may be so intimidated that 'consent' to a search may be granted out of fear of police retaliation.").

17 *See infra* note 31 (cases outlining Court of Appeals for the Federal Circuit's approach under which a patent claim is proved obvious if there is "some motivation or suggestion to combine the prior art teachings"). *See also In re* Dembiczak, 175 F.3d 994, 999 (Fed. Cir. 1999).

18 *See, e.g.*, Daralyn J. Durie & Mark A. Lemley, *A Realistic Approach to the Obviousness of Inventions*, 50 WM. & MARY L.R. 989, 1016–19 (2008) (advocating for a PHOSITA standard that enquires into both what the PHOSITA knows, "but also into what limits there are on that PHOSITA's knowledge" because researchers in the real world "certainly don't have access to every piece of prior art," particularly because some of this art is "secret at the time of invention").

19 *See In re* Merck & Co., Inc., 800 F.2d 1091, 1096–97 (Fed. Cir. 1986) (sustaining the PTO Board's rejection of plaintiff's claimed invention – a method of treating depression in humans using amitriptyline – as unpatentable due to obviousness under 35 U.S.C. § 103 because the prior art of record taught that imipramine was known to treat depression, and these two drugs were both psychotropic drugs and "unquestionably closely related in structure." The Court reasoned that the claimed invention would be obvious to the PHOSITA since there was a reasonable expectation of success that amitriptyline, like imipramine, would treat depression, reiterating that "[o]bviousness does not require absolute predictability.").

20 Robert Ehrlich, *Experiments with "Newton's Cradle,"* 34 PHYSICS TEACHER 181 (1996). The invention of Newton's cradle is commonly attributed to the scientists who conducted critical research and experiments on the underlying physics behind the device – namely John Wallis, Christopher Wren, Christiaan Huygens, and Edme Mariotte – and is said to be named after Sir Isaac Newton. *See, e.g.*, Rodd Cross, *Edme Mariotte and Newton's Cradle*, 50 PHYSICS TEACHER 206 (2012); Piyush Patel, *What is Newton's Cradle and How Does It Work?*, SCIENCE ABC (Oct. 19, 2023), https://www.scienceabc.com/pure-sciences/what-is-newtons-cradle-and-how-does-it-work.html; Stefan Hutzler, Gary Delaney, Denis Weaire, & Finn MacLeod, *Rocking Newton's Cradle*, 72 (12) AM. J. PHYS. 1508 (2004).

21 *See, e.g.*, *Newton's Cradle*, HARV. NAT. SCIS. LECTURE DEMONSTRATIONS, https://sciencedemonstrations.fas.harvard.edu/presentations/newtons-cradle (last visited Mar. 10, 2025); *Newton's Cradle*, VA. TECH DEP'T PHYSICS, https://www.phys.vt.edu/outreach/projects-and-demos/demonstrations-wiki/mechanics/newtons-cradle.html (last visited Mar. 10, 2025).

22 Merit Mfg. Co. v. Hero Mfg. Co., 185 F.2d 350, 352 (2d Cir. 1950).
23 Joseph P. Meara, *Just Who Is the Person Having Ordinary Skill in the Art? Patent Law's Mysterious Personage*, 77 WASH. L. REV. 267, 290 (2002) (discussing the importance of the characterization of PHOSITA and concluding that "[a]lthough the Federal Circuit has developed a six-factor test for defining [PHOSITA], several factors have proven to be unnecessary or unhelpful. Others require further development before they can be properly applied. The Federal Circuit should continue to develop the [PHOSITA] factors to more accurately reflect the level of ordinary skill in the art.").
24 *See* Dennis Crouch, *Person (Having) Ordinary Skill in the Art*, PATENTLYO (Nov. 30, 2018), https://patentlyo.com/patent/2018/11/person-having-ordinary.html (describing the different terms and those who use them).
25 *See, e.g.*, Al-Site Corp., v. VSI Int'l, Inc., 174 F.3d 1308, 1323–24 (Fed. Cir. 1999); *In re* Rouffet, 149 F.3d 1350, 1355 (Fed. Cir. 1998); *In re* Geiger, 815 F.2d 686, 688 (Fed. Cir. 1987).
26 KSR Int'l Co. v. Teleflex Inc., 550 U.S. 398, 421 (2007) (obviousness case involving an adjustable pedal system for cars).
27 *See id.*
28 *Id.* at 418 (explaining that "the analysis need not seek out precise teachings directed to the specific subject matter of the challenged claim, for a court can take account of the inferences and creative steps that a person of ordinary skill in the art would employ").
29 *Id.* ("When it first established the requirement of demonstrating a teaching, suggestion, or motivation to combine known elements in order to show that the combination is obvious, the Court of Customs and Patent Appeals captured a helpful insight.... Helpful insights, however, need not become rigid and mandatory formulas; and when it is so applied, the TSM test is incompatible with our prior precedents.").
30 *Id.* at 419.
31 *See* Bilski v. Kappos, 561 U.S. 593 (2010); Mayo Collaborative Serv. v. Prometheus Labs., Inc., 566 U.S. 66 (2012); Ass'n for Molecular Pathology v. Myriad Genetics, Inc., 569 U.S. 576 (2013); Alice Corp. Pty. Ltd. v. CLS Bank Int'l, 573 U.S. 208 (2014). *See also* Robin Feldman, *Coming of Age for the Federal Circuit*, 18 GREEN BAG 2D 27 (2014) (analyzing the sequence of patentable subject matter decisions).
32 *Cf. KSR Int'l Co.*, 550 U.S. at 418 (explaining that an obviousness analysis "need not seek out precise teachings directed to the specific subject matter of the challenged claim, for a court can take account of the inferences and creative steps that a person of ordinary skill in the art would employ") *with* Millenium Pharms., Inc. v. Sandoz Inc., 862 F.3d 1356, 1362, 1364 (Fed. Cir. 2017) (in overturning a district court finding of obviousness, the Federal Circuit explained that the district court relied on the Sandoz witness' expert testimony that the relevant information was "well-known in the field" and

was considered an obvious alterative but ultimately concluding that "Sandoz identifies no reference or combination of references that shows or suggests a reason to make the claimed compound").

33 *See Justices 1789 to Present*, S. CT. U.S., https://www.supremecourt.gov/about/members_text.aspx (last visited Mar. 10, 2025).

34 Susan Y. Tull & Paula E. Miller, *Patenting Artificial Intelligence: Issues of Obviousness, Inventorship, and Patent Eligibility*, 1 J. ROBOTICS, A.I. & L. 313 (2018).

35 *See* 35 U.S.C. § 102(a)(1) (defining prior art for the purposes of novelty as "patented, described in a printed publication, or in public use, on sale, or otherwise available to the public"); 35 U.S.C § 103 (defining an invention as obvious if the "differences between the claimed invention and the prior art are such that the claimed invention as a whole would have been obvious before the effective filing date of the claimed invention to a person having ordinary skill in the art to which the claimed invention pertains."); DONALD S. CHISUM, *§ 5.03 Factual Inquiries: The Pertinent Art (5.03[3]), in* 2 CHISUM ON PATENTS § 5.03 (2024) (explaining that while "[s]ection 103 does not expressly define what sources must be looked to as 'prior art' to determine obviousness ... the opening phrase clearly implies that the provisions of Section 102 are to be the guide."). *See also id.* at n.2 (explaining that courts rely on the section 102 novelty definition of prior art in applying the obviousness requirement of section 103).

36 Stephen Yelderman, *Prior Art in the District Court*, 95 NOTRE DAME L. REV. 837, 863 (2019).

37 *Id.* at 863–64 (including the examples cited in a category of "other" types of prior art in examining patent litigation, and noting that "[t]he accessibility of these various documents ranges somewhat (and, in some cases, might be debatable), but none of them can be described as a regularly published book or journal.").

38 *See, e.g.*, Millennium Pharms., Inc. v. Sandoz Inc., 862 F.3d 1356, 1361, 1364 (Fed. Cir. 2017) (after explaining that the district court's finding of obviousness, as explained in *supra* note 32.).

39 Dan L. Burk, *AI Patents and the Self-Assembling Machine*, 105 MINN. L. R. HEADNOTES 301, 309–10 (2021) (noting that as with any tool, the use of AI depends on the skill of the person setting the query and parameters).

40 *See* Ryan Abbott, *I Think, Therefore I Invent: Creative Computers and the Future of Patent Law*, 57 B.C. L. Rev. 1079, 1083–91 (2016).

41 This example could raise the concern that patented invention might become limited to those who have access to AI systems; those who don't will be hampered by the ability of AI to invalidate their ideas. However, as modern AI becomes publicly available at a rapid pace, the argument may lose force.

42 *See* 35 U.S.C. § 103 (emphasis added); U.S. PAT. & TRADEMARK OFF., PUBLIC VIEWS ON ARTIFICIAL INTELLIGENCE AND INTELLECTUAL PROPERTY POLICY 12–13 (2020) (citing public comments suggesting that artificial general intelligence machines "are not persons and, therefore, would not affect the legal standard of a 'person' of ordinary skill in the art"); Shlomit Yanisky-Ravid & Regina Jin, *Summoning a New Artificial Intelligence Patent Model in the Age of Crisis*, 2021 MICH. ST. L. REV. 811, 833 (2021) (citing *KSR International Co.* and italicizing the word *person* to support the notion that AI cannot be PHOSITA: "a *person* of ordinary creativity, not an automaton").

43 *See* Connor Romm, Note, *Putting the Person in PHOSITA: The Human's Obvious Role in the Artificial Intelligence Era*, 62 B.C. L. REV. 1413, 1445 (2021) (suggesting that "once AI is common in a given industry, inventors will have to meet the heightened burden of showing nonobviousness based on what a PHOSITA aided by AI – as well as any other widely available technology – would find reasonably pertinent to the problem solved by the invention"); Kay Firth-Butterfield & Yoon Chae, *Artificial Intelligence Collides with Patent Law*, 12 WORLD ECON. F. (2018) (white paper ahead of its time mentioning the possibility that if AI becomes more prevalent in certain industries, the definition of POSITA could be "adjusted" or "chang[ed]" to include the use of AI, but suggesting that over time, this could render all invention obvious); Liza Vertinsky & Todd M. Rice, *Thinking About Thinking Machines: Implications of Machine Inventors for Patent Law*, 8 B.U. J. SCI. & TEC. L. 574, 595 (2002). On the "all-invention-obvious" point, *see also* Lexi Heon, Comment, *Artificially Obvious but Genuinely New: How Artificial Intelligence Alters the Patent Obviousness Analysis*, 53 SETON HALL L. REV. 359, 380 (2022) (comment noting that "the fear of AI creating a world where everything is obvious is impending, if not already at least partially present"); *but see* Burk, *supra* note 39, at 302, 308–12 (responding to everything-is-obvious concerns by noting that patent law has proven "surprisingly adaptable," calling them magical thinking, and noting that if AI were able to invent so easily, all risk would eliminated and there would be no need for a patent reward, anyway). Relatedly, whether an AI is included as a skilled person itself or merely a tool raises problems in the assessment of obviousness. Rätz and Block explain: "While an AI would basically consider any improvement that advances the assessed technology area or makes the production/deployment of devices and services more cost-effective, independent from where it derived this conclusion, a human would only consider and explore thought provoking impulses within her/his area of technical expertise." Benjamin Rätz & Jonas Block, *Killed in the Art? How Artificial Intelligence Challenges the Fictional Concept of the Skilled Person in Patent Law*, 56 LES NOUVELLES J. LICENSING EXEC. SOC'Y 68, 72 (2021). In response,

they classify such distinction as "obsolete if it can be shown (and evidenced in court) that a skilled person would have combined the same two pieces of prior art even without the aid of an AI." *Id.*

44 Yanisky-Ravid & Jin, *supra* note 42. Yanisky-Ravid and Jin use the term "creative AI" to refer to that are "capable of generating new inventions themselves" *id.* at 818. Although not necessarily a term of art, the Article will use the term similarly. Firth-Butterfield & Chae, *supra* note 43 (citing the same Supreme Court and Federal Circuit case language as Yanisky-Ravid to reach a similar conclusion); *cf.* U.S. PAT. & TRADEMARK OFF., *supra* note 42, at 13 (citing public comments suggesting that artificial general intelligence machines "are not persons and, therefore, would not affect the legal standard of a 'person' of ordinary skill in the art").

45 KSR Int'l Co. v. Teleflex Inc., 550 U.S. 398, 421 (2007) (emphasis added).

46 Standard Oil Co. v. Am. Cyanamid Co., 774 F.2d 448, 454 (Fed. Cir. 1985).

47 *Id.* at 454.

48 *Id.*; *see also KSR Int'l*, 550 U.S. at 420 ("The second error of the Court of Appeals lay in its assumption that a person of ordinary skill attempting to solve a problem will be led only to those elements of prior art designed to solve the same problem.").

49 *See KSR Int'l*, 550 U.S. at 420.

50 *Id.* at 421.

51 Standard Oil Co. v. Am. Cyanamid Co., 774 F.2d 448 (Fed. Cir. 1985).

52 *See, e.g.*, Romm, *supra* note 43, at 1431 (arguing that the Federal Circuit had considered PHOSITA "an unimaginative worker devoid of anything resembling creativity," but that *KSR Int'l* endowed PHOSITA with "both ordinary skill and creativity"); Joseph Scott Miller, *Remixing Obviousness*, 16 TEX. INTELL. PROP. L.J. 237, 249–50 (2008) (explaining that in *KSR*, the Court "banished the dullard PHOSITA of *Standard Oil*, just as the Federal Trade Commission recommended in its 2003 report and as two amici, including the United States, urged") (citations omitted).

In an earlier paper, Shlomit Yanisky-Ravid and Jackie Liu interpreted *KSR* in a different manner, one that could suggest the Supreme Court had moved away from the Federal Circuit's notion of PHOSITA as one who follows conventional wisdom, rather than innovating. *See* Shlomit Yanisky-Ravid & Xiaoqiong (Jackie) Liu, *When Artificial Intelligence Systems Produce Inventions: An Alternative Model for Patent Law at the 3A Era*, 39 CARDOZO L. REV. 2215, 2248 (2018) (arguing that "[b]y far the most important development of the PHOSITA standard also came in *KSR*, with the Supreme Court transforming the PHOSITA requirement from a mere 'automaton' to a person with ordinary creativity levels"). *See also supra* notes 45–51 and accompanying text (discussing the Court's decision in *KSR* and the Federal Circuit's decision from two decades before in *Standard Oil*). Despite these suggestions from an earlier paper, Yanisky-Ravid and Jin's later paper seems to focus on the notion of PHOSITA as conventional and ordinary, rather than applying creativity, and ignores any tension between the older Federal Circuit line of cases and *KSR*. *See* Yanisky-Ravid & Jin, *supra* note 42, at 833 ("A better way to assess the obviousness requirement may be to answer the question in the negative or to look at who cannot be a P[H]OSITA. The Supreme Court defines the POSITA as 'a person of ordinary creativity, not an automaton.' The Federal Circuit provides that the POSITA 'is also presumed to be one who thinks along the line of conventional wisdom in the art and is not one who undertakes to innovate.' Under these two opinions, it seems a creative AI system cannot be the POSITA.") (citations omitted).

53 *See* 35 U.S.C. § 103.

54 *See* U.S. PAT. & TRADEMARK OFF., *supra* note 42, at 12–13 (citing practitioner Edward Ryan, and noting that many of the public comments "asserted that AI has the potential to affect the level of ordinary skill in an art").

55 *Artificial Intelligence and Intellectual Property: Part III – IP Protection for AI-Assisted Inventions and Creative Works: Hearing Before the Subcomm. on Cts., Intell. Prop. & the Internet of the H. Comm. on the Judiciary*, 118th Cong. 6 (2024) (written testimony of Joshua Landau, Senior Counsel, Computer & Communications Industry Association). Firth-Butterfield & Chae, *supra* note 43, at 12 ("Revising the definition to encompass a person's use of AI would substantially raise the bar for nonobviousness."); Abbott, *supra* note 40, at 1124–25.

56 *See* Mark A. Lemley, *The Myth of the Sole Inventor*, 110 MICH. L. REV. 709, 715–33 (2012) (describing the history behind some of the most pioneering modern inventions, such as: lightbulb, steam engines, telephone, and telegraph, and noting that the vast majority of the important inventions were either done simultaneously and independently by different inventors, or they resulted from a gradual and communal effort where different key components of the invention were conceived by multiple researchers working independently and almost simultaneously). Firth-Butterfield & Chae, *supra* note 43, at 12.

57 *See* Firth-Butterfield & Chae, *supra* note 43, at 12 ("Some even argue that traditional patent law is irrelevant, and that other, non-patent incentives should be used to provide the gatekeeping function of nonobviousness.") (citing Yanisky-Ravid & Liu, *supra* note 52, at 2215).

58 *See, e.g.*, Ryan Abbott, *Everything Is Obvious*, 66 UCLA L. REV. 2 (2019) (hypothesizing machines as inventors, suggesting a trajectory in which machines are eventually better at inventing than humans, and proposing that

one would need different standards to evaluate patents – one for ordinarily skilled machines and one for expert machine); Yanisky-Ravid & Jin, *supra* note 42, at 834 (suggesting a two-track patent examination model "to separate the examination of AI inventions from that of human-made inventions."). For a different perspective, Lucas Yordy suggests that doctrines surrounding prior art should be changed so that publicly available information about AI-generated inventions may only serve as prior art if they fully enable the public to make the invention. *See* Lucas R. Yordy, *The Library of Babel for Prior Art: Using Artificial Intelligence to Mass Produce Prior Art in Patent Law*, 74 VAND. L. REV. 521, 558 (2021).

59 This is not to suggest agreement with the argument that invention is more difficult and expensive today because all of the easy invention has already occurred. *See* Robin Feldman et al., *Challenges with Defining Pharmaceutical Markets and Potential Remedies to Screen for Industry Consolidation*, 47 J. HEALTH POL. POL'Y L. 583, 587 (2022) (highlighting research refuting the claim that recent consolidation trends in the pharmaceutical industry are the result of rising costs of developing new drugs). In fact, the introduction of AI may reduce the time and cost of invention. It may, however, increase the necessary complexity to a level at which human contribution shrinks.

60 *See, e.g.*, Andrew A. Schwartz, *The Corporate Preference for Trade Secret*, 74 OHIO STATE L.J. 623, 627 (2013) ("Intellectual property (IP) law offers two alternative methods for protecting a novel and useful invention, patent or trade secret.... Both patent and trade secret offer an exclusive right over the invention, but the protection they offer differs in important ways."); W. Nicholson Price II, *Expired Patents, Trade Secrets, and Stymied Competition*, 92 NOTRE DAME L. REV. 1611, 1615 (2017) ("Trade secrets, unlike patents, can persist indefinitely; some last for many decades."); Daniel C. Munson, *The Patent-Trade Secret Decision: An Industrial Perspective*, 78 J. PAT. & TRADEMARK OFF. SOC'Y 689, 690 (1996) ("[I]nvention must concern patentable subject matter. Many valuable trade secrets do not involve patentable subject matter at all...."); W. Nicholson Price II, *Regulating Secrecy*, 91 WASH. UNIV. L. REV. 1769, 1776 (2016) (highlighting the legal differences between patents and trade secrecy, such as (1) disclosure of the subject matter of the claimed invention, (2) the scope of protection, and (3) the duration of protection).

61 *But see* Robin Feldman, *Trade Secrets in Biologic Medicine: The Boundary with Patents*, 24 COLUM. SCI. & TECH. L. REV. 1, 26–27 (2022) (explaining that patent holders are able to file patents on biologic medicines that do not disclose how to make the invention); Sonia K. Katyal, *The Paradox of Source Code Secrecy*, 104 CORNELL L. REV. 1183, 1222 (2019) (citing Greg R. Vetter, *Are Prior Use Rights Good for Software?*, 23 TEX. INTELL. PROP. L.J. 251 for the point that software patents do not disclose the code: "all that is needed is a description of the process implemented"). For an explanation

of the history of patent law and how judicial decisions evolved to allow software patents to include only broad, high-level descriptions of what is accomplished, rather than the details of how the software accomplishes the task, *see* ROBIN FELDMAN, RETHINKING PATENT LAW 104–12 (Harvard University Press 2012).

62 18 U.S.C. § 1839(3) (including the cited language within "the term 'trade secret' means"). The Uniform Trade Secrets Act, which has been adopted by nearly all states, defines the term "trade secret" in a similar manner as the federal statute. UNIFORM TRADE SECRETS ACT § 1(4) (1985); *see also* Robin Feldman & Charles Tait Graves, *Naked Price and Pharmaceutical Trade Secret Overreach*, 22 YALE J.L. & TECH. 61, 128 n. 53 (2020) (explaining that the language of the federal act is the same as "almost all state versions of the Uniform Act"). For variations in state trade secret laws, *see* Grant Cole, Note, *Secrets, Sovereigns, and States: Analyzing State Government's Liability for Trade Secret Misappropriation*, 28 J. INTELL. PROP. L. 131 (2020); *see also* Sid Leach, *Anything but Uniform: A State-By-State Comparison of Differences in the Uniform Trade Secrets Act*, SNELL & WILMER, LLP (Oct. 23, 2015), https://www.swlaw.com/firm_news/anything-but-uniform-a-state-by-state-comparison-of-the-key-differences-of-the-uniform-trade-secrets-act.

63 Michael Risch, *Why Do We Have Trade Secrets?*, 11 MARQ. INTELL. PROP. L. REV. 1, 6–7 (2007).

64 Richard F. Dole Jr., *The Uniform Trade Secrets Act – Trends and Prospects*, 33 HAMLINE L. REV. 409, 425 (2010) (noting as an exception to a Uniform Trade Secrets Act misappropriation violation a "person who obtained subsequent knowledge or reason to know that he or she acquired knowledge of a trade secret by accident or mistake").

65 *See, e.g.*, David S. Levine, *Generative Artificial Intelligence and Trade Secrecy*, 3 J. OF FREE SPEECH L. 559, 582–83 (2023).

66 *See* Cameron Coles, *11% of Data Employees Paste Into ChatGPT Is Confidential*, CYBERHAVEN (Feb. 28, 2023), https://www.cyberhaven.com/blog/4-2-of-workers-have-pasted-company-data-into-chatgpt (presenting this and other hypothetical examples, along with evidence suggesting actual disclosures).

67 *See id.*; *see also* Levine, *supra* note 65, at 575–80.

68 *See* Levine, *supra* note 65, at 575–80.

69 Levine, *supra* note 65, at 577 (citing Emily Forlini, *Samsung Software Engineers Busted for Pasting Proprietary Code into ChatGPT*, PC MAG. (Apr. 7, 2023), https://www.pcmag.com/news/samsung-software-engineers-busted-for-pasting-proprietary-code-into-chatgpt).

70 *See, e.g.*, Levine, *supra* note 65, at 577–78; Ana Nordberg, *Trade Secrets, Big Data and Artificial Intelligence Innovation: A Legal Oxymoron?*, in THE HARMONIZATION AND PROTECTION OF TRADE SECRETS IN THE EU: AN APPRAISAL OF THE EU DIRECTIVE (Jens Schovsbo, Timo Minssen, &

Thomas Riis eds., 2020). *See also* Ameya Paleja, *Alpaca AI: Stanford Researchers Clone ChatGPT AI for Just $600*, INTERESTING ENG'G (Mar. 21, 2023, 6:45 AM EST), https://interestingengineering.com/innovation/stanford-researchers-clone-chatgpt-ai (giving an example of reverse engineering a generative AI product inexpensively); Joshua Weigensberg & Kate Garber, *Risks that Generative AI Poses to Trade Secret Protections*, LEGALTECH NEWS (June 9, 2023, 9:17 AM), https://www.law.com/legaltechnews/2023/06/09/risks-that-generative-ai-poses-to-trade-secret-protections/?slreturn = 20240009151845 (noting that if a company employee uses third-party generative AI that allows for iterative training on prompts, that use may count against claims of trade secrets); Commentary, *Trade Secrets and Generative AI: Protective Measures In an Evolving Technological Landscape*, JONES DAY (June 9, 2023), https://www.jonesday.com/en/insights/2023/06/trade-secrets-and-generative-ai (describing concern that trade secrets may accidentally end up on AI and suggesting measures to ensure against it).

Other scholars have addressed concerns about the ability of AI to reverse engineer software and even other AI, rendering those areas difficult to protect by trade secret, which permits reverse engineering. *See, e.g.*, Shawn Bayern, *Reverse Engineering (by) Artificial Intelligence*, *in* RESEARCH HANDBOOK ON INTELL. PROP. & ARTIFICIAL INTELLIGENCE 391, 396 (Edward Elgar 2022) (explaining that reverse engineering is simply the process of figuring out how something works by exposure to the finished product and noting that machine learning can dramatically reduce the costs of reverse engineering software, both in terms of software in general and AI software itself); Erik Weibust & Dean A. Pelletier, *Protecting AI-Generated Inventions as Trade Secrets Requires Protecting the Generative AI as Well*, IP WATCHDOG (July 24, 2022, 12:15 PM), https://ipwatchdog.com/2022/07/24/protecting-ai-generated-inventions-trade-secrets-requires-protecting-generative-ai-well/id = 150372 (raising concerns that if the AI is reverse engineered, it may not be protectible as a trade secret); *see also* Ashraf Tarek, Intellectual Property Implications of Artificial Intelligence and Ownership of AI-Generated Works 29–31 (June 28, 2023) (unpublished manuscript) (SSRN), https://ssrn.com/abstract = 4494640 (discussing ownership of AI-generated works and noting that those may not be subject to trade secret if the AI can be reverse engineered).

71 *See* Nordberg, *supra* note 70, at 211–12; *see also* Levine, *supra* note 65, at 578 (including a slightly expanded version of the Nordberg quote and noting that "Nordberg's analysis predates ChatGPT's launch").

72 This book uses the term "creative AI" to describe types of AI that can generate inventions themselves, following Yanisky-Ravid & Jin, *supra* note 42.

73 *Id.*

74 *See* Chapter 2.3 (describing the requirements for secrecy, including that the information cannot be generally known or readily ascertainable).

75 *Cf.* Burk, *supra* note 39, at 309–10 (noting in the context of patent law that "machine learning systems find only what humans design them to find, within statistical parameters that humans must specify. Indeed, AI outputs are so copious and non-discriminating that humans must specify which algorithmic outcomes are sufficiently 'interesting' to merit inclusion in the pool of viable results"); Email from George W. Jordan III, Chair, ABA Section of Intell. Prop. L., to WIPO Secretariat, WORLD INTELL. PROP. ORG., at 6 (Feb. 12, 2020) https://www.wipo.int/export/sites/www/about-ip/en/artificial_intelligence/call_for_comments/pdf/org_american_bar_association.pdf (explaining that "the elements of an AI invention will be some combination of features that underlie, engender, and/or utilize the *human-simulation aspects* of the AI invention") (emphasis added).

76 *See, e.g.*, AvidAir Helicopter Supply, Inc. v. Rolls-Royce Corp., 663 F.3d 966, 973 (8th Cir. 2011) (upholding the district court's finding that AvidAir misappropriated Rolls-Royce's trade secrets, specifically details about its overhaul procedure for the Model 250 engine, because "[t]he fact that information can be ultimately discerned by others – whether through independent investigation, accidental discovery, or reverse engineering – does not make it unprotectable.... Instead, the court must look at whether the duplication of the information would require a substantial investment of time, effort, and energy."); MicroStrategy Inc. v. Bus. Objects, S.A., 331 F. Supp. 2d 396, 417 (E.D. Va. 2004) (noting that whether a trade secret is readily ascertainable is "heavily fact-dependent and simply boils down to assessing the *ease* with which a trade secret could have been independently discovered") (emphasis added); Liberty Am. Ins. Grp., Inc. v. WestPoint Underwriters, L.L.C., 199 F. Supp. 2d 1271, 1287 (M.D. Fla. 2001) (concluding that the plaintiff's park list and park data, which consisted of publicly available information that could observed by any visitor to the parks, were not trade secrets because the defendant compiled their own list in two days from the same information).

77 *Cf. AvidAir*, 663 F.3d, *supra* note 76, at 973 ("[T]he fact that information can be ultimately discerned by others – whether through independent investigation, accidental discovery, or reverse engineering – does not make it unprotectable [but rather] the court must look at whether the duplication of the information would require a substantial investment of time, effort, and energy").

78 Michael Carley, Deepak Hegde, & Alan Marco, *What Is the Probability of Receiving a U.S. Patent?*, 17 YALE J.L. & TECH. 203, 209 (2015) (finding that "only 55.8% of progenitor applications emerged as patents without the use of continuation procedures" to create related applications).

79 The Copyright Act of 1976, 17 U.S.C. § 101.

80 Feist Publ'n, Inc. v. Rural Tel. Serv. Co., 499 U.S. 340, 345, 362–63 (1991) (noting that "the requisite level of creativity is extremely low; even a slight amount will suffice" and so Rural's white pages directory "lack[ed] the modicum of creativity necessary to transform mere selection [of facts] into copyrightable expression.").

81 Mazer v. Stein, 347 U.S. 201, 217 (1954) ("Unlike a patent, a copyright gives no exclusive right to the art disclosed; protection is given only to the expression of the idea – not the idea itself."); *see also*, *e.g.*, Christopher A. Cotropia & Mark A. Lemley, *Copying in Patent Law*, 87 N.C. L. REV. 1421, 1423, 1426–28 (2009) ("To infringe a copyright or trade secret, defendants must copy the protected IP from the plaintiff, directly or indirectly. But patent infringement requires only that the defendant's product falls within the scope of the patent claims.").

82 For the seminal case on fair use and the transformativity of criticism, *see* Campbell v. Acuff-Rose Music, Inc., 510 U.S. 569, 578–79 (1994) (asking whether a rap group's commercial parody of "Oh, Pretty Woman" – with the lyrics "big hairy woman" – added "something new, with a further purpose or different character, *altering the first with new expression, meaning, or message*; it asks, in other words, whether and to what extent the new work is 'transformative.'") (emphasis added).

83 Feist Publ'n, Inc. v. Rural Tel. Serv. Co., 499 U.S. 340, 347 (1991) ("It is this bedrock principle of copyright that mandates the law's seemingly disparate treatment of facts and factual compilations. 'No one may claim originality as to facts.'") (citations omitted).

84 Nichols v. Universal Pictures Corp., 45 F.2d 119, 122 (2d Cir. 1930) ("We have to decide how much, and while we are as aware as any one that the line, wherever it is drawn, will seem arbitrary, that is no excuse for not drawing it; it is a question such as courts must answer in nearly all cases. Whatever may be the difficulties a priori, we have no question on which side of the line this case falls.").

85 *Id.* ("A comedy based upon conflicts between Irish and Jews, into which the marriage of their children enters, is no more susceptible of copyright than the outline of Romeo and Juliet.")

86 *See, e.g.*, Abdin v. CBS Broad. Inc., 971 F.3d 57, 68 (2d Cir. 2020) (holding that, because "ideas are not copyrightable," the *Star Trek: Discovery* television series did not infringe upon plaintiff's video game featuring a tardigrade, as "the extension of tardigrades' known ability to survive in space into the ability to travel in space is an unprotectible idea.").

87 ROBERT P. MERGES, PETER S. MENELL, & MARK A. LEMLEY, INTELLECTUAL PROPERTY IN THE NEW TECHNOLOGICAL AGE 446 (5th ed. 2010) ("The most challenging aspect of applying the idea-expression dichotomy is determining where to draw the line between idea and expression.").

88 Baker v. Selden, 101 U.S. 99 (1879) (explaining that a template in a bookkeeping manual is not copyrightable if those "ruled lines and headings of accounts must necessarily be used as incident" to the practice of bookkeeping).

89 Morrissey v. Proctor & Gamble Co., 379 F.2d 675 (1st Cir. 1967) (discussing merger doctrine for sweepstakes rules).

90 *See* Hoehling v. Universal City Studios, Inc., 618 F.2d 972, 979 (2d Cir. 1980) ("These elements, however, are merely scenes a faire, that is, 'incidents, characters or settings which are as a practical matter indispensable, or at least standard, in the treatment of a given topic.'")

91 Skidmore v. Led Zeppelin, 952 F.3d 1051, 1064 (9th Cir. 2020) ("In cases such as this one where there is no direct evidence of copying, the plaintiff "can attempt to prove it circumstantially by showing that the defendant had access to the plaintiff's work and that the two works share similarities probative of copying." (quoting Rentmeester v. Nike, Inc., 883 F.3d 1111 (9th Cir. 2018)).

92 *See id;* Ninth Circuit Jury Instructions Comm., Manual of Model Civil Jury Instructions for the District Courts of the Ninth Circuit § 17.17 (2017) ("The plaintiff can prove that the defendant copied from the work [by proving by a preponderance of the evidence that the defendant had access to the plaintiff's copyrighted work and that there are substantial similarities between the defendant's work and original elements of the plaintiff's work] [*brackets in original text*]"); Three Boys Music Corp. v. Bolton, 212 F.3d 477, 482 (9th Cir. 2000), overruled by Skidmore v. Led Zeppelin, 952 F.3d 1051 (9th Cir. 2020) ("Circumstantial evidence of reasonable access is proven in one of two ways: (1) a particular chain of events is established between the plaintiff's work and the defendant's access to that work (such as through dealings with a publisher or record company), or (2) the plaintiff's work has been widely disseminated.").

93 *See, e.g.*, Three Boys Music Corp. v. Bolton, 212 F.3d 477 (9th Cir. 2000)), overruled by Skidmore v. Led Zeppelin, 952 F.3d 1051 (9th Cir. 2020) ("Subconscious copying has been accepted since Learned Hand embraced it in a 1924 music infringement case: 'Everything registers somewhere in our memories, and no one can tell what may evoke it ... Once it appears that another has in fact used the copyright as the source of this production, he has invaded the author's rights. It is no excuse that in so doing his memory has played him a trick.'") (citing Fred Fisher, Inc. v. Dillingham, 298 F. 145, 147–48 (S.D.N.Y.1924)).

94 *Id.* at 481 ("Absent direct evidence of copying, proof of infringement involves fact-based showings that the defendant had "access" to the plaintiff's work and that the two works are 'substantially similar.'").

95 Bright Tunes Music Corp. v. Harrisongs Music, Ltd., 420 F. Supp. 177 (S.D.N.Y. 1976).

96 *See Three Boys Music Corp.*, 212 F.3d at 483–85. *See also Skidmore*, 952 F.3d 1051, 1068 (9th Cir. 2020) ("As a practical matter, the concept of 'access' is increasingly diluted in our digitally interconnected world. Access is often proved by the wide dissemination of the copyrighted work. Given the ubiquity of ways to access media online, from YouTube to subscription services like Netflix and Spotify, access may be established by a trivial showing that the work is available on demand.") (citations omitted); Brooks Barnes, *The Streaming Era Has Finally Arrived. Everything Is About to Change*, N.Y. TIMES (Nov. 19, 2019), https://www.nytimes.com/2019/11/18/business/media/streaming-hollywood-revolution.html (cited in the Ninth Circuit's opinion to show sheer number availability of access in the Internet Age).

97 *History: Charles Dickens (1812–1870)*, BBC, https://www.bbc.co.uk/history/historic_figures/dickens_charles.shtml (last visited Mar. 10, 2025).

Chapter 7

1 35 U.S.C. § 154(a)(1) ("Every patent shall contain . . . a grant to the patentee, his heirs or assigns, of the right to exclude others from making, using, offering for sale, or selling the invention . . .").

2 17 U.S.C. § 106(1) ("[T]he owner of copyright . . . has the exclusive rights . . . to *reproduce* the copyrighted work[]") (emphasis added). *See also* Robin C. Feldman & John Newman, *Copyright at the Bedside: Should We Stop the Spread?*, 16 STAN. TECH. L. REV. 623, 631 (2013) (stating that copyright provides the authors with the exclusive rights to make copies of their copyrighted works, as well as to create derivative works). The technical term for "copying" is "reproduction," although the courts and common legal parlance frequently use the term "copying." *Cf.* 17 U.S.C. § 106(1) *and* 17 U.S.C. § 101 ("'Copies' are material objects, . . . from which the work can be perceived, *reproduced*, or otherwise communicated, . . .") (emphasis added) *with* Hanagami v. Epic Games, Inc., 85 F.4th 931, 941 (9th Cir. 2023) (using the term "copying" throughout the Ninth Circuit's legal analysis of copyright infringement) *and* Authors Guild v. Google, Inc., 804 F.3d 202, 212 (2d Cir. 2015) ("The ultimate goal of copyright is to expand public knowledge and understanding, which copyright seeks to achieve by giving potential creators exclusive control over *copying* of their works, thus giving them a financial incentive to create informative, intellectually enriching works for public consumption." (emphasis added)).

3 *See* 18 U.S.C. § 1832(a) ("Whoever, with intent to convert a trade secret . . . steals . . . such information[,] . . . shall . . . be fined under this title or imprisoned not more than 10 years, or both"), *and see* 18 U.S.C. § 1839(3) ("the term 'trade secret' means all forms and types of financial, business, scientific, technical, economic, or engineering information . . . whether

tangible or intangible ... [that] the owner thereof has taken reasonable measures to keep such information secret").

4 15 U.S.C. § 1125(1) (establishing "dilution by tarnishment of the famous mark" as a condition for injunction against those using a trademark, with a § 1125(1)(C) defining that dilution as "association arising from the similarity between a mark or trade name and a famous mark that harms the reputation of the famous mark").

5 MILTON FRIEDMAN, MONEY MISCHIEF: EPISODES IN MONETARY HISTORY 10 (1st ed. 1994).

6 *Id.*

7 *See* 1 *Timothy* 6:10 (quoting St. Paul) (King James).

8 *See* CABARET (ABC Pictures Corp. 1972).

9 CHRIS JANSON, *Buy Me a Boat*, *on* BUY ME A BOAT (Warner Bros. Nashville 2015).

10 *See, e.g.*, Oliver R. Mitchell, *The Fictions of the Law: Have They Proved Useful or Detrimental to Its Growth?*, 7 Harv. L. Rev. 249, 264–65 (1893) ("[I]t seems clear that the common law is much indebted to fictions, considered as a whole, for its rapid development and ability to follow closely the wants of men. . . . The last vestige of the fictitious principle will die out when the need to resort to it has ceased. When in the fulness of time the law has achieved its full stature; when every great principle has been not merely dotted out, but firmly outlined; when what is apparently conflicting has been harmonized, and what is left to do is but a process of amplification and refining, – fictions and the fictious principle itself will cease to be used, because they will have ceased to be useful."). *Cf.* Dan L. Burk, *Cheap Creativity and What It Will Do*, 57 Ga. L. Rev. 1669, 1690 (2023) (in the context of arguing that AI will increase the interest in authentic works, explaining that authenticity is "not a natural or native characteristic in any circumstance, but arises out of human interaction, imagination, and performance in every circumstance. Most importantly, it is not an inherent property of any object or occurrence but arises from a confluence of social perception and cultural practices." (citations omitted)).

11 *See* Christopher K. Odinet, *Data and the Social Obligation Norm of Property*, 29 Cornell J.L. & Pub. Pol'y 643, 643, 660 (2020) (discussing a trend in the Supreme Court "toward a more robust conception of data as property" using the example of *South Dakota v. Wayfair*, a tax case concerning the taxability of online retailers with no physical presence in the State of South Dakota).

12 *See also* Martin Petrin, *Reconceptualizing the Theory of the Firm – From Nature to Function*, 118 Penn St. L. Rev. 1 (2013) (discussing the historical legal theories of conceptualizing the firm by fiction, aggregate, and reality theories and arguing for a conceptualization based on the function of the firm rather than by its nature).

13 Frances D'Emilio, *Exhibit Explores Ancient Roman "Designer" Labels, Trademarks*, The Seattle Times (June 16, 2016, 6:13 AM); *cf. A History of*

Trademarks: From the Ancient World to the Nineteenth Century, WIPO. https://www.wipo.int/web/podcasts/madrid/transcripts/international_trademark_system_talk_01 (stating that there has been evidence of trademarks being used dating back to prehistoric times. Further, there have also been trademarks attributed to ancient Egyptian masons). *See also The Fascinating History of Trademark Law*, L.A. Tech & Media Law, https://techandmedialaw.com/the-fascinating-history-of-trademark-law/ (attributing trademark law history to ancient Indian craftsmen).

14 *See* text accompanying notes 19–20, *infra* (discussing exacerbations caused by concerns over the reliability of training data given misinformation and disinformation on the Internet).

15 This book focuses on ways in which AI reduces the value of the trademark system itself, or the value of items protected by the trademark system given uncertainties. Other scholars explore additional ways AI may weaken the trademark system. For example, citing a study of global trademark applications, Katyal and Kesari explain that rising submission numbers are preventing examiners from doing a thorough job of evaluating applications for trademark registration, reducing the quality of trademarks registrations granted. Sonia K. Katyal & Aniket Kesari, *Trademark Search, Artificial Intelligence, and the Role of the Private Sector*, 35 Berkley Tech. & L.J. 501, 505–06 (2020) (suggesting that if governments use high-efficacy AI for evaluating trademark applications, quality would improve; failure to do so could "exacerbate market inefficiencies stemming from information asymmetries"); *see also id.* at 570 (evaluating efficacy of private-sector and government trademark search tools).

16 *See* Sarah Berry, *What Is Amazon Listing Hijacking? (And How to Protect Your Listings)*, WebFX (Mar. 13, 2023, 12:23 PM), https://www.webfx.com/blog/marketing/amazon-listing-hijacking (last visited October 24, 2024) (describing listing hijacking as a third-party seller offering "a counterfeit version of [an original seller's] product on [the original seller's] listing, which can decrease … sales and number of positive reviews" because consumers believe the counterfeit version is the original seller's product); *Listing Hijacked! What to Do, and How to Do It?*, Seller Snap (Feb. 23, 2023), https://www.sellersnap.io/amazon-listing-highjack (explaining the financial and reputational detriment caused by hijackers who "target popular products in order to reproduce cheaper knockoffs, disguising them as originals"); Jeff Bercovici, *Amazon's Counterfeit Crackdown: What It Really Means*, Inc. (Feb. 28, 2019), https://www.inc.com/jeff-bercovici/amazon-project-zero.html (explaining that hijacking involves scammers "flag[ging] legitimate sellers as offering counterfeit or defective goods in order to get [legitimate sellers'] privileges suspended" so hijcakers can get to their valuable product listings); Andrea B. Taylor, *10 Worst Things to Buy on Amazon*, Kiplinger (Sept. 21, 2018), https://www.kiplinger.com/slideshow/spending/t062-s001-worst-things-to-buy-on-amazon-com/index.html; *cf.* Alexandra Berzon,

Shane Shifflett, & Justin Scheck, *Amazon Has Ceded Control of Its Site. The Result: Thousands of Banned, Unsafe or Mislabeled Products*, Wall St. J. (Aug. 23, 2019, 8:56 AM ET), https://www.wsj.com/articles/amazon-has-ceded-control-of-its-site-the-result-thousands-of-banned-unsafe-or-mis labeled-products-11566564990 (identifying counterfeit products as potentially containing dangerous materials or lacking proper warning labels); *see also* Daniel Seng, *Detecting and Prosecuting IP Infringement with AI: Can the AI Genie Repulse the Forty Counterfeit Thieves of Alibaba?*, in Artificial Intelligence and Intellectual Property, 292, 310 (Jyh-An Lee, Reto M. Hilty, & Kung-Chung Liu eds., 2021) (noting that automated trademark infringement detection algorithms "can only *approximate* the probability that a seller or a listing is counterfeit").

17 Fed. Trade Comm'n, *FTC Warns Two Trade Associations and a Dozen Influencers About Social Media Posts Promoting Consumption of Aspartame or Sugar*, FTC (Nov. 15, 2023), https://www.ftc.gov/news-events/news/press-releases/2023/11/ftc-warns-two-trade-associations-dozen-influencers-about-social-media-posts-promoting-consumption; Katherine Tangalakis-Lippert, *The $21 Billion Influencer Industry Has an Ad Fraud Problem*, Business Insider (May 1, 2024), https://www.businessinsider.com/influencer-industry-marketing-fraud-discrimination-unethical-deals-content-creators-brands-2024-4; Sara Morrison, *TikTok Is Full of Shady Secret Advertisements*, Vox (July 11, 2022, 4:30 AM PDT), https://www.vox.com/recode/23197348/tiktok-ad-sponcon-influencers.

18 Elijah Clark, *The Ethical Dilemma of AI in Marketing: A Slippery Slope*, Forbes. (Mar. 14, 2024, 9:15 AM EDT), https://www.forbes.com/sites/elijah clark/2024/03/14/the-ethical-dilemma-of-ai-in-marketing-a-slippery-slope/.

19 Fed. Trade Comm'n, *FTC Consumer Protection Staff Updates Agency's Guidance to Search Engine Industry on the Need to Distinguish between Advertisements and Search Results* (June 25, 2013), https://www.ftc.gov/news-events/news/press-releases/2013/06/ftc-consumer-protection-staff-updates-agencys-guidance-search-engine-industry-need-distinguish (noting that, since 2002, the FTC has required online companies to "distinguish[] paid search results and other forms of advertising from natural search results"; Fed. Trade Comm'n, *.com Disclosures: How to Make Effective Disclosures in Digital Advertising* (Mar. 2013), https://www.ftc.gov/sites/default/files/attachments/press-releases/ftc-staff-revises-online-advertising-disclosure-guidelines/130312dotcomdisclosures.pdf (explaining the disclosure requirements for products sold online); Cat Zakrzewski & Jay Greene, *Amazon's Search Results Full of Ads That May Be "Unlawfully Deceiving" Consumers, Complaint to FTC Claims* (Dec. 8, 2021, 4:35 PM), https://www.washingtonpost.com/technology/2021/12/08/amazon-search-results-ftc-complaint/.

20 *See, e.g.*, A. W. Ohlheiser, *Google Examines How Different Generations Handle Misinformation*, MIT TECH. REV. (Aug. 11, 2022), https://www

.technologyreview.com/2022/08/11/1057552/gen-z-misinformation/ (finding that younger generations are more adept at identifying misinformation and disinformation online); Quinn Mason, *In-Store vs. Online Retail Media: How Each One Impacts the Consumer Shopping Experience*, BROADSIGN (Feb. 27, 2023), https://broadsign.com/blog/in-store-vs-online-retail-media-how-each-one-impacts-the-consumer-shopping-experience/ (stating that online retailers mislead by placing ads in spaces people usually assume to contain trustworthy and independent information); Roscoe B. Starek, III, *Myths and Half-Truths About Deceptive Advertising*, FTC (Oct. 15, 1996), https://www.ftc.gov/news-events/news/speeches/myths-half-truths-about-deceptive-advertising; Selena Templeton, *Common Types of Misleading Statistics in Advertising – And How to Spot Them*, SINGLE GRAIN (Nov. 2024), https://www.singlegrain.com/blog/a/misleading-statistics-in-advertising/.

21 Jon M. Garon, *The Revolution Will be Digitized: Generative AI, Synthetic Media, and the Medium of Disruption*, 20 OHIO ST. TECH. L.J. 139, 205 (2023).

22 *Id.*

23 *See* Chelsea El-Azzi, *Verification of Third-Party Online Marketplace Sellers: Protecting Consumers Against Counterfeits*, 45 HOUS. J. INT'L L 207, 212 (noting that it's fairly easy to hijack listings on online marketplaces to sell low-quality or counterfeit products); Berry, *supra* note 16 (last visited Oct. 24, 2024, 12:23 PM) (describing listing hijacking on Amazon).

24 Krystal Hu, *Investigation: How Sellers Exploit Amazon's Loopholes to Sell Unsafe Products*, YAHOO! FINANCE (Sept. 6, 2019), https://finance.yahoo.com/news/amazon-sellers-exploit-loopholes-to-sell-unsafe-products-144130664.html (noting that victims of listing hijackings "leave the bad review for the seller with the original listing who is not responsible for the defective product").

25 *See supra* Chapter 2, note 19 and accompanying text.

26 *See* text accompanying notes 19–20, *supra* (discussing exacerbations caused by concerns over the reliability of training data given misinformation and disinformation on the Internet).

27 *See, e.g.*, ERIC SCHMIDT ET AL., FINAL REPORT: NATIONAL SECURITY COMMISSION ON ARTIFICIAL INTELLIGENCE 45 (2021) (highlighting concerns that adversaries may use AI-powered misinformation to "create systems to manipulate citizens' beliefs and behavior").

28 *See* Michael R. Grynberg, *AI and the "Death of Trademark,"* 108 KENTUCKY L.J., 199, 209, 238 (2019).

29 *Id.* at 209, 238.

30 *Id.* at 209; *see also* Garon, *supra* note 21, at 206 (noting that AI systems can help simplify consumers' decision-making process by sorting through vast amount of information and thus reduce the utility of trademarks).

31 Seng, *supra* note 16, at 305.

32 *See* Garon, *supra* note 21, at 44–45.; *cf.* Dan L. Burk, *AI Patents and the Self-Assembling Machine*, 105 MINN. L. R. HEADNOTES 301, 302 (2021).

33 *What Is BookTok? Understanding the TikTok Trend That's Bringing Books to Life, SocialPilot*, https://www.socialpilot.co/social-media-terms/what-is-booktok (last visited Mar. 11, 2025) ("BookTok came into existence when TikTok and the world of books collided. It refers to a community of readers and authors passionate about literature and books, which typically interacts with the use of the hashtag. The readers on BookTok recommend, review, and discuss books by making engaging videos about them.").

34 PWC UK, THE MACROECONOMIC IMPACT OF ARTIFICIAL INTELLIGENCE 12 (Feb. 2018), https://www.pwc.co.uk/economic-services/assets/macroeconomic-impact-of-ai-technical-report-feb-18.pdf ("AI technologies could reduce the search costs, or general effort involved in identifying the ideal product or service, therefore reducing friction in the purchasing process leading to more consumption or greater utility derived from existing consumption."); Adam Alexander Buick, *In Search of Value: Trade Marks and Search Costs in the Age of the Internet*, 15 LAW, INNOV. & TECH. 435, 436 (2023) ("[A]dvances in information technology [] have dramatically lowered consumer search costs in many areas . . . this general reduction in consumer search costs facilitated by information technology has also resulted in a reduction in the value of well-known trade marks, at least in some areas, and that this decline in value is likely to continue."). *But see* USPTO, PUBLIC VIEWS ON ARTIFICIAL INTELLIGENCE AND INTELLECTUAL PROPERTY POLICY 33 (Oct. 2020) ("Most commenters . . . noted that . . . AI software would have no impact on trademark law or, alternatively, that the existing statutory and common law framework for trademarks in the United States is sufficiently flexible to address any such impact.").

35 *See, e.g.*, ROBIN FELDMAN, RETHINKING PATENT LAW 13–15 (Harvard University Press 2012) [hereinafter FELDMAN, RETHINKING] (discussing the philosophical roots of this concept in the context of intellectual property); JEROME S. BRUNER, JACQUELINE J. GOODNOW, & GEORGE A. AUSTIN, A STUDY OF THINKING 12–13 (2d ed., Transaction Publishers 1986) (explaining the various achievements of categorizing, which is "essential to life" because it helps to identify events "as *sure* as possible as *early* as possible"); Ronald de Sousa, *The Natural Shiftiness of Natural Kinds*, 14 CANADIAN J. PHIL. 561, 562 (1984) (describing "natural kinds" philosophy, which is concerned with categorization based on natural properties).

36 *See* FELDMAN, RETHINKING, *supra* note 35, at 14 (comparing belief in the concept of a divine and belief in the existence of water).

37 *See, e.g.*, FELDMAN, RETHINKING, *supra* note 35, at 15–18 (discussing the limitations of language); Rex A. Collings Jr., *Unconstitutional Uncertainty – An Appraisal*, 40 CORNELL L.Q. 195, 195 (1955) ("There is no sharp line

between language which is uncertain and language which is certain. What is uncertain at one time may be certain at another.").

38 *See, e.g.*, F. Max Müller, *My Predecessors*, *in* LAST ESSAYS 54 (London, 1901) ("[N]othing is more certain than that two people hardly ever take the same word in the same sense."); ALFRED SIDGWICK, ELEMENTARY LOGIC 192–94 (Cambridge University Press 1914) (arguing that as a tool for reasoning, the "fundamental defect of language is its necessary indefiniteness . . . indefiniteness belongs to all *description* – to every word when and while its function is to describe."); JACQUES DERRIDA, OF GRAMMATOLOGY 6 (Gayatri Chakravorty Spivak trans., 1976) ("[L]anguage itself is menaced in its very life, helpless, adrift in the threat of limitlessness, brought back to its own finitude at the very moment when its limits seem to disappear, when it ceases to be self-assured, contained, and *guaranteed* by the infinite signified which seemed to exceed it.").

39 *See* FELDMAN, RETHINKING, *supra* note 35, at 16.

40 *See* ROBIN FELDMAN, THE ROLE OF SCIENCE IN LAW 183 (Oxford University Press 2009) (discussing language in the context of describing the benefits and limitations of mandating plain-language patents).

41 *Cf.* Lawrence Lessig, *Fidelity and Constraint*, 65 FORDHAM L. REV. 1365, 1373 (1997) (arguing one must reconstruct the original constitutional context surrounding a meaning in order to clarify that original meaning); Robert J. Pushaw Jr., *Talking Textualism, Practicing Pragmatism: Rethinking the Supreme Court's Approach to Statutory Interpretation*, 51 GA. L. REV. 121, 133–78 (2016) (outlining constitutional statutory interpretive approaches).

42 *See, e.g.*, Richard Craswell, *Do Trade Customs Exist?*, *in* THE JURISPRUDENTIAL FOUNDATIONS OF CORPORATE AND COMMERCIAL LAW 118, 132–33 (Jody S. Kraus & Steven D. Walt eds., 2000) (describing the difficulty of fixing meaning with legal rules); Alan Schwartz & Robert E. Scott, *Contract Theory and the Limits of Contract Law*, 113 YALE L. J. 541, 570–73 (2003) (expounding on the challenges of linguistic interpretation in contract law); MARGARET JANE RADIN, THE LINGUISTIC TURN IN PATENT LAW 6 (unpublished manuscript on file with author) (noting the problems of having to define "new" invention with "old" words in patent law); *cf. In re* Bridgeford, 357 F.2d 679, 682 (C.C.P.A. 1966) ("[T]he right to a patent on an invention is not to be denied because of the limitations of the English language").

43 Robin Feldman & Gideon Schor, *Dance of the Biologics*, 39 BERKELEY TECH. L.J. 841 (2024).

44 *See* KIRSTI KNOLLE, *Publishers Need to Know Their Readers to Survive in Digital Era*, REUTERS (Oct. 21, 2013, 3:03 AM), https://www.reuters.com/article/technology/publishers-need-to-know-their-readers-to-survive-in-digital-era-idUSDEE99K072/.

45 WSJ Staff, *Inside TikTok's Algorithm: A WSJ Video Investigation*, WALL ST. J. (July 21, 2021, 10:26 AM), https://www.wsj.com/articles/tiktok-algorithm-video-investigation-11626877477.

46 *See supra* Chapter 6 (discussing an argument that the definition of PHOSITA should be expanded to include "a person using AI as a tool"); *see also* Katyal & Kesari, *supra* note 15, at 509–14 (explaining Stigler's 1961 framing of advertising as reducing consumer search costs and the theory's subsequent migration to trademark theory).

47 *See* Section 6.1; *Contra* Henry Du, *Can AI Tame the Metaverse's Wild West?*, 15 LANDSLIDE 14, 15, 17 (2023) (listing recent developments in using AI to protect trademarks and arguing that AI is "increasingly proving to be a valuable tool globally for protecting brand owners, including the surveillance to detect trademark infringement and to fight bad faith trademark registrations"); Ani Khachatryan, *The Digital Dilemma: Counterfeit Culture and Brand Protection Reform in the E-Commerce Era*, 43 LOY. L.A. ENT. L. REV. 247, 284 (2023) (listing examples of AI companies whose products aim at detecting trademark infringement); Daryl Lim, *Trademark Confusion Simplified: A New Framework for Multifactor Test*, 37 BERKELEY TECH. L.J. 871, 927, 930–32 (2022) (suggesting positive roles AI can play in trademark law, including for predictive trademark classification, robot adjudication, and weighing likelihood-of-confusion factors); Anke Moerland & Conrado Freitas, *Artificial Intelligence and Trademark Assessment*, *in* ARTIFICIAL INTELLIGENCE AND INTELLECTUAL PROPERTY, 266–91, 278, 291 (Jyh-An Lee, Reto M Hilty, & Kung-Chung Liu eds., 2021) (empirically testing AI tools for trademark infringement detection and predicting that complex or substantive tasks will remain in human hands while administrative tasks like registration, examination, opposition, and judicial procedures are, and will increasingly, fall to an AI).

48 The problem may be less acute than with copyright, although trademark protection can go hand in hand with copyright protection. In addition, some authors have claimed overlapping copyright protection for works. For example, the Walt Disney Company holds a trademark for Mickey Mouse. MICKEY MOUSE, Registration No. 0247156; *see also* Feldman and Newman, *supra* note 2, at 625–26 (discussing authors of the Mini Mental State Exam (MMSE), a ubiquitous set of questions evaluating a patient's mental state for the purposes of research or treatment, claiming both copyright and trade secret protection and questioning the validity of those claims).

49 Arnstein v. Porter, 158 F.2d 795 (2d Cir. 1946) (denying dismissal on summary judgment regarding whether Cole Porter copied the song "Begin the Beguine" from a prior author's song, "My Heart Belongs to Daddy."); Bright Tunes Music Corp. v. Harrisongs Music, Ltd., 420 F. Supp. 177 (S.D.N.Y. 1976) (holding defendant liable for copyright infringement due to unconscious copying).

50 *See* notes 57–58 and accompanying text (discussing ubiquitous warnings that are ignored).

51 *See, e.g.*, Tabrez Y. Ebrahim, *Artificial Intelligence Inventions & Patent Disclosure*, 125 PENN STATE L. REV. 147, 205 (2020) (proposing that

Congress "enact reforms to the patent system to require greater disclosure of AI-generated output of inventions that were hardly (or never) developed or were effectively concealed through an unexplainable algorithmic inventive process").

52 H.R. 3831, 118th Cong. (2023) ("Generative artificial intelligence shall include any output generated by such artificial intelligence the following: 'Disclaimer: this output has been generated by artificial intelligence.'").

53 The EU AI Act also requires providers of generative AI systems to mark system outputs as artificially generated or manipulated. *See* 2024 O.J. (L) (EU) 2024/1689.

54 *See* 37 C.F.R. § 202.

55 *E.g.*, Katie Notopoulos, *A Tech News Site Has Been Using AI To Write Articles, So We Did the Same Thing Here*, BUZZFEED NEWS (Jan. 12, 2023), https://www.buzzfeednews.com/article/katienotopoulos/cnet-articles-written-by-ai-chatgpt-article (describing CNET's use of the following disclaimer: "This article was generated using automation technology and thoroughly edited and fact-checked by an editor on our editorial staff.").

56 CAL. HEALTH & SAFETY CODE § 25249.5–25249.14 (West 1986).

57 *See, e.g.*, Clifford Rechtschaffen, *The Warning Game: Evaluating Warnings under California's Proposition 65*, 23 ECOLOGY L.Q. 303, 340 (1996) (noting that "[m]any warnings go unnoticed, fail to inform the public adequately about its exposure to listed chemicals, and fail to communicate effectively the risk levels involved").

58 Geoffrey Mohan and Mark E. Potts, *You See the Warnings Everywhere. But Does Prop. 65 Really Protect You?*, L.A. TIMES (July 23, 2020 6:00 AM) (also highlighting that most Proposition 65 enforcement is driven by "a handful of attorneys and their repeat clients").

59 *See* Section 4.3.

60 *See, e.g.*, David De Cremer & Garry Kasparov, *AI Should Augment Human Intelligence, Not Replace It*, HARV. BUS. REV. (Mar. 18, 2021), https://hbr.org/2021/03/ai-should-augment-human-intelligence-not-replace-it (noting that AI is useful in organizational settings because it can quickly identify informational patterns, but explaining that human intelligence possesses the ability to "imagine, anticipate, feel, and judge changing situations"); Lance Whitney, *Are Computers Already Smarter Than Humans?*, TIME (Sept. 29, 2017, 10:09 AM), https://time.com/4960778/computers-smarter-than-humans/ (highlighting several advantages that computers have over humans, such as better memories, faster processing speed, and a lack of physical constraints such as tiredness).

61 *But see* USPTO, PUBLIC VIEWS ON ARTIFICIAL INTELLIGENCE AND INTELLECTUAL PROPERTY POLICY 33 (Oct. 2020) ("Most commenters ... noted that ... AI software would have no impact on trademark law or, alternatively, that the existing statutory and common law framework for trademarks in the United States is sufficiently flexible to address any such impact.").

Chapter 8

1 *See Bridgerton* (Shondaland & CVD Productions 2020) (a television series surrounding the Bridgerton family and set in a racially integrated society whose issues are, at times, pre-Victorian and, at times, decidedly modern).

2 Loree Seitz, *'Bridgerton' Season 3 Cracks Top 10 Most-Watched Netflix Series Ever With 92 Million Views*, THE WRAP (July 2, 2024, 12:00 PM), https://www.thewrap.com/bridgerton-season-3-netflix-top-10-most-popular.

3 Thomas Moore, *Lab Grown Diamonds Almost Impossible to Differentiate from Real Gems*, SKY NEWS (May 3, 2018), https://news.sky.com/story/lab-grown-diamonds-almost-impossible-to-differentiate-from-real-gems-11356476.

4 Thomas Biesheuvel, *The Diamond Industry Is Coping with a 20% Price Drop and Worries Gen Z Isn't All That Interested in Its Stones*, FORTUNE (Nov. 11, 2023), https://fortune.com/2023/11/11/diamond-industry-faces-price-plunge-gen-z-uncertainty.

5 Samantha Simma, *Alternative Gemstones: A Girl's Other "Best Friends,"* GRAND WEDDING, https://jacksonholewedding.com/alternative-gemstones (last visited Jan. 30, 2024) (citing reports that a quarter of brides-to-be are leaning toward alternative gemstones).

6 *But cf.* Paul Zimnisky, *Lab-Diamond Sales Grow as Prices Fall* (Jan. 2, 2023), https://www.paulzimnisky.com/Lab-Diamond-Sales-Grow-as-Prices-Fall ("[A]s the price point between natural and lab-diamonds continues to widen, consumer's intuitive perception of the two products is also likely to naturally diverge).

7 *See, e.g.*, Jessica Keech, Maureen Morrin, & Jeffrey Steven Podoshen, *The Effects of Materialism on Consumer Evaluation of Sustainable Synthetic (Lab-Grown) Products*, 37 J. CONSUMER MKTG. 579, 585 (2020) (finding that consumers tend to perceive lab-grown diamonds as inferior, but emphasizing the ethicality of lab-grown diamonds can positively influence consumer perception and preference of these diamonds). *Cf.* Humberto Fuentes, Jorge Vera-Martinez, & Diana Kolbe, *The Role of Intangible Attributes of Luxury Brands for Signaling Status: A Systematic Literature Review*, 47 INT'L J. CONSUMER STUD. 2747, 2754 (2022) (highlighting that some consumers prefer luxury brands as a means of self-expression).

Chapter 9

1 Richard A. Posner, *Natural Monopoly and Its Regulation*, 21 STAN. LAW REV. 548, 563 (1968) (describing the classic image of a monopolist who "forces up the price by withholding an adequate supply"); JOAN ROBINSON, THE ECONOMICS OF IMPERFECT COMPETITION 143–58 (1933).

2 *See* G. Ariovich, *The Economics of Diamond Price Movements*, 6 (4) MANAGERIAL & DECISION ECON. 234, 236 (1985) (noting that De Beers, one of the largest

supplier of diamonds, influences prices by "tuning the volume of supply."); Phoebe Shang, *The Fifth C: What Determines Diamond Cost?*, INT'L GEM SOC'Y, https://www.gemsociety.org/article/what-determines-diamond-cost (last visited Mar. 2, 2024) (explaining that De Beers controls the market value of diamonds by decreasing supply when prices begin to fall).

3 *Paradym AI Smoke Family*, CALLAWAY, https://www.callawaygolf.com/aismokeclubs (last visited Oct. 23, 2024) (advertising golf clubs of "Paradym AI Smoke Family").

4 On the flip side, AI can also facilitate better detection of intellectual property infringement. *See* Henry Du, *Can AI Tame the Metaverse's Wild West?*, 15 (3) Landslide 14, 15, 17 (2023) ("AI/ML is increasingly proving to be a valuable tool globally for protecting brand owners, including the surveillance to detect trademark infringement and to fight bad faith trademark registrations."); Ani Khachatryan, *The Digital Dilemma: Counterfeit Culture and Brand Protection Reform in the E-Commerce Era*, 43 LOY. L.A. ENT. L. REV. 247, 284–85 (2023) ("Various companies, like Entrupy, Red Points, and Cypheme, provide solutions for companies and brands. These companies use artificial intelligence to 'analyze materials, colors, packaging and other attributes to spot fakes.'"); Shine Sean Tu, *Use of Artificial Intelligence to Determine Copyright Liability for Musical Works*, 123 W. VA. L. REV. 835, 858–59 (2021) (proposing AI as an expert witness "to help the court dissect [] work and determine if there is a 'similarity of ideas' between the two works.... [alternatively,] AI could dissect the reference work in a fashion where the non-copyrightable portions of the reference work are extracted and only the expressive portions of the work are shown to the trier of fact."); *e.g.*, *Revolutionizing Patent Infringement: Role of AI in Patent Infringement Detection and Monetization*, XLSCOUT (Jan. 24, 2024), https://xlscout.ai/revolutionizing-patent-infringement-role-of-ai-in-patent-infringement-detection-and-monetization (providing patent infringement detection software as a service).

5 *See, e.g.*, Mark A. Lemley, *Romantic Authorship and the Rhetoric of Property*, 75 TEX. L. REV. 873, 898 (1997) ("[T]here is currently a strong tendency to 'propertize' everything in the realm of information. Intellectual property law is expanding on an almost daily basis as new rights are created or existing rights are applied to give intellectual property owners rights that they never would have had in an earlier time."); *see also* Shubha Ghosh, Foreword, *Why Intergenerational Equity*, 2011 WIS. L. REV. 103, 106 (2011) ("[T]he structure of intellectual property rights needs to reflect concerns other than wealth because a focus solely on wealth maximization invariably leads to a proliferation of intellectual property rights. Wealth maximization is a blunt tool that offers little guidance to structuring intellectual property rights other than more is better.").

6 *See* Ben Depoorter, *The Several Lives of Mickey Mouse: The Expanding Boundaries of Intellectual Property Law*, 9 VA. J.L. & TECH. 4, 15–16 (2004)

(highlighting "three main strands of criticism" on the proliferation of intellectual property rights: (1) favoring the protection of producers over the protection of incentives of authors, (2) private control rights hindering technological innovation and artistic creativity, and (3) expanding copyright protections to include control of the content itself.)

7 Feist Publ'n, Inc. v. Rural Tel. Serv. Co., 499 U.S. 340, 346–47 (1991).

8 *See, e.g.*, Adithya Vikram Sakthivel, *Emails and Copyright*, MEDIUM (Dec. 12, 2019), https://medium.com/ip-weekly/emails-and-copyrights-14e673f0e89c; U.S. COPYRIGHT OFF., CIRCULAR 61, COPYRIGHT REGISTRATION OF COMPUTER PROGRAMS (Mar. 2021), https://www.copyright.gov/circs/circ61.pdf; *Terms of Service*, Instagram (last visited Mar 14, 2025), https://help.instagram.com/581066165581870 ("We do not claim ownership of your content that you post on or through the Service and you are free to share your content with anyone else, wherever you want."); *Terms of Service*, YouTube (Dec. 15, 2023), https://www.youtube.com/static?template = terms ("You retain ownership rights in your Content."); *Terms of Service*, TikTok (Nov. 2023), https://www.tiktok.com/legal/terms-of-service ("[Y]ou or your licensors will own any User Content … you upload or transmit through the [platform]."); *Terms of Service*, Meta (Jan. 1, 2025), https://www.facebook.com/terms.php?ref = pf ("You retain ownership of the intellectual property rights (things like copyright or trademarks) in any such content that you create and share on Facebook and other Meta Company Products. …"); *Terms of Service*, X (Sept. 29, 2023), https://x.com/en/tos ("You retain your rights to any Content you submit, post or display on or through the Services.").

9 *See, e.g.*, Robin Feldman & Charles Tait Graves, *Naked Price and Pharmaceutical Trade Secret Overreach*, 22 YALE J.L. & TECH. 61, 84 (2020) (expressing skepticism over claiming pharmaceutical pricing as a trade secret because "[i]t is not an idea, and it certainly is not the product of innovation"); Peter S. Menell, *Tailoring a Public Policy Exception to Trade Secret Protection*, 105 Cal. L. Rev. 1, 37, 45–46 (2017) (advocating for a public policy exception to trade secret protection because "overly broad trade secrecy protection interferes with law enforcement"); Charles T. Graves & Sonia K. Katyal, *From Trade Secrecy to Seclusion*, 109 Geo. L. J. 1337, 1342 (2021) (noting that trade secrecy has moved beyond its use as a tool against misappropriation and has expanded "into nontraditional subject matter with only attenuated connection to a competitive advantage in research and development, sales, or marketing"); Deepa Varadarajan, *Trade Secret Fair Use*, 83 FORDHAM L. REV. 1401, 1405 (2014) (highlighting that instead of using trade secret law to keep confidential information from bad actors, "companies increasingly use trade secret law to shield information from potential 'right' hands – e.g., the scrutinizing eyes of government regulators, consumers, public watchdog groups, and significant improvers" due to the "lack of ex post limiting doctrines").

10 U.S. PAT. & TRADEMARK OFF., U.S. PATENT ACTIVITY: CALENDAR YEARS 1790 TO THE PRESENT, https://www.uspto.gov/web/offices/ac/ido/oeip/taf/h_counts.html (last accessed Mar. 7, 2024).

11 *See, e.g.*, Matthew Sag & Kurt Rohde, *Patent Reform and Differential Impact*, 8 MINN. J.L., SCI. & TECH. 1, 2 (2007) (highlighting that many industry leaders have "expressed concern that too many patents are issued for 'inventions' that are obvious, vague or already widely used"); KSR Int'l Co. v. Teleflex Inc., 550 U.S. 398, 427 (2007) ("[T]he results of ordinary innovation are not the subject of exclusive rights under the patent laws. Were it otherwise patents might stifle, rather than promote, the progress of the useful arts."); Paul R. Gugliuzza, *The Procedure of Patent Eligibility*, 97 TEX. L. REV. 571, 573–74 (2019) (noting that the Court has recently "reinvigorated the patent-eligible subject matter requirement" and discussing *Bilski* and *Alice Corp.*); Bilski v. Kappos, 561 U.S. 593, 609 (2010) (denying a patent application for "the concept of hedging risk and the application of that concept to energy markets" for failure to be a patentable subject matter because these claims are "abstract ideas"); Alice Corp. Pty. Ltd. v. CLS Bank Int'l, 573 U.S. 208, 2355 (2014) (denying a patent application for computer software to mitigate settlement risk for failure to state a patentable subject matter because it lacks an "'inventive concept' – *i.e.*, an element or combination of elements that is sufficient to ensure that the patent in practice amounts to significantly more than a patent upon the ineligible concept itself"); Alan Devlin, *The Misunderstood Function of Disclosure in Patent Law*, 23 HARV. J.L. & TECH. 401, 404 (2010) ("The sheer volume of outstanding patents, coupled with the lack of specificity in many claims ... makes an exhaustive search of the prior art expensive."); Note, *The Disclosure Function of the Patent System (or Lack Thereof)*, 118 HARV. L. REV. 2007, 2024 (2005) (discussing flaws in patent disclosures).

12 *See* Aaron S. Kesselheim & Jonathan J. Darrow, *Hatch-Waxman Turns 30: Do We Need a Re-designed Approach for the Modern Era?*, 15 YALE J. HEALTH POL'Y, L. & ETHICS 293, 304 (2015) ("[S]econdary patented structures may not add to the efficacy or safety of the original drug. Moreover, the patents themselves are more likely to be invalid as lacking novelty or for being obvious improvements on prior patented structures.").

13 *See, e.g.*, Dan L. Burk, *Cheap Creativity and What It Will Do*, 57 GA. L. REV. 1669, 1706–07 (2023) (referencing "the frequently lamented expansion of trademark law to situations that have little to do with consumer confusion") (citing Rochell C. Dreyfuss, *Expressive Genericity: Trademarks as Language in the Pepsi Generation*, 65 NOTRE DAME L. REV. 397, 398 (1990)). *See also id.* at 1707 ("Despite the repeated mantra of 'confusion' and 'source,' trademark doctrine is being continually stretched and manipulated to try to fit modern branding practices") (citing Mark A. Lemley & Mark P. McKenna, *Irrelevant Confusion*, 62 STAN. L. REV. 413, 414 (2010) and Glynn S.

Lunney Jr., *Trademark Monopolies*, 48 EMORY L.J. 367, 371–72 (1999)). *See also* Lemley & McKenna, *supra* (analyzing modern cases as an improper expansion of trademark beyond likelihood of source confusion); Lunney, *supra* (arguing that modern trademark law has shifted from a doctrine for the protection of consumer interests to a form of property right for trademark holders); Ann Bartow, *Likelihood of Confusion*, 41 SAN DIEGO L. REV. 721, 737, 744–48, 817 (2004) (discussing the lack of clarity for evaluating consumer confusion and arguing that this lack of clarity has enabled mark holders to expand and broaden their rights under the guise of protecting consumers).

14 *See generally* ROBIN FELDMAN, RETHINKING PATENT LAW 157 (Harvard University Press 2012) (explaining the dangers of letting parties contract around the restrictions of the patent system and citing several cases where the Supreme Court showed willingness to allow that practice); Robin C. Feldman and John Newman, *Copyright at the Bedside: Should We Stop the Spread?*, 16 STAN. TECH. L. REV. 623, 626–27, 651 (2013) (documenting case where the authors of a cognitive function assessment exam claimed copyright and trade secret protections even though the exam was widely and freely distributed for decades and stating, "In copyright as well as in patents, rights are being systematically stripped from any underlying product, grouped and repackaged, and then traded much like a commodity."); Robin Feldman & Gideon Schor, *Dance of the Biologics*, 39 BERKELEY TECH. L.J. 841, 862 (2024) (explaining how pharmaceutical companies improperly claim trade secrets and "confidential commercial information" protections in order to fend off competition).

15 *See e.g.*, ROBERT H. FRANK & BEN S. BERNANKE, PRINCIPLES OF MICRO-ECONOMICS (4th ed. 2009); OPENSTAX, PRINCIPLES OF MICROECONOMICS 47–77 (3d ed. 2022).

16 U.S. CONST. art. I, § 8, cl. 8.

17 Patent Act of April 10, 1790, ch. 7, 1 Stat. 109–12 (repealed 1793) (declaring that anyone who has "invented or discovered any useful art, manufacture, engine, machine, or device" may be granted a patent if evaluation panel "deem[s] the invention or discovery sufficiently useful and important").

18 35 U.S.C. § 101.

19 *See* Michael Risch, *Reinventing Usefulness*, 2010 BYU L. REV. 1195, 1199 (2010) (recommending utility be defined as "commercial utility," which would "seek[] to ensure that inventions are worth more to the public than they cost"); *see id. at* 1197 n.5 & 6 (citing the works of other modern scholars noting the anemic quality of the doctrine, with some recommending ways to revitalize it: DAN L. BURK & MARK A. LEMLEY, THE PATENT CRISIS AND HOW THE COURTS CAN SOLVE IT 110–11 (University of Chicago Press 2009); Rebecca S. Eisenberg & Robert P. Merges, *Opinion Letter as to the Patentability of Certain Inventions Associated with the Identification of Partial cDNA Sequences*, 23 AIPLA Q.J. 1, 4 (1995); Phanesh Koneru, *To Promote the*

Progress of Useful Art[icle]s?: An Analysis of the Current Utility Standards of Pharmaceutical Products and Biotechnological Research Tools, 38 IDEA 625, 641 (1998); Note, *The Utility Requirement in the Patent Law*, 53 GEO. L.J. 154, 156 (1964)); *see also* USPTO, 2107 GUIDELINES FOR EXAMINATION OF APPLICATIONS FOR COMPLIANCE WITH THE UTILITY REQUIREMENT [R-11.2013], https://www.uspto.gov/web/offices/pac/mpep/s2107.html (collecting cases and endorsing the Federal Circuit's position that an invention lacks utility only when the claimed device is "totally incapable of achieving a useful result" (citing Brooktree Corp. v. Advanced Micro Devices, Inc., 977 F.2d 1555, 1571 (Fed. Cir. 1992)); Christopher Buccafusco & Jonathan S. Masur, *Drugs, Patents, and Well-Being*, 98 WASH. U.L. REV. 1403, 1407 (2021) (proposing that policymakers remove many of the legal protections for patents with "an *insubstantial* effect on human welfare" so they are easier to challenge and therefore invalidate) (emphasis in original); E.I. du Pont De Nemours and Co. v. Berkley and Co., 620 F.2d 1247, 1260 n.17 (8th Cir. 1980) (noting in the context of the subcategory of utility regarding whether an invention is inoperable, "[a] small degree of utility is sufficient"); *In re* Brana, 51 F.3d 1560, 1566–67 (Fed. Cir. 1995) (holding that an invention only partially successful in achieving a useful result remains patentable under the utility doctrine).

20 *See, e.g.*, Brenner v. Manson, 383 U.S. 519 (1966); *In re* Fisher, 421 F.3d 1365 (Fed. Cir. 2005); *In re* Ziegler, 992 F.2d 1197 (Fed. Cir. 1993).

21 *See* Robin C. Feldman et al., *Negative Innovation: When Patents Are Bad for Patients*, 39 NATURE BIOTECHNOLOGY 914, 915 (2021) ("One avenue for [patent] reform might be to enforce a more rigorous utility requirement for pharmaceutical patents, demanding that they actually improve social welfare relative to the prior art"); *see also* Buccafusco & Masur, *supra* note 19, at 1411 (proposing that the USPTO and courts could interpret § 101's useful requirement as entailing "an affirmative requirement that patent applicants establish that their inventions are likely to improve social welfare relative to the status quo").

22 *See* Michael Risch, *Why Do We Have Trade Secrets?*, 11 MARQ. INTEL. PROP. L. REV. 1, 39–40 (2007).

23 Kay Firth-Butterfield & Yoon Chae, *Artificial Intelligence Collides with Patent Law*, 12 WORLD ECON. F. 10 (2018) ("[T]here may be grounds for raising the bar for utility. . .so that only the truly 'useful' inventions by AI would be eligible for patent rights.").

24 *Cf.* Teo Susnjak, *ChatGPT: The End of Online Exam Integrity?*, 14 EDUC. SCI. 656 (considering oral exams in response to ChatGPT's current uni-modal capabilities – it can currently only accept text-inputs); Michael Neumann, Maria Rauschenberger, & Eva-Maria Schön, *"We Need To Talk About ChatGPT": The Future of AI and Higher Education*, IEEE 3 (2023) (citing Susnjak and recommending complimentary oral examinations to ensure response is human-based, not AI-generated). Of course, with humans, one

always risks reducing the evidence to a battle of the experts, perhaps even featuring the usual suspects.

25 *See* Feist Publ'n v. Rural Tel. Serv. Co., 499 U.S. 340, 345 (1991) (holding, nevertheless, that alphabetical residential telephone listings do not satisfy the modicum of creativity standard).

26 *See id.*; Russ VerSteeg, *Rethinking Originality*, 34 WM & MARY L. REV. 801, 818–24 (1993) (discussing these quotes in describing the *Feist* case).

27 *Id.* at 827–33.

28 *See id.* at 858 ("In order to ascertain whether a compilation meets the requirement of Type II originality, the decisionmaker must determine that the author's selection, coordination, or arrangement ... of the preexisting elements or works is a distinguishable variation of the elements or works as they had existed prior.").

29 *See* Justin Hughes, *Restating Copyright Law's Originality Requirement*, 44 COLUM. J. LAW & ARTS 383, 390 (2021). In discussing and criticizing the ongoing Restatement of Copyright project, Hughes then argues that the Restatement reporters are perhaps too faithful to *Feist*, and that shifts in terminology among the different subparts of the draft Restatement reflect *Feist* on one hand and what courts are actually doing on the other, while failing to explain what the lower courts are doing. *See id.* at 390, 392.
In the interests of full disclosure, the author notes that she serves as an advisor on the Restatement of Copyright project. Her explorations in this chapter reflect her personal musings and are unrelated to any drafts or discussions within the Restatement project.

30 *But cf. Artificial Intelligence and Intellectual Property: Part III – IP Protection for AI-Assisted Inventions and Creative Works: Hearing Before the Subcomm. on Cts., Intell. Prop. & the Internet of the H. Comm. on the Judiciary*, 118th Cong. 2 (2024) (written testimony of Sandra Aistars, Clinical Professor, George Mason University Antonin Scalia Law School) (explaining that "*Feist* should continue to apply in the context of AI-assisted creative works").

31 *See, e.g.*, Robert C. Denicola, *Ex Machina: Copyright Protection for Computer-Generated Works*, 69 RUTGERS UNIV. L. REV. 251, 267 (2016); Annemarie Bridy, *Coding Creativity: Copyright and the Artificially Intelligent Author*, 2012 STAN. TECH. L. REV. 5, 50–51 (2011).

32 *See* Graves & Katyal, *supra* note 9, at 1337.

33 Feldman & Graves, *supra* note 9, at 81.

34 *See id.* at 64, 97–99.

35 If AI can develop a list of solutions that includes the one being claimed as a trade secret, but doesn't specify which one, a challenger might claim that there is no secret. After all, the solution was "readily ascertainable by AI." In that case, the trade secret response could be that perhaps part of the value is the human's ability to identify, among a sea of options, the one that will actually work.

Chapter 10

1 Marc Andreessen, *The Techno-Optimist Manifesto*, ANDREESEN HOROWITZ (Oct. 16, 2023), https://a16z.com/the-techno-optimist-manifesto.

2 *See* Chapter 1 (describing the remarkable capability of many current-generation AI systems, including improving on surgical outcomes, and making vehicle transportation much safer).

3 *See, e.g.*, Peter Mullen, *Why Customer Service Needs Its Own 'Good Housekeeping'-Style Seal Of Approval*, FORBES (Jan. 5, 2023, 07:30 AM), https://www.forbes.com/sites/forbescommunicationscouncil/2023/01/05/why-customer-service-needs-its-own-good-housekeeping-style-seal-of-approval; Carleigh Stiehm, *Celebrating 110 Years of the Good Housekeeping Seal*, HEARST (Aug. 22, 2019), https://www.hearst.com/-/celebrating-110-years-of-the-good-housekeeping-seal; *Good Housekeeping Institute Product Reviews*, GOOD HOUSEKEEPING, https://www.goodhousekeeping.com/institute/about-the-institute/a19748212/good-housekeeping-institute-product-reviews/#seals (last visited Mar. 14, 2025).

4 *See* discussion in Chapter 6. One should note that the theoretic underpinnings of the intellectual property regimes do not include the perpetuation of the regimes themselves. One could scour the various existing, historic, and potential utilitarian and non-consequentialist perspectives on each regime as described in Chapter 2, but one would be hard-pressed to find any notion of perpetuation of the intellectual property system itself as a goal. Obviously, the systems have to function effectively *if* we have them, but the various theoretical views generally lack the notion that the systems themselves are needed. Rather, the regimes are needed to accomplish something else; we need them to do their jobs. As Burk noted in a humorous aside, if AI truly could make innovation cheap and instantaneous, we wouldn't need the cumbersome patent system. In other words, we don't value them per se, we need them to do a job, and the job is defined by whatever theoretical perspective one holds about the particular regime – whether one views the job as promoting the progress of innovation and creativity for society, following an author's moral rights, preserving a producer's property rights, or ensuring the morality of the marketplace, Whatever the job, these systems cannot carry it out if the value myth evaporates. And if it does, things subject to intellectual property will be left unprotected, that is, unless the AI revolution somehow manages to replace the systems with something else.

5 Lexi Heon, Comment, *Artificially Obvious but Genuinely New: How Artificial Intelligence Alters the Patent Obviousness Analysis*, 53 SETON HALL L. REV. 359, 384 (2022) (proposing that patent applications should require disclosure of the involvement of AI in the invention process and that there should be a separate standard of obviousness for AI inventions); Jessica A. Caso, Note, *AI Inventorship: It's Time to Cache in the Latest Challenge to Patentability in the*

Modern Era, 35/36 N.Y. INT'L L. REV. 53, 73–74 (2023); *see also* Tim W. Dornis, *Artificial Intelligence and Innovation: The End of Patent Law as We Know It*, 23 YALE J.L. & TECH. 97, 150 (2020) (suggesting that AI-generated inventions receive a lower level of patent protection because "it will be less costly to artificially invent"). Mehdi Poursoltani, *Disclosing AI Inventions*, 29 TEX. INTELL. PROP. L.J. 41, 59–64 (suggesting "AI patents should be held to a higher standard of disclosure"). *Cf.* Dan L. Burk, *Cheap Creativity and What It Will Do*, 57 GA. L. REV. 1701 (2023) (arguing that intellectual property will shift toward regimes that can confirm authenticity, meaning human-created, and suggesting that "trademark may come to support a somewhat orthogonal marketing position, fostering an artificial scarcity that identifies otherwise indistinguishable goods produced by human creativity rather than AI generativity"); Tabrez Y. Ebrahim, *Artificial Intelligence Inventions & Patent Disclosure*, 125 PENN STATE L. REV. 147, 194 (2020) (proposing enhancement of disclosure requirements for AI-generated output of invention that were "hardly (or never) developed" or which were "concealed through an unexplainable algorithmic inventive process").

6 SB 1047, 2023–2024 Leg., Reg. Sess. (Ca. 2024) (establishing the Board of Frontier Models to oversee regulations pertaining to advanced AI models). European Union also established a similar body, called the European AI Office, that monitors and supervises AI affairs across all member states of the European Union. *See* 2024 O.J. (L)(EU) 2024/1689.

7 *See, e.g.*, RESPONSIBLE AI INST., THE RESPONSIBLE AI CERTIFICATION PROGRAM – WHITE PAPER (2022) (rationalizing "[f]irst [i]ndependent [a]-ccreditation [c]ertification [p]rogram for [r]esponsible AI"); Daniel Seng, *Detecting and Prosecuting IP Infringement with AI*, *in* ARTIFICIAL INTELLIGENCE AND INTELLECTUAL PROPERTY 292, 305 (Jyh-An Lee, Reto Hilty, & Kung-Chung Liu eds., 2021) (lauding a joint project of the Chinese-government-owned Alibaba company and rights holders including "online enforcement practices, offline investigations such as conducting investigation purchases from suspect sellers, litigation strategies and tactics, and IPR-protection efforts" and arguing that "[t]he problem of counterfeits and fake goods can only be solved with greater transparency and cooperation between right holders, intermediaries, and public institutions"). *See also* Carlos I. Gutierrez, Gary Marchant, & Lucille Tournas, *Lessons for Artificial Intelligence from Historical Uses of Soft Law Governance*, 61 JURIMETRICS 133, 147 (relaying a "well-known characteristic of soft law: its voluntary nature. As a governance alternative that lacks a means of regulatory enforcement, its compliance is contingent on the alignment of incentives").

8 Petroc Taylor, *United States: Number of Fixed Broadband Subscriptions 1998–2023*, STATISTA, https://www.statista.com/statistics/187145/number-of-fixed-broadband-subscriptions-in-the-united-states-since-2000/ (last visited Mar.14, 2025).

9 Petroc Taylor, *Number of Mobile Cellular Subscriptions in the United states 1984–2023*, STATISTA, https://www.statista.com/statistics/186122/number-of-mobile-cellular-subscriptions-in-the-united-states-since-2000/ (last visited Mar. 14, 2025).

Conclusion

1 *See* ALEXANDER POPE, AN ESSAY ON CRITICISM (1711).

2 *See id.* ("a little learning is a dangerous thing").

INDEX

For EU product safety concerns, contact us at Calle de José Abascal, 56–1°,
28003 Madrid, Spain or eugpsr@cambridge.org.

www.ingramcontent.com/pod-product-compliance
Ingram Content Group UK Ltd.
Pitfield, Milton Keynes, MK11 3LW, UK
UKHW022353190926
475702UK00015B/2258
* 9 7 8 1 0 0 9 6 4 6 8 4 0 *